Paris-Bucharest, Bucharest-Paris

D1796524

FAUX TITRE

367

Etudes de langue et littérature françaises
publiées sous la direction de

Keith Busby, †M.J. Freeman,
Sjef Houppermans et Paul Pelckmans

Paris-Bucharest, Bucharest-Paris

Francophone writers from Romania

Edited by
Anne Quinney

AMSTERDAM - NEW YORK, NY 2012

Cover illustrations: Dambovita River, Bucharest (1924) and Ile de la Cité, Paris (1998). © www.pozeleonline.ro and Richard Quinney

Cover design by Inge Baeten

The paper on which this book is printed meets the requirements of 'ISO 9706: 1994, Information and documentation - Paper for documents - Requirements for permanence'.

Le papier sur lequel le présent ouvrage est imprimé remplit les prescriptions de 'ISO 9706: 1994, Information et documentation - Papier pour documents - Prescriptions pour la permanence'.

ISBN: 978-90-420-3451-8
E-Book ISBN: 978-94-012-0737-9
© Editions Rodopi B.V., Amsterdam - New York, NY 2012
Printed in The Netherlands

Table of Contents

List of Illustrations

Acknowledgments

I would like to thank the Department of Modern Languages and the Office of Research and Sponsored Programs at the University of Mississippi for supporting this project financially since its inception. Departmental chair and editor of *Balkanistika*, Donald Dyer, deserves special recognition for offering his editorial skills and his expertise in the area of Romanian scholarship, as well as for suggesting certain members of this community of scholars now represented together in this volume. Several individuals were also instrumental in the initial conception and ultimate completion of this book. Contributor Monique Yaari offered her vision and insight into the phenomenon of Romanian Francophonia and helped define this project in numerous ways as it shifted and changed its ideological, geographical, and historical range over the last decade. Doina Pasca Harsanyi and Nicolae Harsanyi provided excellent guidance in regard to the subject in general and generously shared their first-hand knowledge and appreciation of Romanian Francophilia on many occasions over the years. I speak for all the authors of this work in expressing gratitude to our copy editor, Nicola McCarthy, who painstakingly read and re-read, corrected, formatted, and proofread this manuscript written by ten different authors in six different countries and in French, English, and Romanian. Christa Stevens at Rodopi was especially helpful in all matters related to publishing a multi-authored book. Finally, I am indebted to each of the contributors for their excellent work, enthusiasm, and patience as our collaborative efforts evolved to produce this unique volume.

Introduction

Just 250 years ago most people living in what is present-day Romania had not even heard of France. The Romanian Principalities, i.e., Wallachia and Moldavia, were considered the cultural heirs of Greece, Russia, and Turkey rather than of Europe.[1] Transylvania, the Western arm of Romania, joined Romania as late as 1919 and Transylvanians were in part responsible for renewed interest in the Latin origins of Romania. And yet from the mid-eighteenth century forward, Romanians began to cultivate an intense and complex connection with France marked by serious efforts to emulate the French in everything from political philosophy to cultural tastes and habits to artistic and literary conventions. Why such a sudden shift to Western sources in their search for redefinition? More importantly, why France in particular, and not, for example, Italy, England, or Germany? In the words of one historian, "Romanians identified with the Latinity of French culture, which they recognized as being akin to their own, and endeavored to realize some of the romantic and radical notions they had encountered in Parisian salons…. Romanians [were convinced] that France was truly a reliable friend, ready to sponsor their quest for statehood."[2]

This relationship was and is far from one-sided. It must be emphasized that while Romania has long enjoyed its ties to France, France also depended on Romania as a satellite of its cultural empire in the nineteenth century. The French, for their part, hoped to enhance their country's international prestige by preserving the balance of power in Eastern Europe. Around 1848, France's interest in Romania reached an unprecedented peak, and at the beginning of the twentieth century, in particular, Romania became a pivotal figure in this equation.

It bears repeating that the Romanian language developed in much the same way that French developed; that is to say, both languages evolved from the moment in history, around the time of the Roman

---

[1] Doina and Nicolae Harsanyi, "The Discreet Charm of the Little Sister: France and Romania," *East European Quarterly*, XXVIII, no. 2, June 1994, 183.
[2] Frederick Kellogg. *The Road to Romanian Independence*. (West Lafayette: Purdue University Press, 1995), 6.

expansion east and north when its influence in those provinces from 74 BC to around 245 AD was gradually taking hold. Romans brought their imperial culture and civilization to these areas. But more importantly, they brought their most "powerful Romanizing instrument, the Latin Language."[3] The Romanian language today is largely what remains of the vulgar Latin spoken in the province of Roman-occupied Dacia, in the Balkans, along the Black Sea. Its other identifiable influences include elements of the Thracian idiom (linguists say they are able to identify only 80–110 words of this language) and Slavic lexical elements. The grammatical structure of Romanian, which has remained more or less unchanged, is decidedly Latin.[4] That Romanian was a Latin language at once divorced Romania and Romanians from their Slavic neighbors and put them in direct familial relationship with other Latin countries and cultures.

To focus entirely on the linguistic alliance between France and Romania would be to eclipse the cultural legacy as well as the political structures and ideas of France that Romanians were eager to embrace. During the Russian and Turkish wars, the local Romanian aristocracy aligned itself with the language and culture of France. Around 1820 and later, in 1848, the search for a unified Romanian national and cultural identity led the young "revolutionaries" to Paris. There they hoped to find, under the influence of the French Enlightenment and the French Romantic poets, the guidance necessary in their struggle for self-definition and national consciousness. Napoleon III was particularly sensitive to efforts to construct what would become the Romanian nation state. He supported the reorganization of Europe through the Treaty of Paris in 1856, which resulted in the union of Moldova and Wallachia into a single state. Ultimately, they would officially be known as Romania in 1861, with complete inde-

---

[3] Vlad Georgescu, *The Romanians: A History*. Edited by Matei Călinescu, translated by Alexandra Bley-Vroman (Columbus: Ohio State UP, 1991), 6.

[4] Georgescu notes in his study of the Romanian language that "recent research has calculated that from 16 to 20 percent of the words in the basic vocabulary are of Slavic origin. The language continued to evolve until, at the Slavic invasion, the Daco-Roman dialect began to separate from the three dialects spoken south of the Danube, Macedo-Romanian, Istro-Romanian, and Megleno-Romanian. It is likely then that the four dialects became fully distinct during the ninth and tenth centuries, when the Romanians emerged as a people and began to appear in the sources" (*The Romanians: A History* 13).

pendence proclaimed in 1877. In the nineteenth century, France symbolized the "soul sister" of Romania at a time when Romanians were searching to define their collective identity in such a way as to unify the disparate communities in the Romanian Territories. France was viewed as a cultural beacon, signifying at once the site of status and prestige and a culture clearly distinct from that of Romania's Eastern European neighbors.

This volume considers the cultural and artistic links between France and Romania in the twentieth century from the perspective of writers of Romanian cultural heritage who chose French as a literary language. However, this heritage in some cases was mixed—their influences were sometimes German, Russian, Ottoman—and many were multilingual. Thus, their adoption of French represents a hybrid form of *francophonie*. While many scholars of French literary studies have given much attention to twentieth-century literary production emerging from the former French colonies, few have considered such writers within the domain of Francophone literature. Given that Romanian is itself a Romance language and given the long history of Franco–Romanian ties, it is time to consider these writers who made a choice to express themselves in French within the contemporary understanding of Francophone literary production. It is also important to note the influence that Romanian artists and writers have had on intellectual life in Paris. What would Dada be without Tristan Tzara? French theatre without Ionesco? Or, contemporary poetry without Isou? The nature of Franco–Romanian relations is one of exchange, borrowings, and crossovers, rather than a relationship based on a hierarchy characterizing the colonial and postcolonial experience underwriting other Francophone literatures.

The recent changes to the European political and economic landscape make it imperative to consider the notion of national boundaries in a new way, that is, with an increased appreciation for the historical permeability of those boundaries. It is equally important to consider the possibilities of a Francophone literary tradition that extends beyond the colonial dimension. The essays in this book question the idea of a *francophonie roumaine* by showing how the hybrid cultural identity developed for French writers of Romanian heritage, whether geographically established on French or Romanian soil. Rather than summarily adding Romania to the list of Francophone writers' diverse national origins, these rich and varied essays reflect an inquiry into the commonalities with and differences from works written in French produced in various geographical spaces. And, based on these, they seek to establish the ways in which the writers whose mother tongue was Romanian are or are not to be considered in a separate category.

This volume is particularly rich because of the variety of genres analyzed and discussed: poetry, drama, fiction, and non-fiction. The chapters cover a wide terrain of literary currents from the traditional narrative to avant-garde texts, and they also treat a considerable range of ideological orientations over an extended chronological span. Furthermore, the chapters offer the voices of authors who hail from six countries writing in French, English, and Romanian. Given this range and the importance of the authorial voice to the overall subject of this volume, a rigid standardization of the French and Romanian conventions in regard to matters such as capitalization of titles and movements has not been enforced. Instead, many of the individual preferences of the authors have been allowed to stand in an effort to preserve signs of the genesis and style of each author.

Monica Spiridon opens this collection with her essay, "'Bucharest-on-the-Seine': The Anatomy of a National Obsession," which explores the many faces of Romania's obsession with Paris as a space of cultural identification. Throughout the nineteenth and twentieth centuries, debates concerning Romania's national identity focused repeatedly on the cultural heritage of the Roman Empire and the Romance origins of the Romanian language. Membership in the club of Romance languages was considered irrefutable proof of a Western European identity and allegiance. Eventually, for most Romanians, Romance came to mean that France (and French) was regarded as the most dignified heir of the late Roman Empire, not only economically and politically, but especially culturally. As a consequence, France and its capital city became (and have remained) a Mecca for young Romanian intellectuals seeking a Western European education. Their fascination with Paris and French cultural models, as well as their efforts to transplant French culture to Bucharest (and Romanian culture to Paris), has taken many different forms from the Romantic period to the present: it has been a place of nostalgia, a place of stolen memory. And, after the Soviet takeover of Romania, the French capital became a mythical space situated somewhere between fiction and reality. The author argues that Romanians have constructed and reconstructed Paris as an imaginary Eastern European city for over two centuries. There are several versions of a Romanian Paris, totally non-coincident, heterogeneous, and discontinuous, regardless of their topographical starting points. Almost every generation and every group of Romanians—exiled, displaced, traveling, writing fiction, diaries, and/or memoirs—has had a Paris of its own, complete with a unique historical narrative, nostalgic sentiments, and recollections. Consequently, as a "Bucharest-on-the-Seine," Paris seems to be a typical *non-lieu* and in this respect a typical *lieu de mémoire* as well.

Chapter 2 by Ferdâ Asya entitled "The Orientalism of Anna de Noailles" examines the literary production of Anna de Noailles (1876–1933), one of the most accomplished, prolific, and charismatic writers of the France of the first half of the twentieth century. She was the first woman to receive the rank of commander in the Legion of Honor. In her almost forty-year career, Noailles produced nine volumes of poetry, a book of prose poems, three novels, a collection of novellas and essays, an autobiography, and countless articles, prefaces, and essays. Yet, less than a century later, she appears in literary scholarship more often than not as one of the writers of the "Forgotten Generation." Today, Noailles's works are out of print, inaccessible to general readers and hardly available to scholars. Recent critics, who have overcome these conditions, firmly locate the writer in her deserved place in literary history and scholarship. However, always finding that Noailles's art has a Western pedigree, these critics overlook her Oriental inheritance as the most prominent factor guiding the direction of her life and shaping the intellectual paradigm of her art. Asya claims that Sufism was an unmistakable force that fueled the artistic creativity of Anna de Noailles. As revealed in her autobiography, *Le livre de ma vie*, and her poem, "Constantinople," she was inspired to write poetry at the age of nine during a visit to Istanbul, her mother's native city, where Sufism formed the essence of the Ottoman intellectual life and literature. Noailles's Oriental inheritance is evident in her entire œuvre. That is, she appropriates some of the esoteric concepts of the Sufi creed as tropes for devising her own particular literary lexicon, thereby evoking mystic images that yoke erotic *amour* with emotional love, life with death, and death with immortality. This chapter examines some of Anna de Noailles's poetry and prose to demonstrate that she used these tropes as vehicles to control, compose, and convey her intense emotions about life, love, and death as profoundly as the Sufi poets did.

In Chapter 3, "Before They Were Famous: Tristan Tzara, Nation-hood, and Poetry," Stephen Forcer deals with the French translations of Tzara's first and only collection of Romanian-language poems, which he wrote before his ascendancy to Dadaist-in-chief in the Zur-ich of World War I. Through close textual analysis of these and later poems, Forcer demonstrates that Tzara, in general greatly underesti-mated as a poet, undertakes an exceedingly dense lyric mourning for his native Romania and offers a more surface-level engagement with nations and nationhood. He points, in particular, to Tzara's critique of "nationality" as a totalitarian concept used to help gain consensus for armed conflict, including the Spanish Civil War. By reading Tzara closely and in the terms set out by his poems, we can in turn distin-guish an instructive contrast between, on the one hand, the complex formal play of Tzara's poetic mediation of nationhood and, on the other, the biographical events for which Tzara is more commonly re-membered (the Dadaist rejection of national identity, his support of the Spanish Republicans, and his rupture with the Surrealists, as well as his divorce from Greta Knutson). In contrast to previous critiques of Tzara's poetry that tend to read authorial and historical "essences" in his verse, the author looks at the ways in which Tzara's diverse relationships with nation, language, identity, and selfhood may or may not play out at the level of the poetry itself. By focusing on the French translations of Tzara's first published poems—the first and last body of work to be published by Tzara in Romanian—Forcer establishes a productive tension between, on the one hand, the textual mediation of self and nationhood in the verse and, on the other, the personal and historical issues for which Tzara is more commonly remembered, i.e., his departure from Romania, the Dadaists' rejection of national identi-ty, his support of the Republicans during the Spanish Civil War, and his French naturalization. Curiously, Tzara has been neglected by lit-erary criticism; Forcer makes the case that some of this neglect stems precisely from Tzara's status as an ethno-national hybrid, and that his Franco–Romanian status brings into instructive relief a set of funda-mental issues to do with cultural belonging, collective memory, and the curation (or not) of literary legacies.

Monique Yaari offers, in Chapter 4, "The Surrealist Group of Bu-charest: Collective Works, 1940–1947," an insightful examination of the question of language in the short life of this group, whose literary component was by and large of French expression and whose artistic production straddled verbal and visual languages. This group, formed in 1940, was quickly forced to go underground at the onset of the war, especially as three of its five members were Jewish. It resurfaced for a fleeting period of liberty under the young communist regime (1945–1947) with a flurry of publications and three exhibitions, only to be forced to cease its activity when the regime tightened its grip. Shortly afterwards it dispersed, leaving only traces of the unique friendships that had been at its heart. Most of its members continued their literary and artistic activity with various degrees of intensity. Some remained in Bucharest and had to conform to the diktats of Jdanovism. Others left at different times, for Paris, Chicago, or Haifa—this displacement allowing them to continue writing freely, in French, and producing visual art. One distinguishing trait of the group during the 1940s is their collective activity—texts signed by two to five group members and sets of individual short texts published together. Another characteristic is their effort to set themselves apart from French surrealism, even as they borrowed its language. Indeed, in addition to two 1945 manifesto-like texts, starting in 1946 all the group's collective texts were written in French (not without some opposition within the group), and some of its members individually adopted this language as their exclusive mode of expression.

Why French? Was this a case of snobbism or the result of a hegemonic French cultural presence in Central and Eastern Europe? Yaari argues that the answer is more complex, and specific. Naturally, French was a vehicle allowing a marginal culture to reach a wider audience. But this was only a condition of possibility. Beyond that, French was the language of deep cultural affinities that transcended national borders, and it was the idiom through which important friendships and intellectual exchanges could be maintained, established, and cultivated. Moreover, in the political situation of the time, caught between two totalitarianisms, fascism on the one hand and communism on the other, it was a language that served as a means and a space of resistance to both. These last three factors, contends Yaari, were intellectual, psychological, and political imperatives. Thus, it would be improper to consider this choice of language as a form of cultural exile. Rather, it may have been a way to reconstruct an identity that conditions in the homeland aimed to suppress.

Chapter 5, "The Trans-cultural Journey of Benjamin Fondane" by Monique Jutrin provides an overview of the work of Fondane from

his early years in Romania through his sojourns in France. His body
of work is marked by a migration through cultures and languages and
by a dialogue between forms of knowledge. In his polymorphic
œuvre, he easily shifted between writing poetic, philosophical,
and critical texts, as well as works for the theatre and the cinema.
Fondane was passionate about all the innovative aspects of his era's
thinking, and not afraid to venture down the paths of anthropology,
psychoanalysis, logic, and physics. Thus, he maintained an intellectual exchange with the likes of Lévy-Bruhl, Caillois, Artaud, Wahl, and
Maritain, to list only a few. The authors who were influenced by him
are numerous: for example, Cioran, Lupasco, Celan, and Jean
Lescure. Situated at the crossroads of Romanian, French, and Jewish
cultures, Fondane enriched French poetry with a new tonality that
cleared a new path for today's readers. His essays on Rimbaud and on
Baudelaire and his *Faux Traité d'esthétique* (1938) remain reference
works and stirred up a revival of interest in the postmodern era. His
existential thought, well appreciated in the 1930s but forgotten after
the war, has re-emerged in the philosophical debates of our time. This
chapter will familiarize readers with his vast and varied body of work
and contextualize it within his tripartite orientation as Jewish, as Romanian, and as a writer of French.

    In Chapter 6, "French as the Language of *Libre Échange* in the
Works of Panaït Istrati," Catherine Rossi discusses the position of
Panaït Istrati within the field of Francophonie. Self-taught in French,
Istrati wrote his entire literary œuvre in his second language. True, his
native city, Braïla, was an urban milieu that championed French and
French culture; however, his decision to write exclusively in French
had nothing to do with necessity or obligation, and even less to do
with the will to assimilate into French culture. For Istrati, French was
the language that expressed the Revolution and the Rights of Man and
Citizen, not to mention the great ideas found in fiction, which he read
quite voraciously in Romanian translation. For Istrati, to write in
French, therefore, was to represent in language "l'idéal." Aside from
his exposure to works in French by Rousseau, Fénelon, Montesquieu,
and others, Istrati's encounter and friendship with Romain Rolland
ultimately proved to be the catalyst for his first literary experiments in
French. Istrati's appropriation of French is highly original. Rather
than abandoning his initial culture, Istrati reinforced his Romanian
identity in French. Rather than seek assimilation in literature (to read

and to write like a Frenchman), he sought distinction. Istrati made use of the French language in a particular way: he misconstrued it and invented turns of phrase that are disconcerting and irregular for standard speech. Istrati's French belongs to him alone, yet it is understood by all. As a tentative reconciliation between East and West, his work is not so much a fusion of cultures as an exchange between the men who constitute the "nouveaux gentilshommes du XXe siècle."

In "Home Is Elsewhere: Exile in the Theatre of Ionesco," Ingrid Chafee (Chapter 7) demonstrates that, though Eugène Ionesco's theatre is viewed as Francophone as it is written in French, it actually bridges two cultures while belonging entirely to neither. Born to a Romanian father and a French mother, he lived in France until age thirteen, then after his parents' divorce was summarily relocated to Bucharest. He learned Romanian, changed cultural identity and language, and completed his education. He wrote poetry and criticism in Romanian and taught French in the secondary school system, but in the late 1930s he became appalled over the growth of fascism in Romania. He broke definitively with his father over this question, and managed to leave for France together with his Romanian wife, having won a scholarship to write a dissertation on French poetry. A more compelling motive for leaving was his distaste for the fascist regime in Romania. With one brief interruption, he would spend the remainder of his life in France, writing in French and becoming a widely acclaimed pioneer of the French theatre of "the absurd." His first plays, parodies of the efforts to make language and meaning coincide, were praised as brilliant deconstructions of naive belief in words; they were reflections of a mixed cultural identity in which time, place, and names all seem ambiguous and uncertain. Over time, his plays became self-conscious theatre with protagonists who were would-be playwrights trying to oppose the script and the other characters. Then *Rhinocéros* and *Le Roi se meurt* earned Ionesco international fame and a place among the "immortals" of the Académie Française. His last works were surrealist, autobiographical, and political in tone. And, though they received adverse criticism because of contemporary critical trends, his place in world theatre now seems assured, and his literary achievement is claimed in both France and Romania.

Ashby Crowder's essay in Chapter 8, "Traditionalism and Protochronism in the European Context," compares two cultural movements among two different groups of Romanian writers at two different points in the twentieth century and situates these movements in a context at once Romanian and European. The first group considered here consists of several interwar writers broadly categorized as the "traditionalists" or "indigenists," including Lucian Blaga, Nichifor Crainic, and Constantin Radulescu-Motru. The second group is composed of the Ceauşescu-era "protochronists" who rose to fame in the 1970s and 1980s. The writers discussed from this category are Edgar Papu, Ilie Purcaru, Mihai Ungheanu, and Dan Zamfirescu. Although these traditionalists and protochronists published fiction and poetry, this essay examines their backgrounds and their political writings to gain an understanding of the external influences on their intellectual development. The essay critiques Keith Hitchins's and Katherine Verdery's discussions of traditionalism and protochronism. It points to shortcomings in Hitchins's portrayal of "traditionalism" as incompatible with "Europeanism"; this formulation is problematic as the interwar indigenists were part of a reaction against modernity that was broadly European. The essay then suggests problems with Verdery's claim that Ceauşescu-era protochronism was a resuscitation of the interwar polemic between traditionalists and Europeanists. Its argument is that protochronism should be seen as quite separate from, and not as a continuation of, interwar traditionalism. In support of the position that each movement should be understood as a product of its own time, the essay discusses the influences of French and German philosophy on the interwar and Ceauşescu-era debates on cultural philosophy. While the traditionalists wrote under strong German influence, the protochronists rejected German philosophy altogether. This negation of German influence is a main point in arguing against the continuity of the traditionalists' and the protochronists' conceptions of national ideology.

In "Isidore Isou's Spirited Letters" (Chapter 9), Jean-Jacques Thomas discusses the phenomenon that was Ioan-Isidor Goldstein, better known as Isodore Isou, who founded the two literary and artistic movements, Letterism [*lettrisme*] and Metagraphy [*métagraphie*], in mid-twentieth-century France. An extremely well-read intellectual, an indefatigable writer and thinker, Isou devoted his intellectual attention to the breadth of human knowledge, focusing on letters, arts, and sciences, at one point or another in his life. Yet his megalomania coupled with a sharp and relentless criticism ("chiseling" would be his word in its literal sense) of the mediocrity of the other intellectuals, writers, and thinkers of the immediate post–WW II period in France compromised his reputation. Thomas first illustrates Isou's paradoxi-cal status as a marginal intellectual generally at odds with different intellectual and literary movements that span the period of 1945–1970 in France. He explains in great depth Isou's remarkable originality in regard to a radically new vision of what poetry looked like on the page and the kinds of meanings that could be created with these novel forms. With a view toward Isou's beginnings as the child of Jewish parents in Botoşani, an important center for Judaic life in North-Eastern Romania, and his youthful membership in an international Zionist movement, this chapter frames Isou's contributions to the in-tellectual landscape in his adopted city (Paris) in terms of his renunci-ation of his Romanian roots. That his mother destroyed his early work when she feared the police of the Antonescu regime would question his involvement with the Communist Party further hardened Isou's position that he would never have the artistic freedom in Romania that he could have in France. What he could not have anticipated was the resistance in France on the part of the rather institutionalized Parisian avant-garde to his ideas about the importance of poetic graphic plas-ticity. The reasons for this resistance to Isou's ideas are multiple and complex as Thomas delineates, and they have as much to do with his outsized egomania as with the radical nature of the ideas themselves. Regardless, we are at present just beginning to understand, fifty years after Isou's first Parisian appearance, the extent to which his work still earns him a place at the very core of the most extreme contemporary Parisian reflections on poetry and symbolic representation.

In the final chapter, "Emile Cioran and the Politics of Exile," Anne Quinney treats the work of the philosopher and aphorist, Emile Cioran, a Romanian who lived in France from the late 1930s until his death in 1995. Cioran was a self-identified exile and iconoclast, whose work varies in form from meandering philosophical essay to terse aphorism. He refused to belong to any literary or philosophical movement in France although he lived in the heart of the literary sixth *arrondissement* in Paris for over fifty years and counted Eugène Io-nesco and Samuel Beckett among his close friends. He preferred soli-tude to affiliation, and he cultivated a reputation for mystery and noto-riety as a literary genius, a Romanian transplant, and a misanthropic *penseur d'occasion*. Recent revelations about his experiences in Ro-mania in the early part of this century, however, have shattered this image of the reclusive, timid philosopher. More precisely, his partici-pation in the Iron Guard movement, a proto-fascist, anti-democratic movement inspired by mysticism and German National Socialism that reached its zenith during his adolescence and years as a college stu-dent in Bucharest, has caused a buzz of speculation and outrage. The extent to which Cioran became an enthusiast, for a time, of the movement serves as an important metric for his capacity for negative passions, as his writing from this period demonstrates. Quinney hy-pothesizes that the body of his work written in French after 1937 was a response to his involvement in the fascist movement in Romania during his thirties. Although undeclared as such, his post-Romania writing served as a lifelong attempt to rewrite thoughts once ex-pressed publicly (which he regretted later) and as an attempt to exor-cise demons that never ceased to plague him.

Each chapter of this book treats the stakes involved in writing in a language that is not one's mother tongue and the advantages, both political and psychological, that result from this choice. To write in French, and in many cases, to immigrate to France, presented certain difficulties to these writers; yet, it signified particularly liberating conditions as well. That there was so large a community of such writ-ers of Romanian origin qualifies their experiences as a phenomenon unique to the nineteenth and twentieth centuries, in a category that divorces theirs from other literatures currently designated as Fran-cophone that developed within this period. The case of Romanian writers illustrates an alternative to the postcolonial paradigm that re-cent movements such as the manifesto for *littérature-monde* wish to topple in order to free language, once and for all, from its exclusive relationship to nation. From these examples, we have much to gain as they offer new ways to conceptualize the literary uses of a specific linguistic idiom like French beyond the limiting notion of national boundaries.

—Anne Quinney
University of Mississippi

"Bucharest-on-the-Seine": The Anatomy of a National Obsession

Monica Spiridon
University of Bucharest

France: The Hospitable Land

Starting with the 1848 bourgeois uprisings—that to a great extent were just political replicas imprinted by the myth of the Great Revolution—for several waves of Romanian intellectuals exiled in Paris, the French metropolis became the starting point of a tortuous process of cultural projection, being constantly (re)built, in slightly different versions, as an imaginary East European city. Despite their unique topographical starting points, there have been successive non-coincident, heterogeneous, and discontinuous versions of "the Romanian Paris." Almost every generation and sometimes every group of Romanians—exiled, displaced, traveling, writing diaries or memories, nurturing nostalgic sentiments and recollections—had a Paris of its own, disguising particular agendas and distinct historical narratives. The following pages explore the many faces of the national obsession with Paris as a space of cultural identification throughout the process of Romania's modernization.

Throughout the nineteenth and twentieth centuries, the debates concerning Romania's national identity repeatedly focused on the cultural heritage of the Roman Empire and on the Romance origins of the Romanian language. At that time, membership in the club of Romance languages was the irrefutable proof of a Western European identity and allegiance. Eventually, for most Romanians, Romance came to mean French. Economically, politically, but first and foremost culturally, France was regarded as the most dignified heir of the late Roman Empire. Consequently, France and its capital city became the Mecca for young Romanian intellectuals seeking a Western European education.

From the Romantic period to the present time, their obsession with Paris and with French cultural models as well as their efforts to transplant Romanian culture to Paris and, reciprocally, French culture

to Bucharest, has taken different forms. Paris was a place of emulation, of memory, and of nostalgia, and especially after the Soviet
takeover of Romania, it became a mythical space situated somewhere
between fiction and reality.

Paris as a Jerusalem of Liberty

Let us begin with the first generation of Romanian intellectuals
who, around 1840, started going to Paris to seek higher education and
top professional training. For several reasons that I will develop below, this early brand of Romanian Francophilia should be evaluated
as an elitist and anti-Russian option. In the first half of the nineteenth
century, Paris was primarily an exclusive cultural option, insofar as
only the economically privileged could afford to study abroad. Romanians enrolled in French universities, kept abreast of public life, were
regularly seen in literary salons, and even started to build family alli-
ances. The French–Romanian connection often took an unmediated,
personalized, and even affectionate form.

On a political level, the Great French Revolution was perceived in
Bucharest as the starting point of a mythical process that claimed to
build an imaginary France, a Jerusalem of liberty and eternal revolution. While lecturing at the Collège de France, Jules Michelet himself
chose "revolution" as the defining feature of French identity, the very
name of France (Roman 76–79). Eventually, for the Romanians, Paris, the capital city of this mythical realm, seemed to be "such stuff as
dreams are made of."

Romanian intellectuals of the time also tried to assimilate romantic Herderian ideas, then fashionable in Paris. This led to a Romanian
revival of the vernacular language and of oral culture, to an emphatic
interest in national history, in local color if not in pure exoticism and
in the rural tradition. In retrospect, the national poet Mihai Eminescu
critically portrayed this period, detecting in the ideological and revolutionary discourse of the 1848 generation a certain *naiveté* and above
all a strong mimetic impulse.

In the wake of the so-called 1848 imitative revolutions *à la française* in the Romanian Principalities, in a letter published by the
Courrier Français, C.A. Rosetti and Ion C. Brătianu, prominent liberal political leaders of the time, urged Edgar Quinet:

> Rappelez encore à la France que nous sommes ses fils; que
> nous avons combattu pour elle sur la barricade. Ajoutez que
> ce que nous avons fait, nous l'avons fait à son exemple.
>
> [Help France remember that we are her sons and that we
> have fought for her in the streets. Add to this that every-
> thing we did, we did following her example.]
>
> (Anghelescu 49)

In 1853, Brătianu wrote to Napoleon III asking for his support in favor of uniting the two Romanian Principalities, to be discussed in the near future in Paris. The paradoxical claim of his petition was that the forthcoming political union could pass for a veritable "French Conquest." The Romanian army, he maintains in his letter, would become a French army, and the Romanian harbors on the Black Sea and on the Danube banks would be the warehouses of the French market, and so on. In this way, France would have all the profits of a real colonization minus its numerous discomforts (Brătianu 31).

From a certain point of view, this emphatic pro-French yearning was also an anti-Russian option, as after the treaty of Andrianople, Romania had been placed under the double control of Turkey and Russia. When compared to the declining Ottoman Empire, Russia, whose power at this time was on the rise, acted economically, administratively, and politically in an intrusive and hostile way towards Romania. At about the same time, the French Marquis de Custine made stark revelations about Russia, which nourished an anti-Russian West European romanticism, steadily opposing the religious and communitarian spirit of Russia. Consequently, the Romanians quite naturally adopted France as a providential cultural alternative to the encroaching political and cultural power of their oppressive and greedy Eastern neighbor.

Post-1848 Paris: A Nostalgic Retreat

After the defeat of the 1848 revolutions in the Romanian Principalities, many liberal Westernizers were forced into exile and went to Paris. Among them were both writers and political leaders, including C.A. Rosetti, Brătianu, Vasile Alecsandri, A. Russo, Mihail Kogălniceanu, Cezar Bolliac, Ion Ghica, and Ioan Heliade Radulescu. The evolution of the latter, whose exile lasted for nine years, was highly significant for the messianic rhetoric adopted by the 1848 Romanian intellectuals and for their fascination with the Christian–socialist models provided by Felicité Robert de Lamennais, Pierre Leroux, and François Marie Charles Fourier, among others.

Paradoxically enough, Paris, which was perceived by Romanian intellectuals as the very cradle of the Romance culture and the epitome of Romania's Latin heritage, became, among post-1848 exiles, the subject of a nostalgic literary stuff following not the model of the Roman poet Ovidius exiled by the Black Sea, but the well-known "down the rivers of Babylon" model of the Jewish diaspora, celebrated by the Bible. It was also during this period that the tradition of Romanian literature written in French, or of the "Romanian francophonie," began. In this respect the 1848 generation were pioneers, especially in the epistolary genre. During his exile in Paris, Heliade wrote *Souvenirs et impressions d'un proscrit* [Recollections and Impressions of an Outcast] (1850) and *Mémoires sur l'histoire de la régénération roumaine* [Memoirs on the History of Romanian Regeneration] (1851). Simultaneously, Alecu Russo produced and published in French the first version of his prose poem *Cântarea României* [Hymn for Romania], portraying a mythic rather than a real Romanian homeland.

In the aftermath of the 1848 exile, in certain intellectual circles in Bucharest, the use of French prevailed, being ascribed the role of a cultural idiom. After his studies in Paris, Alexandru Macedonski, founder of the Romanian symbolist movement, published poetry in Romanian and in French in Bucharest as well as French-language prose poems in Paris, some of which were occasionally reviewed in French literary journals. In the early twentieth century, Romanian symbolist poets were quite familiar with the Parisian artistic milieu. Overall, the recollection of this particular experience developed on the banks of the Seine stimulated the modernization of Romanian poetic expression and enhanced Romania's national self-awareness.

A close scrutiny of this poetic production would detect a subtle nostalgia obviously nourished by displacement: the melancholy of the Romanian writers lusting after Paris, the city of the *flâneurs*, and displaying obvious symptoms of marginality. As a matter of fact, such writers were uncomfortable both in Bucharest and in Paris, which progressively emerged as a "Bucharest-on-the-Seine." In the twentieth century, two distinct faces of this Bucharest on the Seine became quite salient: an aulic and an insurgent one.

Aulic Bucharest-on-the-Seine

Ever since the mid-nineteenth century, several Romanian aristo-
cratic families had settled on the Seine and entered mixed marriages.
Among them, the related princely families of Brancovan and Bibesco
managed in various ways to make their names distinctly resound in
the Parisian cultural milieu. Anna-Elisabeta Brancovan, married as
"comtesse Mathieu de Noailles," was totally assimilated as a French
poet and also did the best she could to ensure that her Romanian origins would go unnoticed. Her first cousin Antoine Bibesco is the author of a drama, *Le Jaloux*, staged in Paris and reviewed by Marcel
Proust himself in *Le Figaro*.

However, perhaps the most fascinating member of the clan was
Marthe Bibesco, wife of the prince Georges-Valentin Bibesco, distinguished pilot in the French army during the First World War,
cousin of countess Anna de Noailles and of Hélène Vacaresco as well.
Marthe Bibesco was an heiress of the Byzantine Mavrocordats
and through her mother-in-law, the princess of Caraman-Chimay,
she was related to a Napoleonian general. Contends one of her
contemporaries,

> Dans ses veines coulait le sang roumain, français, grec, ita-
> lien et, par un long effort d'anamnèse, elle s'était rémémo-
> rée l'histoire de toutes les familles, de principautés et des
> peuples de l'Europe qui avaient partagé la créativité de ses
> ancêtres.
>
> [In her veins was flowing Romanian, French, Greek and
> Italian blood and by an intense anamnesis she had remem-
> bered the past of all the European families, princip-
> alities and peoples who had nourished the creativity of her
> ancestors.] (Eliade 67)

A frequent guest of the Parisian salons, she was also acquainted
with military and political personalities such as Ramsay MacDonald,
Neville Chamberlain, and Winston Churchill (to whom she dedicated
a monograph). As a written testimony to her distinguished Parisian
friendships, we could mention her public epistolary exchange with
Paul Claudel and her well-known book *Au bal avec Marcel Proust* [In
the Ballroom with Marcel Proust] (Bibesco 1928).

Thoroughly assimilated into French literature, by the end of her
life Marthe Bibesco had published more than thirty volumes in Paris

and in Bucharest, some of which were prizewinners of the French Academy. Of her most well-known French writings at least these should be mentioned: *Isvor, le pays des saules*, *Le Perroquet vert*, *Portraits d'Epinal*, *Les huit paradis* (a travel diary), *Catherine-Paris* (swiftly translated in the US), and *La vie d'une amitié* (three volumes of her exchange of letters with Father Mugnier). She was elected as a member of the Belgian Academy succeeding Anna de Noailles and followed by Mircea Eliade. After the Second World War, General Charles de Gaulle awarded her the Légion d'Honneur for her literary endeavors in French.

Mircea Eliade, among others, draws attention to Marthe Bibesco's prominence, insisting on her role as a cultural mediator:

> Peu de temps avant sa mort, on a dit de la princesse Marthe Bibesco qu'elle était le dernier témoin de l'avant-dernière Europe. En effet elle avait connu le dernier tsar et tous les souverains de l'Europe; elle comptait parmi ses amis aussi bien le roi Ferdinand et la reine Marie de Roumanie, que la comtesse Anna de Noailles, Marcel Proust, Paul Claudel ou l'abbé Mugnier; elle fréquentait non seulement les salons et les écrivains parisiens, mais aussi les hommes politiques et les grands chefs militaires, les artistes, les savants, les princes de l'église partout en Europe.

> [Just before her death, the princess Martha Bibesco was perceived as the last witness of an earlier Europe. The fact of the matter was that she had been an acquaintance of the last tsar and of all the European sovereigns; among her closest friends she could count King Ferdinand and Queen Maria of Romania, as well as Marcel Proust, Paul Claudel and Father Mugnier; she frequented not only the Parisian literary salons and writers, but also politicians, military leaders, artists, scientists, and priests, from all over Europe.] (Eliade 67)

As regards the double identity of Marthe Bibesco, Eliade reports that her close friends saw her as another goddess Proserpine, living six months of the year above the earth and the other six underground, which meant that she usually spent half of her life in Paris and the other, the mysterious half, on her properties in Romania (Eliade 72). For these Romanian aristocrats who were easily integrated into French culture, Paris was somehow a second Bucharest: "Rien ne pourra faire de moi une exilée en France!" [Nothing could make me feel exiled in France!], Marthe Bibesco used to say, according to her friends (Eliade 76).

The scenery of *Isvor, le pays des saules*, her most cherished and most acclaimed book, is a profound, half-imaginary and half-real Romania, an entirely built-up territory. Isvor, the name of the narrator's properties in Romania, means *spring*. As an identity space, Isvor is the emblem of a reflective, mirroring, even narcissistic universe. At once author and narrator of this literary text, Marthe Bibesco is obviously in search of her hybrid cultural identity through which, as she contends, the profound common grounds of European spirituality could be grasped. Both in France and in Romania, she seems to have been continuously haunted by this amniotic spirituality—at the same time Celtic, Slavic, Greek, and Romanian, etc. In this particular way, Marthe Bibesco figures herself as the emblem of a particular "idea of Europe" based on a staunch unity as well as on rich differences.

Marthe Bibesco devoted the last thirty years of her life to a massive book never finished: *La Nymphe Europe*. Its title is highly suggestive, as it uses a feminine effigy to embody the European idea. *À la recherche de l'Europe perdue* [In Search of Lost Europe] or even *L'Europe retrouvée* [Europe Recaptured] would have also been appropriate titles for such a book, where Marthe Bibesco endeavors to build up Europe mostly in the same way as her friend Marcel Proust strived to regain the past. In her book, this specific way of representing Europeanism progressively evolves into an autobiographical discourse. In this respect, her exchange of letters with Father Mugnier is quite insightful.

Marthe Bibesco's destiny and her cultural heritage are utterly representative of an entire generation of intellectuals who, by the simple fact of being born Romanian, perceived Europe as their own homeland. They left Bucharest for larger and more provocative horizons and firmly decided to behave and to create in any circumstances as plain Europeans. Highly symbolic, their Europeanism transgressed and made irrelevant the narrowly topographical sense of belonging.

Among them, Hélène Vacaresco, a Romanian writer who wrote in French, also occupies a well-deserved and prominent place. To quote from a speech given by the Brazilian ambassador in Paris in her presence: "C'est que, ma chère amie, vous n'êtes pas une femme roumaine, vous n'êtes pas une femme européenne, vous êtes une femme universelle!" [You, my dear friend, are not a Romanian woman, you are not a European woman, you are a universal woman!] (Vacaresco and Turcu 178). Vacaresco was a manifold personality who perfectly managed to accommodate several distinct if not opposite dimensions. On the one hand, she was a "pure" Romanian, a descendant of an old princely Romanian family, and at the same time of a series of kings of Romanian poetry and founders of Romanian literary language: "The Vacaresco poets." On the other, she was a distinguished writer who published in French, and in France, poetry, prose, and drama. Her poems in particular were highly acclaimed by her contemporaries: She won two prizes from the French Academy for her books of poetry *Les Chants d'Aurore* and *Le Rhapsode de la Dâmbovitza*. In 1927, the French minister of foreign affairs, Aristide Briand, awarded her the prestigious Légion d'Honneur.

When compared to other of her illustrious compatriots, such as Mircea Eliade or Marthe Bibesco, Hélène Vacaresco draws everybody's attention with her pragmatism and her militant, efficient, strenuous activity—in one word with her "*radio-activité*"—to quote one of her contemporaries. Her presence in Francophile Europe had a conspicuous institutional dimension. She was the founder, president, and a notorious member of a whole series of political and cultural European institutions, as well as a professional diplomat representing Romania in Paris at the Institut pour la Coopération Intellectuelle and in Geneva at the Société des Nations. Forerunner of our times as a (proto)feminist, Vacaresco founded in Paris the study circle La Femme et l'univers, and was a jury member for the literary award, Femina. In no way disconcerted by her Romanian origins, this born orator and internationally acclaimed lecturer was convinced that the visibility of Romania beyond its borders needed to be enhanced by all available means.

As she eventually got the best of all the circumstantial details of her life, beyond the boundaries of her country and especially in Paris, Hélène Vacaresco managed to embody a necessity, something at the same time essential and permanent. Paul Morand paid public tribute to her in Paris in 1937:

> Hélène Vacaresco a quitté les eaux patriarcales du Danube littéraire et est venue sur les bords de la Seine recevoir droit de cité. Elle y a vu finir l'époque 1900 et naître celle d'aujourd'hui; elle a assisté à la cassure de deux mondes et elle a fait la guerre aux côtes de la France. J'ai recontré

Hélène Vacaresco pour la première fois ... au fait, l'ai-je
rencontrée quelque part pour la première fois? Non, je l'ai
toujours connue.

[Hélène Vacaresco left the patriarchal waters of the literary
Danube to settle on the banks of the Seine and to be accepted as one of us. She saw the end of the era of 1900 and the
beginning of our contemporary era; she witnessed the split
between two worlds and she went to war on the side of the
French. I met Hélène Vacaresco for the first time ... as a
matter of fact, did I ever meet her for the first time? No, I
have always known her.] (Vacaresco and Turcu 189)

"Rebellious" Paris

The rebellious face of "Romanian Paris" was associated with historical vanguards. Avant-garde Romanian writers saw Paris as a stage
upon which they were able to present their programs regardless of
whether they settled there or continued to commute between Paris and
Bucharest. According to Marcel Cornis-Pope, the Romanian vanguard
tried to fight the Romanian *time lag*, a complex and perpetual sense of
cultural belatedness. Some Romanian writers managed to anticipate
some of the West European vanguard movements. Tristan Tzara, for
example, left Romania in 1915, after publishing ironic poems that
mocked both traditional and symbolist poetry. His presence in Zurich
and later in Paris managed to stir up Western poetry as well, launch-
ing the Dadaist and Surrealist experiments. Ilarie Voronca had a similarly interesting evolution. After contributing in the 1920s to the
modernist circles in Bucharest, he left for Paris to study for a doctoral
degree in law. Contaminated by the experimental virus he had picked
up in the artistic quarters of Paris, he made frequent trips to Bucharest
to act as a catalyst for a new wave of experimentation. Together with
the painter Victor Brauner, he founded *75HP*, a dadaist–constructivist
literary magazine. A real wanderer from one editorial board to another, either as an editor or as a contributor, he settled in Paris in 1933,
and produced more than a dozen volumes introduced to the public by
Eugène Ionesco himself.

The most impressive feature of this type of Bucharest-on-the-
Seine was the two-way traffic of values between France and Romania
and the reciprocal exchange of cultural artifacts. Some Romanians
started writing in French while still in Romania. Others left for Paris
to produce literature in an adopted language. On their return to Roma-

nia, they did or did not keep up their French writing. Some of them, like Ilarie Voronca, simultaneously inhabited the two cities. All mediated the cultural dialogue between French models and local forms of modernism, and their Paris became a cosmopolis and the main knot of an intense process of artistic networking.

Which was the real equation between this emphatic experimentalism and Romanianness? This question has been raised in connection with the modernist Romanian-born sculptor Brâncuşi, who spent most of his life in Paris. Significantly enough, Mircea Eliade raised this in the opening essay of an insightful volume, *Briser le toit de la maison: La créativité et ses symboles*, published in Paris in 1986 at the end of his cosmopolitan life.

Eliade notices that the already existing interpretations regarding the aesthetic roots of Brâncuşi are unnecessarily divided into two belligerent camps. The adherents of the first one equate the creative options of Brâncuşi to the formal and axiological universe of the Parisian vanguard of his time, whereas their opponents do not spare any efforts to cloister the vision of the artist within the archaic Romanian world from which he came. Eliade does not sympathize with any of these polar views. As he maintains, flying away to Paris to get acquainted with contemporary experimentalism was Brâncuşi's great chance to plunge into his deep creative self and to recapture his roots. Even if we admit the major influence of the École de Paris on his artistic achievement, the solidarity of Brâncuşi's masterpieces with the old Romanian mythology is still conspicuous. The external pressures, Eliade concludes, would have boosted a particular type of anamnesis that guided the artist toward self-awareness and self-discovery. His encounter with the contemporary vanguard in Paris would have kicked off his return to his secret and profound imaginative world.

In order to validate his hypothesis, Eliade points to the house of the artist. According to him, the famous residence situated in Impasse Ronsin has the typical foundations of any archaic Romanian home and at the same time a roof wide open to all creative horizons. Built with his own hands, the peculiar home of Brâncuşi in Paris is the most eloquent emblem of his universe. Consequently, we are not entitled to treat it as a duplicate of some pre-existing model, as a typical archaic Romanian house, or as the workshop of a Parisian vanguard artist.

In the second half of the twentieth century, the Soviet takeover of Romania and the imposition of communism in the country pushed a new generation of Romanian intellectuals into exile. Paris became the center of the Romanian diaspora, organized around a kernel of distinguished friends and writers—Eugène Ionesco, Emile Cioran, and Mircea Eliade—who became its symbolic figureheads.

Although the three undisputed leaders of the Romanian diaspora in Paris, Ionesco, Eliade, and Cioran, have been perceived as a team, in reality they followed rather divergent paths. Ionesco integrated himself completely into his adopted culture, becoming a member of the French Academy and the unanimously recognized founder of Absurdist Theatre. In one of his diary entries, he ironically states that "since culture is a matter of self-estrangement the Romanians who want to do literary criticism must become French" (Ionesco 150).

Cioran was also totally assimilated as a French philosopher and essayist and acclaimed as one of the most accomplished postwar stylists in the French language. This kind of "over-integration" can be viewed as a response to the striking marginality of his native culture. Echoing Montesquieu's famous dilemma, "Comment peut-on être persan?" his essays obsessively raise this question: "Comment peut-on être roumain?" [How can one be Romanian?]. Roughly speaking, the answer bluntly suggested both by his work and his career is that one can be a Romanian precisely by choosing self-exile in Paris. In his turn, Mircea Eliade adopted a particular type of exile. After crossing the Atlantic to found a school in the history of religions at the University of Chicago, he regularly returned to Paris for five months every year, where he published essays and books (in both French and Romanian), participated in the life of the Romanian diaspora, and frequented fashionable intellectual circles. Over several decades, his small apartment at the Place Charles Dulin became a place of cherished Romanian memories for his compatriots. Eventually the Sorbonne honored him with the title Doctor Honoris Causa.

Apart from this acclaimed trinity, the political diaspora in Paris clustered around the Romanian department of Radio Free Europe. This is where for more than 40 years Monica Lovinescu and Virgil Ierunca loudly and successfully preached the principles of intellectual and spiritual liberty. Beginning in the early 1950s, their radio essays presented under the title "Teze şi antiteze la Paris" [Theses and Antitheses in Paris] engaged both Romanian and French cultural phenomena, validating non-dogmatic aesthetic standards. Their talk shows constantly energized the Romanian community and boosted the integration of its products into French cultural life.

During the last and most oppressive years of Ceauşescu's dictatorship, a different sort of exile started arriving in Paris. They were the "undesirables" expelled by Ceauşescu's regime, such as the dissident novelist Paul Goma, an adherent to the Czech militant document called *Charta 77*, and Dumitru Ţepeneag, for a while director of the publication, *Cahiers de l'Est.* They were followed by a wave of intellectual and political refugees, among whom were a few writers (Al. Papillian, Ilie Constantin, and Bujor Nedelcovici) who wrote both in Romanian and in French, contributed to literary periodicals, or studied for doctoral degrees. Their Paris was one of political refuge and resistance, representing a political and cultural alternative to totalitarianism, and at the same time an option for intellectual survival. Thanks to Virgil Ierunca's airing of the forgotten and censured pages of Romania's cultural heritage, Paris became the unique and precious repository of exiled Romanian memory.

By Way of a Conclusion

In Romania, the national obsession with peripheral identity and cultural belatedness developed into a profound interest in Western models and, significantly enough, into symbolic urban topographies endowed with compensatory meanings. Among these, Paris became a stereotype for the European West, even if the influences of Vienna, Berlin, or London were also visible, confirming Foucault's allegation that the so-called *heterotopic spaces* should be seen as a superposition of real heterogeneous spaces.

Within certain contexts, the mental resonance associated by individuals or by groups with real as well as with imaginary cities can be seen as relatively stable. As a principle, the verisimilitude of all ideal urban patterns is rhetorically validated by school textbooks and by travel writing. Nowadays, the mass media plays an utterly important part in such symbolic constructions. The equation *Paris = Bucharest* and the representations of Paris subsequently generated by it emerged with French travelers to Romania, such as Raymond Poincaré, Jules Michelet, Lucien Romier, and Paul Morand, and were carried on by the Romanians themselves. This imaginary match nurtured a fascinating mixture of emotional stereotypes and clichés as well as a number of purely fictitious projections (Spiridon).

As this contribution draws to its close, we might ask ourselves: How real to the Romanians was the so-called *real Paris*? Is there a significant difference between the Romanian versions of Paris and other fictional topographies? Even the Paris of the 1848 generation, the Paris of the *bonjouristes*, was to a great extent a political and cultural fiction, dominated by the myth of the Great Revolution and built out of biblical and messianic materials. This was only the starting point of a long process of imaginative construction.

After the review of this trajectory, the answer to the two questions raised above may seem less puzzling. Roughly speaking, the same Paris as an imaginary East European city has been constantly built and re-built, in slightly different versions, in almost all areas of East-Central Europe. We could conclude that for over two centuries, Romanians have constructed and reconstructed Paris as an imaginary Eastern European city. As a Bucharest-on-the-Seine, Paris was a typical *non-lieu* and, in this respect, also a typical *lieu de mémoire*.

Works Cited

Anghelescu, Mircea. "The Romanian Revolution of 1848: Moving Images." *New International Journal of Romanian Studies* I, 1–2 (1998): 44–51.

Bibesco, Marthe. *Au bal avec Marcel Proust*. 5th ed. Paris: Gallimard, 1928.

_____. *Isvor, le pays des saules*. Paris: Christian de Bartillat, 1994. (See also Sanda Stolojan, "Marta Bibescu sau actualitatea Isvorului" (Marthe Bibesco ou l'actualité d'Isvor) in *Caiete critice. Exil şi literatura*, 1–2 (1993): 48–50.

_____. *La Nymphe Europe: Mes vies antérieures*. Vol. I. Paris: Plon, 1960.

_____. *La Nymphe Europe: Où tombe la foudre*. Vol. II. Paris: Grasset, 1976.

Bratianu, Ion C. *Acte si cuvîntari*. Vols. I–IV. Bucharest: Editura Cartea Românească, 1938.

Brown, Patricia M., and John C. Turner. "The Role of Theories in the Formation of Stereotype Content." *Stereotypes as Explanations: The Formation of Meaningful Beliefs about Social Groups*. Ed. Craig McGarty, Vincent Y. Yzerbyt, and Russell Spears. Cambridge: Cambridge UP, 2002. 67–89.

Cornis-Pope, Marcel. *The Unfinished Battles: Romanian Postmodernism Before and After 1989*. Iasi: Polirom, 1996.

Eliade, Mircea. Briser le toit de la maison: La creativité et ses symboles. Paris: Gallimard, 1986.

Foucault, Michel. *Dits et Ecrits II (1976–1988)*. Paris: Gallimard, 2001.

Goldsworthy, Vesna. *Inventing Ruritania: The Imperialism of the Imagination*. New Haven and London: Yale UP, 1998.

Gregory, Derek. *Geographical Imaginations*. Oxford, UK, and Cambridge, MA: Blackwell, 1994.

Ionesco, Eugène. *Present Past, Past Present: A Personal Memoir*. Trans. Helen R. Lane. New York: Grove Press, 1971.

Nora, Pierre. "Les lieux de mémoire." *Representations* 26 (1989): 7–25.

Roman, Andrea. *Le populisme Quarante-Huitard dans les Principautés Roumaines*. Bucharest: Les Éditions de la Fondation Culturelle Roumaine, 1999.

Spiridon, Monica. *Les dilemmes de l'identité au confins de l'Europe: Le cas roumain*. Paris: L'Harmattan, 2004.

Tzara, Tristan. *First Poems*. Trans. Michael Impey and Brian Swan. Berkeley: New Rivers Press, 1976.

Vacaresco, Hélène, and Constantin Turcu. *Hélène Vacaresco: Une grande européenne*. Bucarest: Les Éditions de la Fondation Culturelle, 1996.

The Orientalism of Anna de Noailles

Ferdâ Asya
Bloomsburg University

Anna de Noailles (1876–1933) was arguably one of the most ac-complished, prolific, and charismatic writers of France in the first half of the twentieth century. In her almost forty-year career, she produced nine volumes of poetry, a book of prose poems, three novels, a collec-tion of novellas and essays, an autobiography, and numerous articles and prefaces. She invariably contributed to the literary periodicals and daily papers and made her voice heard at all times about the social and political issues of her time. In 1921, she was awarded the Grand Prize for Literature by the French Academy. The following year, she was selected as the first female member to the Belgian Royal Acade-my of French Language and Literature and, in 1934, she was honored with the French order of distinction, La Légion d'honneur. Yet, less than a century later, she appears in literary scholarship more often than not as one of the writers of the "forgotten generation."[1]

Today, with the exception of her novel, *Le visage émerveillé*, a second edition of which was published in 2004, Anna de Noailles's works are out of print and inaccessible to general readers and hardly available to scholars. Not surprisingly, since the second half of the twentieth century, few critics have been able to overcome this chal-lenge to complete studies on the writer's work. In Noailles criticism,

---

[1] In *The Forgotten Generation*, Jennifer E. Milligan explains the reasons that pre-vented the interwar female writers from becoming better known. She agrees with Henri Peyre, Hélène Cixous, and Susan Rubin Suleiman that, until the second half of the twentieth century in France, the quality of the work of the interwar female writers did not match the standards of the writers of the second half of the century. Further-more, most women writers who wrote between the wars concealed their identities under pseudonyms. Also, these writers' popular romances, which were produced in inexpensive editions, are not currently accessible at libraries. A more important ele-ment in the poor recognition of these writers was the wider reception of the outgoing activities and innovative works of their contemporary Anglo-American expatriate artists and writers (cf. 3, 6, 38–41). In addition, Catherine Perry posits that "[n]ot only did Noailles' gender present an obstacle in the literary scene, but her ethnic back-ground also provoked resistance to her recognition as a French writer" (*Persephone Unbound* 27).

long volumes are given over to the study of her life. François
Broche's *Anna de Noailles: Un mystère en pleine lumière* (1989) and
Claude Mignot-Ogliastri's *Anna de Noailles: Une amie de la
Princesse Edmond de Polignac* (1987) provide information on the
personal and cultural background of the writer. Elisabeth Higonnet-
Dugua's *Anna de Noailles: Cœur innombrable* (1989) presents
Noailles's correspondence with the writers of her time. Two earlier
and smaller volumes, Louis Perche's *Anna de Noailles* (1969) and
Édmée de la Rochefoucauld's book of the same title (1956), deliver a
mixture of biographical and critical commentary. In conveying valuable information about the personal, historical, and cultural milieu of
the writer, these volumes provide a context for scholarship on her art;
yet, few book-length studies of her art have been published. The volumes cited evidence, as Jennifer E. Milligan posits, that the critics and
average readers have been interested more in Noailles's personal life
than in her literary achievements (cf. 62). Critical studies, such as
Patrick J. Quinn and Steven Trout's *The Literature of the Great War
Reconsidered: Beyond Modern Memory* (2001) and Diana Holmes's
French Women's Writing 1848–1994 (1996), by mentioning Anna de
Noailles's name only in passing, underestimate her considerable contribution to both women's writing and war literature.

Recently, however, some critics have examined the writer's work
with the intention of releasing it from the gender presuppositions of
her time, and they firmly locate Noailles in her deserved place in literary history and scholarship. Among these critics, Mari H. O'Brien
claims that the writer was pushed to the margins of the literature of
the belle époque because of her intrusion, with a female voice, on the
male terrain of Romanticism. Tama Lea Engelking relates Noailles's
under-rated literary status to her being erroneously labeled as an unin-
tellectual feminine writer. She praises the writer's work for appealing
to all kinds of readers: male and female, intellectual and general. In
her article, "In the Wake of Decadence: Anna de Noailles' Revaluation of Nature and the Feminine," Catherine Perry analyzes Noailles's
distinct treatment of the lyric subject and her unusual approach to nature and decides that she was neither like the Romantic nor the post-
Romantic poets. Some of the longer studies of Noailles's work
include dissertations that have inauspiciously remained unpublished.
For example, Harry G. Allard's 1973 Yale University Ph.D. dissertation, "Anna de Noailles, Nun of Passion: A Study of the Novels of

Anna de Noailles," is a remarkable study of the themes in the writer's three novels and one incomplete and unpublished novel.[2] Finally, Catherine Perry's 2003 book, *Persephone Unbound*, examines closely Noailles's poetry in terms of Dionysian aesthetics by relating its inspiration to classical Greek antiquity and the philosophy of Arthur Schopenhauer and Friedrich Nietzsche and by tying its intellectual heritage to writers such as Victor Hugo, Charles Baudelaire, and Alphonse de Lamartine. Nevertheless, this body of criticism fails to bring out some of the most significant influences that compelled Noailles to create her art.

A closer examination of Anna de Noailles's life and art reveals that the philosophy of Sufism was an unmistakable force in her artistic creativity. The interest in Oriental mysticism in the European intellectual circles during the fin de siècle and the early twentieth century is well known. However, unlike the turn-of-the-century upper-class Parisians, Noailles did not have to turn to the mystic traditions of the Near East and the Middle East for a social distraction or a literary diversion. Born to Romanian and Greek parents, as she was growing up, the Eastern lifestyle, tradition, and culture existed in her surroundings as surely as their Western counterparts, constituting an integral part of her familial life. Undoubtedly, she had no need to formally acquire the Near Eastern and Middle Eastern characteristics of life and art, as she inherited them naturally from her family. Indeed, many of Noailles's personal views and literary inclinations mirror significant elements of Sufism and confirm that, for her, Sufism was a way of life as well as a source of inspiration for her art.

Born in Paris, evidently, Noailles was mindful of her French citizenship as much as she was aware of the Eastern ambiance of the immediate world in which she lived. She begins her autobiography, *Le livre de ma vie* [The Book of My Life], proudly declaring, "Je suis née à Paris" [I was born in Paris], and patriotically quoting Verlaine, "L'amour de la patrie est le premier amour" [The love of country is the first love] (11).[3] In the following pages of this book, however, she describes her parents' taste in interior decoration as inclining toward

---

[2] Anna de Noailles began writing a fourth novel, "Octave," as early as 1918, but she never completed it.

[3] Regarding Noailles's mixed ethnicity, Catherine Perry states: "Though born in France, Noailles remained a foreigner, a cosmopolitan by choice and by necessity" (*Persephone Unbound* 28).

Eastern fashions, which resulted in her own early tendency to adopt Oriental trends of living and thinking. From her parents' spacious, high-ceilinged home at 34 avenue Hoche in Paris to their summer chalet, la villa Bassaraba, at Amphion-des-Bains on the shore of Lake Léman (cf. 132), her family's lifestyle reflects the origin of the Eastern edge to Noailles's own taste in both her demeanor and decoration of various dwellings.

In 1902, Noailles was taking her turn to reveal her Orientalism by posing for photographers lying on her couch, "le 'Bain turc'" [the Turkish Bath] (Mignot-Ogliastri n.pag.), and in 1913, in her apartment at 40 rue Scheffer, she would receive journalists, as well as her guests, in Eastern style, stretched out on her bed in the garret, wearing a black silk robe strewn with golden sequins and a rough-cut amber necklace (cf. Broche 304). The penetrating quality of the Orient in her life and art was noticed by many who knew her. In 1897, at her marriage ceremony, the exotic aura she exuded inspired Marcel Proust to immortalize her in his novel, *Le côté de Guermantes* [The Guermantes Way], as the young princess of the Orient who was married to a cousin of Saint-Loup and known to have written poems as beautiful as those of Victor Hugo and Alfred de Vigny (cf. 124–25). In the same year, actress and novelist Simone Benda alluded to her as "'une petite princesse orientale'" [a little Oriental princess] (126). At a gathering in 1902, poet and art collector Robert de Montesquiou praised Noailles: "Elle a doré son génie aux splendeurs de l'Orient" [She has gilded her genius with the splendors of the East] (175). Publishing an interview with her in 1902, the periodical, *La vie heureuse* [The Happy Life], described her as "'une petite princesse byzantine'" [a little Byzantine princess] (183). After the war, observing Noailles's admiration for such men of politics as Briand, Barthou, and Clemenceau, Maurice Barrès famously said that Anna de Noailles was a princess of the Orient who had a high regard for the sultans, whose names now happened to be Waldeck-Rousseau, Clemenceau, Briand, or Caillaux (cf. 326).[4]

---

[4] Anna de Noailles met Maurice Barrès in 1896 (cf. Rouchefoucauld 18). Their intellectual and platonic relationship began in 1903 and stayed so for a long time before it turned into a sexual liaison; it ended with the death of Barrès in 1923. They did not speak to each other from 1909 to 1917. During this period, Barrès blamed Noailles for the death of his nephew, Charles Demange, who committed suicide out of unrequited love for Noailles (cf. Perry, *Persephone Unbound* 279).

Significantly, Barrès's shrewd comment reveals his keen perception of Anna de Noailles's sense of admiration and respect for powerful rulers and their impact on her perspective on life and relations with people. In her autobiography, the writer's first impressions of her mother, Rachel Musurus, correspond to her feeling of "respect envers un tissu bariolé, justement dénomé 'le châle du Sultan'" [respect for a colorful material appropriately called "the shawl of the Sultan"] (*Le livre de ma vie* 20). In the little girl's mind, this beautiful shawl, given to her mother by the Ottoman Sultan, was a symbol of the Sultan's grace and generosity, culminating in her lasting awe of men who were influential rulers.[5] When Noailles was nine years old, she lost her father.[6] Sadly, after her father's death, the little girl fell into such a deep distress that neither the puppet theatres nor the horse carts, nor the parti-colored candy stores with red-and-green barley candy sticks of the Champs-Élysées, nor other children could cheer her up. She felt that her father's death had killed the feeling of love in her (cf. 144). Evidently, her father remained in her memory as a powerful person, "aimé, certes, mais craint, devint l'objet de la dévotion de tous ceux qui l'avaient servi" [loved, certainly, but feared, and turned into an object of devotion for those who served him] (126).

After a long period of mourning, Noailles's mother, Rachel, decided to take her daughters, Anna and Hélène, and her son, Constantin, to Istanbul to visit her family. Her father, Musurus Pasha, ambassador of the Ottoman Sultan to England, had a palace built of blue marble in Arnavutköy on the Bosporus (cf. 146). All at once, the tidings of this trip brought back to the nine-year-old the cheer, happiness, and love of life that she had lost. Noailles remembers that at a time when the family was overwhelmed by sadness, suddenly, "la promesse du Bosphore fit renaître chez moi l'instinct du printemps, de la poésie, le délectable désir de plaire" [the promise of the Bosporus

---

[5] Sultan Abdülhamid II (1842–1918) was the thirty-fourth sultan of the Ottoman Empire. He ruled from 1876 to 1909. The territories of the Ottoman Empire (1299–1922) extended to the Middle East, Northern Africa, and Southeastern Europe. Its capital was Istanbul.

[6] Anna de Noailles's father, Grégoire Bassaraba de Brancovan, was a descendant of Constantin Brancovan II, hereditary prince of the Holy Roman Empire, who was married to Maria de Pospesci.

For the ancestral lines of Noailles's parents, see "Annexe 1: Le Côté de Bucarest" (411–13) and "Annexe 2: Le Côté de Musurus" (414–15) in François Broche's *Anna de Noailles: Un mystère en pleine lumière*.

revived in me the instinct of spring, of poetry, and a delightful desire to please] (147). Upon arriving by sea at the immense port of Galata in Istanbul, Rachel, proud of her Cretan blood and attachment to the city of her birth, called her children to the deck and told them the story of the night, on her honeymoon, during which she visited Sultan Abdülhamid's palace, where she gave him a concert, and in return the Sultan, himself an eminent musician, rewarded her with a dazzling diadem and a precious shawl (cf. 155–56).[7] To the little girl, the Bosporus, invoking the magnificent Sultan whose empire her maternal grandfather had served and whose splendid gift her mother possessed, restored the life of splendor and the feeling of love she had lost with her father. Thus, she was urged to please this liberator: "A qui voulais-je plaire? Au Bosphore" [Whom did I want to please? The Bosporus] (147). Undeniably, as she reveals in her poem, "Constantinople," Noailles's soul was awakened to artistic creativity during her visit to Istanbul, her mother's native city, where Sufism formed the essence of Ottoman intellectual life and literature:

> Je me souviens d'un soir aux Eaux-Douces d'Asie,
>> Soir si traînant, si mou,
> Que déjà, comme un chaud serpent, la Poésie
>> S'enroulait à mon cou.

> [I remember an evening at the Sweet Waters of Asia,[8]
>> Evening so lingering, so listless,
> That already, like a fiery snake, Poetry
>> Coiled around my throat.]
>>> ("Constantinople" 5–8)[9]

---

[7] Ayşe Osmanoğlu, writing about her father's love of music in *Babam Abdülhamid* [My Father Abdülhamid], states that her father had pianos imported from Europe and piano instructors hired from France and Italy for herself and her brothers. Osmanoğlu mentions that Sultan Abdülhamid encouraged his children, and even instructed them himself, to play the piano and other instruments (cf. "Babamın Musikiye Merakı" [My Father's Interest in Music] 25–26).

[8] Les Eaux-Douces (Tatlısu) is a district in the Bosporus.

The fact that some of Noailles's poems in *Les vivants et les morts* [The Living and the Dead] were inspired during her stay in Istanbul is confirmed in Barrès's *Correspondance*. On 19 July 1907, Noailles wrote to Barrès that the fire imagery in "Si vous parliez, Seigneur ..." [If You Spoke, Lord ...] originated during her visit to Istanbul, watching at night the flames from burning Turkish villages on the hills of the Bosporus (cf. 608; cf. Perry, *Persephone Unbound* 339).

[9] In 1888, Noailles wrote the poem, "Idylle" [Idyll], with the subtitle, "La Muse et L'Enfant" [The Muse and the Child], in which she combined her mother's birth place,

It is almost uncanny that none of Noailles's critics or biographers or even the writer herself mentions that she was exposed to the traits of Sufism in Istanbul. In *Le livre de ma vie*, Noailles writes about the impact of the natural beauty of the Bosporus and the Eastern atmos-

---

"l'Orient" [the East], with her mother's name, "Rachel," as divine music, both of which elevated her mother to the level of a demi-god. At the end of the poem, Noailles writes:

> *Mon art est seviteur du sien.*

> [*My art is a servant of hers.*]
> (qtd. in Mignot-Ogliastri 54–55)

For the Sufi poet Jalaluddin Rumi's esteem for the superiority of music over words as a stimulation for meditation, see Friedlander and Uzel, *The Whirling Dervishes*, 131; and for the music, musicians, and instruments of the whirling dervishes, see 127–54 in this book.

For the relationship between Sufism and music, see Seyyed Hossein Nasr, "The Influence of Sufism on Traditional Persian Music."

Annemarie Schimmel posits that "the greatest attraction in Rumi's lyrics is certainly his stress on rhythm in his poetry. Since he initiated the Order of the Whirling Dervishes, it is only natural that his poetry should have been created out of a feeling of music and rhythm" (*Sufi Literature: Special Paper* 6).

Clearly, for Noailles, music had an ecclesiastical mystery that functioned as a link between the worldly and the otherworldly:

> Et cependant c'est vous, Musique, âme excessive,
> Dont le pouvoir s'affirme au-dessus, au-dessous
> De ce que l'homme exhale en syllabes pensives,
> Et seul votre mystère impérieux absout
> L'univers haïssable et sa faute native …

> [And nevertheless it is you, Music, excessive soul,
> Whose power asserts itself above and below
> What man exhales in thoughtful syllables,
> And your compelling mystery alone absolves
> The loathsome universe and its native fault …]
> ("J'ai bien servi le dieu" [I Served God Well] 5–9)

Catherine Perry writes that Barrès often compared Noailles's poetry with music, and as he became older, he used religious imagery to suggest the spiritual quality of her work (cf. *Persephone Unbound* 287). Perry links the religious imagery, with which Barrès identified, to John the Baptist and the harmony, which Noailles created in her poetry, to Schopenhauer's perception of harmony. However, Noailles's association of music with her mother's origin in the Orient suggests that the source of some of the harmony she creates in her poetry is hidden in the Orient.

phere of the city of Istanbul on her senses. She remembers her grandfather's palace on the Bosporus adorned with heavenly trees and
flowers (cf. 163) as creating the most beautiful scenery; her boat out-
ings to Eaux-Douces (Tatlısu); sunset promenades to Bebek; and ex-
cursions to the grand bazaar (Kapalıçarşı), full of jewelry, tobacco,
silk (cf. 164–65).[10] It would be a stretch of the imagination to claim
that, during her three-month-long sojourn in Istanbul, the nine-year-
old Anna instantaneously turned into a mystic poet. Apparently, however, at this time, her admiration for this enchanting city and the
beauty of the Bosporus, reinforced by her exposure to the Eastern elements in her environment in Paris, reached a certain level of exalta-
tion that made Eastern mysticism the source of her inspiration.[11] She
proclaims in her poem the "need" to stay permanently in this artisti-
cally stimulating ambiance, which enabled her to write:

> Peut-être que ma longue et profonde tristesse
> > Qui va priant, criant,
> N'est que ce dur besoin, qui m'afflige et m'oppresse,
> > De vivre en Orient!
>
> [Perhaps my long and profound sorrow
> > Which will pray and cry,
> Is only this unyielding need, afflicting and oppressing me,
> > To live in the Orient!] ("Constantinople" 97–100)

Meanwhile, in Turkey, Sufism was a prominent philosophy influ-
encing the literary and intellectual lives of the people, and its impact
was felt most remarkably in the district of Üsküdar, not far from
Musurus Pasha's palace in Arnavutköy. The geographical position
and the natural beauty of Üsküdar made this district a preferred abode
for Sufi philosophers and poets, who could comprehend nature with a

---

[10] The short essay, "Les Nuits de Turquie" [The Turkish Nights], published in *Exacti-
tude*s [Exactitudes] (105–09) and in *De la rive d'Europe à la rive d'Asie* [From the
Shore of Europe to the Shore of Asia] (7–11) encapsulates the lasting impression that
her three-month-long stay in the Bosporus left on Noailles.

[11] Although, in Noailles's œuvre, the images of the East appear to be of Egypt, Italy,
and Spain, most of these images resulted from the influence of the Eastern atmosphere of Istanbul. Referring to Noailles's trip to this city as a child, Elisabeth
Higonnet-Dugua confirms: "Ce sera le premier et dernier contact concret d'Anna
avec l'Orient, qui inspirera plus tard de nombreux poèmes et proses" [This will be the
first and last tangible contact of Anna with the East, which will be an inspiration for
many poems and prose much later] (19).

divine sensibility and define it as the reflection of the absolute truth, giving Üsküdar a "mystic atmosphere" (cf. Ceylan 122). Moreover, particularly Sultan Abdülhamid, among the Ottoman sultans, was in favor of Sufi philosophy, and in 1891 he donated one thousand Turkish liras to repair the Rumi monastery in Konya (cf. Moyne 76).[12] Noailles's grandfather, Musurus Pasha, was an official of the Ottoman Court and he moved comfortably in Sultan Abdülhamid's close circle so much so that his daughter, Rachel, as noted, entertained the Sultan with her musical talents. Noailles's uncle, Paul Musurus, was a poet and artist. It is inconceivable that the writer's grandfather and uncle, members of an intellectual elite who held important social positions, would have been oblivious to the contemporary cultural, intellectual, and literary currents in the city. Contrary to this seeming silence, however, Noailles's Istanbul relatives were, in fact, immersed in Sufi philosophy. In her autobiography, Noailles vents her frustration about being unable to join, because of her illness, a group of her uncles, wearing fezzes and frock coats, and her exulted aunts, dressed in Parisian style, to go to a sacred seance of "whirling dervishes" (cf. *Le livre de ma vie* 108).[13] The "dervishe" [dervish] would later add a

---

[12] Mevlânâ Celâlleddin Muhammed Rumi (Mawlana Jalaluddin Rumi) was born on September 30, 1207, in Balkh (Afghanistan) and died on December 17, 1273, in Konya (Turkey). He was a mystic and Sufi poet whose importance and influence transcended the Middle East. His most well-known work is *Mesnevi* (*Mathnawî*), which was written in six volumes in twelve years. Although Rumi initiated the *sema* [whirling dance] and founded the Mevlevi Sufi Order, after his death, his son Sultan Veled became the leader of the dervishes and introduced them to the turning (whirling) ceremony in honor of his father. Sultan Veled's son, Ulu Arif Çelebi (Chelebi), established the organization of the Mevlevi Sufi Order. The Mevlevi *tekke* (place where Sufis are trained and where they meet) in Konya prospered as a school of art and culture through many centuries (cf. Friedlander and Uzel 62).

For Rumi's life, see Schimmel, *Rumi's World: The Life and Work of the Great Sufi Poet*; and for Rumi's work, see Schimmel, *The Triumphal Sun: A Study of the Works of Jalāloddin Rumi*.

[13] The whirling dance, also known as *sema* (which means "to hear and to listen" in Arabic), for Sufis, signifies reaching a high level of emotion, excitement, pleasure, and inspiration in the accompaniment of music or divine hymns (cf. Shafii 104). It is also known as the *zikr* in motion (*zikr* or *dhikr*: awareness of God by repetition of divine names).

Harry G. Allard mentions a "cyclic pattern" in Noailles's novels, *La nouvelle espérance* [The New Hope], *Le visage émerveillé* [The Marveling Face], and *La domination* [Domination], in which plots, characters, and moods coincide with the four seasons (cf. 15–36). I believe that this format is reminiscent of the whirling through

mystic image to the serene but sensuous atmosphere of her poem, "Paysage Persan" [Persian Scenery], in her 1925 collection, *Les éblouissements* [The Dazzling Lights]:

> Un jet d'eau, parmi des tulipes,
> Tremble comme un arbuste frais;
> Un dervishe fume sa pipe
> Près d'un mur jaune et d'un cyprès.
>
> [A gush of water, among the tulips,
> Trembles like a cool shrub;

---

which dervishes attain perfection by *zikr*, repetition of divine names. Especially the pattern, Allard discerns with the four seasons of the year as well as the divisions of the day (cf. 26), recalls the "eternal present" that Rumi mentions, where "the past and the future and time without beginning and time without end do not exist" ("The Mouse and the Frog," Book VI: 408). Quoting Rumi, John A. Moyne writes: "When you become naught / in the light of God, / past, present, and future vanish" (72).

Annemarie Schimmel states that dance with religious edification was licit as early as the ninth century, and for Rumi "the whirling movement was an expression of his enraptured interior state which he, in most cases, could not control" (*The Triumphal Sun* 217). Before the dance was institutionalized in the Mevlevi Order, Rumi whirled alone or with a partner (cf. 217).

Dance had a spiritual value for the poet Henri Franck, who was Noailles's close friend from 1907 until his death in 1912: "[D]ance as both prayer and poetry becomes the means to replenish the space left void by the disappearance of God …:

> Si l'arche est vide où tu pensais trouver la loi,
> Rien n'est réel que ta danse:
> Puisqu'elle n'a pas d'objet elle est impérissable.
> Danse pour le désert et danse pour l'espace
> Comme un prophète dans le sable
> Danse dans l'éternel silence
> Avec la gravité d'un roi.

[If the ark, where you searched for the law, is empty, nothing but your dance is real: having no object it is imperishable. Dance for the desert and dance for the void like a prophet in the sands, dance in the eternal silence with the solemnity of a king.] (*La Danse devant l'Arche*; in Higonnet-Dugua, *Anna de Noailles*, 143)" (Perry, *Persephone Unbound* 334, n 47). Especially significant here is the connection of the prophet to the East with the sand, which is the natural setting of the Prophet of Islam, whose native country, Arabia, is in the desert.

The Persian word *darwish* (*derviş* in Turkish) literally means the sill of the door. It also means poor (cf. Gölpınarlı 24), one who is indifferent to being wealthy. Dervish is "the Sufi who is the one who is at the door to enlightenment" (Friedlander and Uzel 15).

A dervish smokes his pipe
Near a yellow wall and a cypress.] (1–4)

Although Noailles's association with Sufism is seldom mentioned
in her autobiography, her modest stance in her personal and artistic
life, her mixed heritage, and her equal allegiance to the traditions of
the East and the West inevitably brought her position close to that of
the Sufis. Noailles states: "Mais oui, je suis avec ceux qui veulent
pour la masse de tous les hommes plus d'équité et plus de bonheur"
[Of course, I am with those who want for the masses of all people
more equality and more happiness] (qtd. in Broche 190). Furthermore,
the writer's declaration to André Lang that she wanted to reach all the
people, the old, the young, and the children (cf. 366 note), strikingly
recalls the widely renowned Sufi poet Rumi's plain style and common
language with which he popularized Sufism (cf. Moyne 27). According to Abdülbâki Gölpınarlı, Rumi wrote in Persian, Arabic, Greek,
and Turkish, and he always used vernacular to reach the common
people, avoiding the jargon of the philosophical theories (cf. 200).
Likewise, Noailles's unbiased attitude toward people transcended ethnic and national differences as well as class considerations. Claude
Mignot-Ogliastri writes that for Anna de Noailles to be French,
Greek, or Persian was not contradictory: she searched ubiquity in
space and time (cf. 225). This existence is analogous to that of the
Sufis, identified by them as the "union with God": "When an attempt
is made to define the state of union [with God] closely, the most that
can be done is to divest it of all the limitations which condition existence. Such limitations have only a sort of 'negative reality,' whereas
in the state of union only positive reality, i.e., God, remains" (Chittick
76). According to scholars Arasteh and Sheikh, one of the dreams of
the Sufis, as voiced by Rumi, was to bring an ecumenical parity to all
religions by closing the mental differences that fed the needs of Muslim, Jewish, and Christian communities. One aspect of Sufi education
centers on this "ideal of healing" (cf. 43). In a poem beginning with
"What is to be done," Rumi says:

What is to be done, O Moslems? for I do not recognise
    myself.
I am neither Christian, nor Jew, nor Gabr, nor Moslem.
I am not of the East, nor of the West, nor of the land,
    nor of the sea;
I am not of Nature's mint, nor of the circling heavens.

. . . .
My place is the Placeless, my trace is the Traceless;
'Tis neither body nor soul, for I belong to the soul of the
        Beloved. (XXXI. "What is to be done" 1–6, 17–19)

As Tama Lea Engelking posits, some contemporary critics reduced Noailles's poetic vision to a "sensual and narcissistic appreciation of nature, coupled by a fear of death," and herself to "an
'inspired' rather than an intellectual writer" (102). Paradoxically,
however, in expressing their unfavorable opinions of Noailles's work,
these critics inadvertently revealed the foremost attributes that rendered her a disciple of the Sufis and her work a representative of Sufi
philosophy. Clearly, the knowledge of Sufi traditions provided the
writer with a method of contemplation of an inward search for her
self. In all likelihood, Noailles was familiar with Sa'd ud din Mahmud
Shabistari's lines, "You are the kernel of the world in the midst there-
of, / Know yourself that you are the world's soul" ("Thoughts on
Souls" Rule IV: 270–71), and Rumi's saying, "There is nothing outside you in the universe, / seek within yourself for whatever you desire" (qtd. in Moyne 14). Nevertheless, being a "mystic without God,"
she pursued a quest that had no inclination toward a religious faith.[14]
Inattentively reading the different influences and nuances of expressions in Noailles's poems addressed to God in her collection *Les vivants et les morts* [The Living and the Dead], Francis Jammes, in a
letter of July 11, 1913, to the writer, blamed her for producing
"d'inconscients blasphemes" [unconscious blasphemies] (Higonnet-
Dugua 241).[15] Concerning similar poems, François Mauriac con-

---

[14] Noailles was a confirmed atheist. She declared to Jean Cocteau her lack of faith in
the concept of God: "'Je suis une mystique sans Dieu'" [I am a mystic without God]
(Mugnier 470; qtd. in Broche 385). In her apartment at 40 rue Scheffer, "'Du reste,
c'est simple, lui [Jean Cocteau] crie-t-elle une fois, si Dieu existe, je serais la première à en être avertie!'" [For the rest, it is simple, she cried out loud once to him
[Jean Cocteau], if God exists, I would be the first person to be informed!] (Cocteau
20; qtd. in Broche 385; Allard 142).
[15] In *Persephone Unbound*, Catherine Perry mentions critics, such as Nicolas Ségur,
who "admired her work" but criticized it for being dominated by "sex—love, sensuality, and fear" (23), and José Ortega y Gasset, who criticized the lyric quality of her
work as private and belonging "to the intimacy of the boudoir rather than the public
forum" (23).
  For anyone, who is uninformed about the impact of Sufi philosophy on Noailles's
life and art, especially during her stay in Istanbul, her poems addressed to God would
seem contradictory to her statement about her lack of faith in God:

demned her with charges of narcissism: "'She remained incurably herself, blinded by her own light' (*Les Nouvelles Littéraires* [6 May 1933]: 1)" (cf. Perry, *Persephone Unbound* 333, n 45). It is possible that Noailles was taking Rumi's advice, "Make a journey out of self into self, O master, / For by such a journey earth becomes a quarry of gold" (XXVII. "If a tree might move" 18–19), as explained by Chittick, "Man must know himself in order that he can escape from himself; all other knowledge is worthless" (98). Overlooking the influence of the Sufi school of thought on Noailles's art, critics were confounded by her expressions, such as "C'est toujours soi qu'on cherche en croyant qu'on s'evade" [It is always for ourselves we are searching when we think we escape] ("Mon Dieu, je ne sais rien …" [My God, I Know Nothing …] 73). In the Sufis' view, only internal knowledge could lead to the path of truth. Rumi asserts: "Every proof (that is) without (a spiritual) result and effect is / vain: consider the (final) result of thyself!"("The Sage and the Peacock" Book V: 567). According to Rumi's perspective, knowledge in the usual sense is useless. He explains that "the great scholars of the age split hairs on all manner of sciences. They know perfectly and have a complete comprehension of those other matters which do not concern them. But as for what is truly of moment and touches a man more closely than all else, namely his own self, this your great scholar does not know" (*Discourses* 30). Unfortunately, during her lifetime, some of

---

> – Ah! puisque vous n'étiez, Dieu des cieux enivrés,
> Qu'un Sultan amoureux des jardins et des arbres,
> Qui, la nuit, contemplez les bleus poissons nacrés
> Que la lune nourrit dans son bassin de marbre,
>
> [– Ah! since you, the God of intoxicated spirits,
> Are only a Sultan in love with gardens and trees,
> Who, at night, contemplate the blue mother of pearl fish
> Which the moon nourishes in his marble pool,]
>   ("O Dieu mystérieux …" [O Mysterious God …] 33–36)

In this poem, from *Les vivants et les morts*, the association of God with the Sultan and the intoxicated spirits, of perhaps the whirling dervishes, is an excellent example of Noailles's adaptation of the Sufi concept of "being in the presence of God in this world," which will be discussed in this article. As its relation to the Sultan denotes, the term "God" refers to the poet's source of inspiration, which at this time of her life happened to be the mystic atmosphere of Istanbul, the city of the Sultan.
  For the Sufi concept of God, see Moyne 21–29; Chittick 71–99.

Noailles's critics underestimated the importance of her Eastern heritage and its impact on her art and mistakenly labeled her looking inward as narcissism.

The preface Noailles wrote for the Iranian poet Saâdi's book, *Le
jardin des roses* [The Rose Garden], in 1912, is a powerful expression
of her admiration for Sufi literature, and it is the only concrete evidence of her preoccupation in her art with Sufi lore.[16] Even so, this
prologue is an inadequate edict to convey the decisive importance of
Sufism in her life and art. Before the writer read the works of such
Sufi philosophers as Saâdi and Rumi, she had been exposed solely to
similar physical and intellectual environments to those that had inspired these poets to conceive a mystic tradition, but she lacked a vehicle to express her intense emotions as emphatically as these poets
did. Following the Sufis' direction, she turned inward and discovered
the wisdom in her heart. As a result, she learned to employ her emotions in making sense of her immediate universe. Then, throughout
her life, the inward peregrination of the Sufi philosophers became a
resource for her to search deeper in her heart and to understand better
her emotions. Her discipleship reveals not only an inadvertent sharing
of the depth of the Sufis' connection with the human and divine spirit
but also a conscious emulation of their work. The nonpareil religious
undertones in Noailles's work disclose her deft use of some of the
esoteric concepts of Sufi mysticism as tropes to evoke her own particular mystic literary universe. Catherine Perry's observation regarding
how Noailles structured her artistic universe on the frames of thought
she appropriated from different worlds sounds just as right for
Noailles's rapport with Sufi philosophy: "While Noailles may have
drawn some authority as a reflective writer from these philosophers,
she also adapted and transformed their thought to suit her own ends"
(*Persephone Unbound* 24).[17] Considering the numerous volumes of

---

[16] Noailles wrote a preface to the 1912 edition of Saâdi's *Le jardin des roses* [The
Rose Garden]. Trans. Franz Toussaint. Paris: L'Édition d'Art H. Piazza, 1912. The
preface is also published in *De la rive d'Europe à la rive d'Asie* under the title "Saâdi
et le jardin des roses" [Saâdi and the Rose Garden] (79–103).

[17] Here the philosophers to whom Catherine Perry refers are Arthur Schopenhauer
and Friedrich Nietzsche. Although Perry convincingly demonstrates the influence of
these philosophers on the specific themes in Noailles's poetry, she still cautions her
reader: "Although Noailles' work manifests the influence of Schopenhauer and Nietzsche, one should keep in mind that she interpreted the ideas of these philosophers
through the transformative medium of her own poetic vocabulary" (*Persephone Un-*

bound 35). At the turn of the twentieth century, in Europe, these two philosophers' thoughts were very much in vogue, and in France, many writers were coming under the influence of their ideas. Certainly, Noailles must have been no exception. However, many writers were reading the work of Eastern philosophers as well. On writing about Stoicism as the common influence on both Nietzsche and Abū Yūsuf Ya 'qūb ibn Işhaq al-Kindī, Peter S. Groff demonstrates the convergence of Greek and Islamic ideas on the theme of *amor fati*. Quoting Nietzsche in *Ecce Homo*, Perry writes: "'My formula for greatness in a human being is *amor fati*: that one wants nothing to be different, not forward, not backward, not in all eternity. Not merely bear what is necessary, still less conceal it—all idealism is mendaciousness in the face of what is necessary—but *love* it' (*EH,* 258)" (55). This idea of accepting, affirming, and celebrating necessity also exists in al-Kindī's thinking: "In good Stoic fashion, al-Kindī admonishes us to be consistent in the way we think about the world. We should not expect things to be as we would like them to be; rather, we should accept things as they are and adjust our desires accordingly" (Groff 145). Groff also points out that some of the vocabulary that al-Kindī used, such as *tarbiya* (to "train someone") and *adab* ("appropriate conduct") "came to be used as technical terms in Sūfism" (166). Although Groff reminds his readers that "these notions should not be seen as the exclusive property of Sūfism" (166), it is clear that one may consider al-Kindī as a prototype Sufi who had been writing before this philosophy was institutionalized under Sufism.

Although Catherine Perry admits that Noailles "inherit[ed] a variety of traditions, [and] she adapted them to her own use and constructed from them a distinctive subjectivity" (*Persephone Unbound* 20), she traces only a Western pedigree of influence on Noailles's poetry. See, for instance, her reading of Noailles's poem, "Nature que je sers …" [Nature Which I Serve …], in *Les éblouissements*, where the female speaker's "simultaneous acceptance and affirmation of life as it is given" ("In the Wake of Decadence" 98), is tied to Nietzsche's "heroic notion of *amor fati*" (98). However, it is equally likely that Noailles might have come across *amor fati* as a basic component of Stoicism in Eastern ethics. One of Noailles's favorite philosophers was Epictetus, and she always kept his *Discourses* next to her bed (cf. Allard 154; cf. Mignot-Ogliastri 402, n 12). In discovering Stoic philosophy as a common source for both Nietzsche and al-Kindī, Peter S. Groff shows Epictetus's *Discourses* as a reference for both writers. See also Groff (25) for Nietzsche's and al-Kindī's familiarity with Stoic philosophy.

In discussing the origins of Sufism, John A. Moyne posits that there are several arguments on the subject: one claiming that it originated during the pre-Islamic era, influenced by Indo-Iranian (Zoroastrian/Vendanta) dogma, and another stating that, later, it was affected by Hellenic and Roman sources, as well as Islam, Christianity, Buddhism and other creeds (cf. 31–39). Moyne explains that the term "*Sufi* is derived from the Arabic *suf* 'wool,' and presumably refers to the coarse woolen garments of the early Muslim ascetics" (21). Ömür Ceylan agrees that Sufi philosophy has many common traits and associations with other philosophies that came before it, and he believes that it would be appropriate to consider Sufi activities in different historical and geographical territories under their local circumstances (cf. 6–7). William A. Chittick concedes to this contention: "From a certain point of view there has indeed been borrowing of forms of doctrinal expression from other traditions and a great

poetry and prose that the leading Sufi writers and Noailles produced, it is impossible to include in this essay all the Sufi convictions that equipped Noailles with a spiritual vision through which she enriched her artistic universe with a mystic dimension. However, it is possible to focus on a few central figures of speech that establish the Orientalism of Anna de Noailles.[18]

Apparently, as Noailles's knowledge of Sufi philosophy was evolving, finding her heart capable of more knowledge and wisdom, she shifted the faculty of her cognizance of the world, both inside and outside herself, from the realm of the mind and the intellect to that of the emotions and the heart. Sufis accept that the true nature of the relationship between God and the world can be discovered only through gnosis—the intuitive apprehension of spiritual truths revealed to them in their hearts—the sole dwelling of knowledge proper to created beings: "To know the heart in its inmost essence is to know God" (Chittick 86).[19] Noailles's concern about such Sufi concepts as heart and love in her life and her emphasis on them in her art coincide with this particular interpretation of gnosis in Sufi philosophy. According

---

amount of development" (15). However, he warns the reader that "to conclude from this in the manner of many scholars that Sufism gradually came into being under the influence of a foreign tradition or from a hodgepodge of borrowed doctrine is to completely misunderstand its nature" (15–16). He concludes: "[I]n essence it is a metaphysics and means of spiritual realization derived of necessity from the Islamic revelation itself" (16). According to Annemarie Schimmel, too, "[i]f we go back to the beginnings of Sufism, we see that this movement grew out of the teachings of the Koran" (*Sufi Literature: Special Paper* 1). Schimmel writes that "Sufism developed during the ninth century almost everywhere in the Muslim world" (2).

For the origins of Sufism, see Reynold A. Nicholson, *The Mystics of Islam*; and Arthur J. Arberry, *Sufism: An Account of the Mystics of Islam*.

[18] It is too obvious that such images as the sun, fire, and gardens in Noailles's poetry and prose are loaded with mystic significance and they were created with the direct influence of the Sufi mysticism of Saâdi and Rumi. For Rumi's imagery, see Schimmel, *The Triumphal Sun* (59–222).

[19] The Sufi concept of *irfān*, "gnosis," which means "[w]isdom made up of Knowledge and Sanctity.... the higher Knowledge which comes of intuition by the Intellect" (Palmer 8), is felt in the heart.

For the significance of the heart in replacing the role of the intellect, see Kemal Sayar's "Geçmişin Bilgeliği Bugünün Psikoterapileriyle Buluşabilir mi? Sufi Psikolojisi Örneği" [Is It Possible for Earlier Knowledge to Meet Present Psychotherapies? An Example of Sufi Psychology] in *Sufi Psikolojisi* [Sufi Psychology] (15–18).

For the relationships among the heart, spirit, and intuition, see İsmail Yakıt's *Batı Düşüncesi ve Mevlâna* [Western Thought and Mawlana] (26–38).

to Sufi tenets, especially in Rumi's view, "Man should never be satisfied to 'know' with the feeble powers of his reason. Rather, he should enter the Path in order to be delivered from the limitations of reason and attain to gnosis" (Chittick 95). The Persian poet of mysticism, Abdur Rahman Jami, confirms: "One must become educated by one's heart to the things which cannot be understood intellectually" (Friedlander and Uzel 24). Chittick also affirms that "gnosis is 'existential' rather than purely mental" (11).

In her novel, *La nouvelle espérance* [The New Hope], Noailles manipulated the esoteric meanings of the heart and love, engaged in the pursuit of God in Sufi philosophy, to create her own special literary lexicon, and she used it in her exploration of the meaning of heart and love. The heart of her heroine-in-love, Sabine de Fontenay, possesses physical attributes. Significantly, Sabine's heart as a tangible object full of perceptible blood debunks the conventional image of the inventive heart replete with imperceptible emotions. For Pierre Valence, whose love Sabine mistakenly believes she possesses, it is hard to comprehend her preoccupation with "the heart":

> – Vouz aimez beaucoup le mot "cœur"?
> – Oh oui! avouait-elle, n'est-ce pas, c'est le mot charnel et
>   sensible, le mot rond dans lequel il y a le sang?
> Et les mouvements de ses mains modelaient ses phrases.
>
> [– You like very much the word "heart"?
>   – Oh yes! she admitted, isn't it, it is a carnal and
>   sensible word, a round word in which there is blood?
> And the movements of her hands shaped her phrases.] (138)

Sabine's hands, gesturing the physical shape of the heart, vividly suggest the impressionistic image of the heart in its earthly existence as a substantial and autonomous part of the flesh and body. The roundness of Sabine's heart denotes a finished perfection in itself. Because of this heart's concreteness, its function is uniquely different from that of its conventional predecessors. Sabine's heart, contrary to its assumed role as the abode of ethereal emotions, constitutes a vessel of physicality and sensual liveliness. Her vision of the heart underscores the importance of the senses over the intellect and discerns the heart as the place of wisdom and knowledge of love. As a singled-out object, this heart is independent of the rest of the body and it displaces rational insightfulness from the mind to the heart. Instead of passive feelings, which are customarily the only substance of the heart in love, the blood in this heroine's heart connotes active cerebral capabilities; her heart is not only capable of feeling but also of analyzing the love it contains. For Pierre, whose emotional quotient is limited to the traditional meaning of love, Sabine's esoteric concept of the "heart" is unfathomable: "[I]l ne cherchait pas à savoir ce qu'elle pensait dans le moment ... il l'avait du fond de son cœur oublié" [[H]e did not try to know what she was thinking at that moment ... he had at the bottom of his heart forgotten her] (138).

Unlike the love in the hearts of Sufi mystics, which guides them to the knowledge and presence of God, however, the love in the hearts of Noailles's poetic personae or fictional characters leads them to both spiritual and emotional cul-de-sacs. For God, who stands for the absolute truth in Sufi philosophy, is substituted by love in Noailles's œuvre. Although Rumi's verses almost always reveal his stimulation by the divine love of God and constantly manifest his aspiration to be one with God, those of Noailles often evoke her desire for an ideal love, which is fashioned by her own interpretation of the mystic order of Sufism and her unique application of Sufi philosophy to her life and art. This love is an end in itself, and it exists neither for a deity nor for another person but only for its own sake. After being deserted by Philippe, her lover, Sabine writes to him: "Ce n'est pas vous que j'aime; j'aime aimer comme je vous aime" [It is not you whom I love; I love to love as I love you] (285). Although at no time did Noailles admit a belief in God, she never showed contrary feelings toward a deity. In fact, she used the concept of God as a means by which to express the extent of power in her emotions or in her heart, as she does in addressing God in her poem "Mon Dieu, je ne sais rien ...": "Votre amour et le mien jamais ne rétrogradent, / Et je m'entoure enfin de mon cœur infini" [Your love and mine are never reactionary, / And finally I surround myself with my infinite heart] (75–76). In *La nouvelle espérance*, Noailles's analysis of love benefits from the double entendre of gnosis. For Sufis, gnosis also means the spiritual realization of the full potentialities of the human state, and it is deemed tantamount to love. They believe that "love is the most direct reflection in this world, or the truest 'symbol' in the traditional sense, of the joy and beatitude of the spiritual world" (Chittick 10–11).

If one takes Noailles to be an artist who simply conveys in her art her emotions enraptured by nature, one may miss the spiritual undertones of her artistic creativity. Noticeably, in some of Noailles's work, nature reveals erotic love. In nature, her poetic personae and fictional characters experience sexual pleasure in love. In the poem, "Azur" [Azure], in her collection *Les éblouissements*, the poet creates a dramatic situation to delineate in nature's terms the actual lovemaking of a couple. As an ardent practitioner of the Sufi tradition in her art, Noailles never abstained from blending the sexual with the spiritual in conveying her strong feelings about nature. In the poem, the speaker describes her sexual pleasure in coupling with a male partner represented by different elements of nature. In this poem of playful erotism, nature's fecundity is depicted with spiritual connotations. In the beginning, the poet's presentation of the morning, "[c]omme un *sublime* fruit qu'on a de loin lancé" [as a *majestic* fruit thrown from afar] (1; emphasis added), foreshadows the possibility of awe-inspiring creation, the nearly certain outcome of the sexual act in the poem. It is this spiritual quality of "[l]a matinée avec son ineffable extase" [the morning with its ineffable ecstasy] (2) that arouses the speaker's heart, who assumes a female personality in her enjoyment, with the "morning," of coitus, as shown by the flow of her female fluids: "Sur mon cœur enivré tombe, s'abat, s'écrase, / Et mon plaisir jaillit comme un lac insensé!" [On my inebriate heart falls, crashes, presses, / And my pleasure gushes forth like an insane lake!] (3–4). Significantly, the pleasure is felt in the speaker's heart, Sufis' lieu for knowledge of God. For Noailles's poetic persona, however, the heart is the place for the cognition of love, where its power is not only felt but also understood. Consequently, in the second stanza, the image of the male partner, as morning, is replaced by the sky, and the "pulpe" [pulp] of the sky symbolizes the male sexual organ: "– O pulpe lumineuse et moite du ciel tendre" [– O sweaty and luminous pulp of the tender sky] (5). Interestingly, Noailles's portrayal of the progenitor with "pulpe" [pulp] (5) and the progeny with "fruit" (1), each as a peculiar synecdoche for morning, reveals the speaker's perception of the morning, as a part of nature, the source of the endless continuity of the universe "sans fin et sans bord" [without end and without boundary] (7). Subsequently, in the last stanza, the male, who has already come out of a "sweaty" climax, is passive; whereas the speaker is still unfulfilled and desires more sex:

Coulez, roulez en moi, détournez dans mon corps
Tout ce qui n'est pas vous, prenez toute la place!
Déjà ce flot d'argent m'étouffe, me terrasse,
Je meurs, venez encor, azur! venez encor …

[Flow, roll in me, push aside in my body
All that is not you, fill all the space!
Already that silver flood suffocates and shatters me,
I vanish, come again, azure! Come again …] (9–12)

The ellipsis at the end portrays the over-familiar sexual insatiability of the female, while the male is reposed after his passion is consumed. Throughout this poem, it is noticeable that the male partner, represented by nature symbols, is free from nature's binary opposite, culture or society, and the lovemaking and the ensuing pleasure occur in the heart, and the natural inevitability of both partners' sexuality is felt, comprehended, and manifested through the heart. Demonstratively, nature inspires Noailles with a spiritual sensibility and a sexual sensation through which to create her art.

Anyone who detects a fear of death or a wish for death in such conceptions as "essential self," "annihilation of self," or "die before you die" in Noailles's art may be misreading her philosophical outlook on love. In some of her work, Noailles uses the Sufi tenet of "becoming one with God," depicted by these terms, to illustrate her discernment of the difference between "self-love" and "true love." In Sufi philosophy, humans have to follow a long and hard path to achieve "perfect or universal existence," in which the possibility of union with God exists. The first step on the path is *fanā*, "annihilation of self," which evolves from the "no" of the *Shahādah*:[20] "'There is *no* god but God,' there is *no* reality but the Reality. Man's self-existence is not real, since he is not God; therefore the illusion that it is real must be annihilated" (Chittick 71). The next step is *baqā*, "subsistence in God," which is taken from the "but" of the *Shahādah*: "'There is no reality *but* the Reality.' Since God alone is real, man's real Self is God. Man attains to Reality only by passing away from his illusory self and subsiding in his real Self" (71). Sufis believe that humans can achieve this state in this life, if they are able to annihilate their false selves and reach their essential nature, which is their total reality derived from God: "[I]t is man's individual self that through

---

[20] *Shahādah*: There is no God but God.

the spiritual method must be transformed in order for man to reassume his rightful place in the Universe" (92).

In Noailles's art, expressions of nihilism by death appear to be contrary to the Sufi notion of *fanā*, "naught" (Moyne 23) or nothingness, expressed by *Mathnawi*'s speaker, who celebrates the perishing of the self in God and being "naught":[21]

> The beloved said, "Thou hast done all this, yet open thine
> ear wide and apprehend well;
> For thou hast not done what is the root of the root of love
> and fealty: this that thou hast done is (only) the branches."
> The lover said to her, "Tell me, what is that root?" She
> said, "The root thereof is to die and be naught.
> Thou hast done all (else), (but) thou hast not died, thou art
> living. Hark, die, if thou art a self-sacrificing friend!"
> ("The Devoted Lover" Book V: 1252–55)

Boldly embracing her own death, the speaker of the poem, "Ils ont inventé l'âme" [They Invented the Soul] (1–2), refuses all hope of eternity and defies survival after death:

> Je refuse l'espoir, l'altitude, les ailes,
> Mais étrangère au monde et souhaitant le froid
> De vos affreux tombeaux, trop bas et trop étroits,
> J'affirme, en recherchant vos nuits vastes et vaines,
> Qu'il n'est rien qui survive à la chaleur des veines!
>
> [I refuse hope, altitude, wings,
> But foreign to the world and desiring the cold
> Of your ghastly tombs, too low and too narrow,
> I affirm, pursuing your vast and empty nights,
> That naught survives the warmth of veins!] (13–17)

Nevertheless, the sensuality of Noailles's expression of love is in no way antithetical to the voluptuous pouring out of the divine love by Sufis for God. For instance, Rumi's father Bahauddin Valad's description of his intimacy with God is deemed by some Western schol-

---

[21] *Fanā*, "annihilation of self" (Chittick 71) or "the doctrine of passing away in God" (Moyne 23) is explained by A.J. Arberry: "By passing away from self the mystic does not cease to exist, in the true sense of existence, as an individual; rather his individuality, which is an inalienable gift from God, is perfected, transmuted and eternalised through God and in God" (58).

For *fanā*, "annihilation of self," see also Gölpınarlı (57–81).

ars to be "shocking, weird, sensuous, preoccupied with praising female beauty" (Moyne 26). Coleman Barks writes that Rumi himself "shows a startling sensual freedom in stating his union with God" (xix).

Charging love with spiritual power, to represent her wavering predilection between "self-love" and "true love" between two individuals, Noailles refashioned in her art a series of images from the Sufi tradition of love. To delineate her preference for the ideal of self-love, in contrast to that of true love, she appropriated from the Sufi doctrine the notion of the "essential self," which is the self that the perfect individual attains after the annihilation of the false self, and through which the Sufis' union with God is accomplished in this world. Toward the end of the long poem, "Le vallon de Lamartine" [The Valley of Lamartine], the impossibility of sharing true love with a beloved is enacted by both the speaker's inability to find true love in the chamber of the "mind" and the futility of searching for a reciprocity for this kind of love in this world. For this speaker, true love, like the essential self, signified by "mes dieux" [my gods] in the last line, is directed toward the self; it cannot be given to another individual. True love is the self-love that is doomed to revert to the possessor:

> Mais moi, dès mon enfance, abîmant ma raison
> Aux luisantes parois du muet horizon,
> J'ai su que tout désir, tout amour, toute flamme
> S'élançait de mon âme et rentrait dans mon âme,
> Que mes dieux sont en moi, qui'ils mourront avec moi,
>
> [But I, since my childhood, have battered my mind
> Against the glowing walls of the silent horizon,
> I have known that all desire, all love, all flame
> Dashed forward from my soul and returned to my soul,
> That my gods are within me, and they will die with me,]
> (131–35)

Noailles illustrates her skepticism regarding true love between two individuals by rendering impossible the idea of "annihilation of self" also in the poem "Mon Dieu, je ne sais rien ...," in the lines, "Jamais un être humain avec plus de constance / N'a tenté de vous joindre et d'échapper à soi" [Never has a human being with more constancy / Attempted to join you and escape from herself] (21–22), the speaker's inability to elude her false self in order to join God represents the po-et's strong desire but failure to obtain true love. Evident from the word "a tenté" [attempted], Noailles illustrates her distrust of the ideal of true love between two individuals by portraying her speaker locked in her self. Later in the same poem, in addressing God, the speaker seems to undergo a fleeting "annihilation," but this experience proves to be only a vision:

> Je ne puis l'expliquer, mais votre éclat suprême
> Semble être mon reflet au lac d'un paradis:
> Un soir je vous ai vu ressembler à moi-même,
> Sur la route où mon corps par l'ombre était grandi.
>
> [I was unable to explain it, but your supreme luminosity
> Seems to be my reflection on the lake of a paradise:
> One night, I saw you appear like me,
> On the way where by my shadow my body had grown.] (69–72)

It seems paradoxical at first glance in Noailles's literary world that love has to rely on a lover to exist as an entity, stimulate a poetic persona or a fictional character, and provide emotional satisfaction for the lover. However, in this aspect of her art, too, Noailles's inspiration stems from Sufi philosophy. Annemarie Schimmel states that "the center of his [Rumi's] thoughts is Love, which is sometimes inter-changeable with the Beloved, and one often wonders whether it is Love or the Beloved that is intended by his words" (*As Through a Veil* 101). Rumi recognized the knowledge of God in his heart through the love he felt for Shamsi Tabrīz.[22] He writes: "I gazed into my own heart; / There I saw Him [Shamsi]; He was nowhere else" (XVII. "I was on that day" 22–23). Rumi admits that he owed to Shamsi this "metamorphosis that shifted his center of manifestation from mind to heart" (Friedlander and Uzel 20). Although the two men

---

[22] Shamsi Tabrīz was born in Tabrīz in Persia. He left his native city in search of ab-solute perfection. One of his teachers was the unique and holy Sheikh Abu Bakr. He also studied with the eminent theosophist Ibn al-'Arabi. He had a great love of God. He arrived in Konya in 1244. Shams, the sun, was known as *parandeh*, winged one, because he wandered in different places seeking spiritual teachers (cf. Friedlander and Uzel 44–55; Moyne 11).

For Rumi and Shamsi's friendship, see Schimmel, *Rumi's World: The Life and Work of the Great Sufi Poet*, and Ira Friedlander and Nezih Uzel, *The Whirling Dervishes*.

seemed thoroughly mesmerized by each other, and they were totally oblivious to the needs and jealousies of Rumi's students during the first three months of their meeting, the true reason for their attraction was more the love each felt for God than for the other. Rumi said: "He [Shamsi] guided me to the path of love and I learned the Truth in his school. I was ravaged by love and became strong. I became a slave to love, and became free. The divine ecstacy in love, which is an attribute of God, led me to the Truth. Every moment that I was with Shams my soul was in a state of adoration and I was in touch with the Supreme Soul. I could clearly see the seat of Creation" (Tadayun in Aflaki qtd. in Moyne 10–11).

The influence of Sufi philosophy on Noailles's life and art is most evident in her relationship with Maurice Barrès. Rumi discovered a flame for God in Shamsi, and Shamsi's companionship made his faith in God stronger. Similarly, the liaison with Barrès kept Noailles's ties with her Oriental origins alive and her artistic prospect intact. In fact, they each found in the other's character the evocation of an Oriental ambiance, which strengthened their attachment to each other and to their art. As Noailles and Barrès occasionally exchanged this passion for Eastern mysticism with their feelings for each other, it is hardly possible to distinguish the object of their love in their work. Evidently, for Barrès, Noailles was a personification of his Oriental heroines: "Soudain, Barrès a pris consience que cette femme était la plus séduisante, la plus stupéfiante incarnation de l'Orient qui n'avait cessé d'habiter ses rêves, de cet Orient mythique qui nourira une grande partie de son œuvre" [Suddenly, Barrès realized that this woman was the most seductive, most stupefying incarnation of the East that never ceased to inhabit his dreams of that mythical East that would nourish a large part of his work] (Broche 193).[23] Noailles's devotion to Barrès, however, transgressed a creative inspiration, for Barrès completed

---

[23] In *Persephone Unbound*, Catherine Perry writes that Maurice Barrès compared Oriante, the female character of his semi-autobiographical last novel, *Un jardin sur l'Oronte* [A Garden on the Orontes], to Anna de Noailles. This novel, published in 1922, was developed from a short story under the title, "La Musulmane courageuse" [The Brave Mussulman] completed in 1904. The setting of the novel includes the River Orontes. The river's name, Orontes, means "the impetuous one, the one that cannot be mastered" (Barrès, *Mes cahiers* 10: 361). The female character's name, Oriante, sounds like *Oronte* and Orient (cf. Perry 295–301). In 1903, Barrès began another novel, whose protagonist, Aïsse, was directly inspired by Noailles (cf. Broche 194). Clearly, to Barrès, Noailles's Orientalism was her most appealing attribute.

the missing part, the place of God, in appropriating Sufi philosophy in her art. In mid-April 1911, Noailles confessed to the abbé Mugnier "qu'elle vénérait Barrès, qu'elle avait pour lui 'la dévotion qu'on a au Seigneur'" [that she revered Barrès, that she had for him "the devotion that one has for God"] (292).[24] The profound reverence for God through a human beloved is one of the concepts of mystic poetry. "When you read the ghazals of Hāfiz, and even of his earlier compatriot Saâdi, you will always find this kind of opalizing quality so that you never know exactly whether the addressee of the poem is the Divine Beloved or a human being" (Schimmel, *Sufi Literature: Special Paper* 2). In Noailles's glossary, Barrès could be defined as the human representation of the divine object, which, for her, was love. The first line of an 1898 poem, "Notre amour" [Our Love], anticipates this formula: "Notre amour sera grave ainsi qu'un Dieu vieilli" [Our love will be as grave as an aged God] (1).

Calling to mind Rumi's identification with Shamsi, Noailles's recreation of Maurice Barrès as her fictional self in some of her art ascertains her familiarity with *fanā*, "annihilation in the Friend," and reasserts the significant place Sufism held both in her life and art. When Shamsi disappeared from Konya for the second time, Rumi was devastated once again and he went to Damascus in search of his friend. He was unable to find Shamsi in Damascus, but he found him in himself:

> Why should I seek? I am the same as
> he. His essence speaks through me.
> I have been looking for myself! (Barks xx)

Albeit inconsistent, Noailles's application of the Sufi notion of "annihilation in the Friend" marks a definite shift of her art toward a closer and deeper level of artistic involvement—if not a personal convic-

---

[24] Harry G. Allard suggests a Freudian reading of the autobiographical components of Noailles's novels: "A Freudian would not hesitate to link the two events, bereavement and the almost automatic turning toward the Muslim *Sublime Porte*" (112). Allard claims that in Noailles's novels, *La nouvelle espérance*, *Le visage emerveillé*, and *La domination*, "all of her major female characters eventually fall in love with an older stranger" (114). Undeniably, Noailles's art was a product of her psychological influences as well as her intellectual world, and it would not be hard to make a connection between the "love" and "fear" she had for her father and similar feelings she might have had for Maurice Barrès. The "religious" undertones of Noailles's adoration of Maurice Barrès, however, exceeded the parameters of Freudian psychology.

tion—in Sufi philosophy. Emulating Rumi's recognition of himself in Shamsi, she created the character of Antoine Arnault, the hero, to portray Maurice Barrès, through whose perspective the third-person narrator tells the story of her 1905 novel, *La domination* [Domination]. The title of the novel boldly epitomizes the egoistic and despotic intellectual attitude of Barrès toward Noailles. Less perceptible in the novel, though, is the writer's definite intention to reveal her awareness of her lover's overbearing attitude toward herself through her fictional character. At about this time, in the letters Noailles was writing to Barrès, she was defining their relationship as "an annihilation of the self overrun by the other" (31 October 1904, *Correspondance* 245–46). Despite this acknowledgment in her letters, in her novel, she still refrained from a total annihilation of her self in Barrès, let alone allowed an "overrun by the other." The distance between the writer and her hero, created by the third-person omniscient narrator of the novel, suggests that Noailles was unable to completely assume her hero's unattractive personality, thereby reflecting only her profound comprehension of her lover's scornful attitude toward herself and her resistance to "losing her self" in him. Clearly, at the end of the novel, the death of Antoine a few days after Elisabeth, the only woman for whom he has feelings, once again, reveals Noailles's lack of faith in the possibility of true love between two individuals in this world. Indeed, the last line of the book reveals Antoine's true sentiment for Elisabeth not as love but as "son amitié, qui était au-dessus de son amour" [his friendship, which was beneath his love] (307).

Enlightened by Rumi's passion for Shamsi, Noailles was gradually persuaded to believe in the possibility of true love between two individuals, and she was impelled to recognize in her art the feeling she had for Maurice Barrès as true love. Her resignation to this feeling is revealed in a short story, "L'Exhortation" [Exhortation], which contains two letters written by an elderly man to a woman, "Lettre de lui à elle" [Letter from Him to Her] and the other by the woman to a younger man, "Lettre d'elle à un autre" [Letter from Her to Another]. In the first of these letters, as apparent from the first-person narrator of the story, at this time, Noailles was able to completely take on the vicious and domineering aspects of Barrès's character and employ them to describe herself, revealing the total "annihilation of [her] self" in her lover in her art:

> J'ai vous ai quittée parce que vous étiez trop gaie. Madame,
> vous ne riez pas pour rire, ni parce que votre sort est léger
> et le plus enviable qu'on puisse imaginer, mais parce
> qu'inconsciemment, —et si digne, si hautaine, —vous sui-
> vez pourtant votre inclination, qui est de provoquer la vo-
> lonté des hommes. Vous sentez que votre étrange rire ouvre
> dans votre âme et dans votre corps un abîme, qui donne à
> ceux qui vous contemplent un singulier vertige.

> [I left you because you were too gay. Madame, you do not
> laugh to laugh, nor because your kind is as light-hearted
> and enviable as one can imagine, but because, unconscious-
> ly, —and so dignified, so haughty, —you somehow follow
> your inclination, which is to provoke the desire of men.
> You are aware that your strange laugh opens in your soul
> and in your body an abyss, which gives to those who expe-
> rience it a singular vertigo.] (192–93)

In this passage, as in the rest of the letter, Noailles allows neither the interference of her own nor a third-person narrator's perspective in viewing and presenting herself. Becoming one with the first-person point of view of the writer of the letter, she eerily looks on herself through Barrès's lens. Although Catherine Perry never alludes to the influence of Sufism on Noailles's life and art, her labeling of this stage of Noailles's life as "A Loss of Self" (*Persephone Unbound* 275–82) and her affirmation that Noailles's letters to Barrès reveal her dependence on him as a man of authority, support my contention that Noailles eventually did admit in her art that she harbored "true love" for Barrès: "[T]he letters often function as the scene in which Noailles appears to have regained an 'essential' self, in contrast to the more problematic selves displayed in her encounters with Barrès" (276). Noticeably, albeit unintentionally, Perry employs the Sufi terminology, "essential self," to describe Noailles's newly acquired self at this time of her life.

According to scholars of Sufism, "annihilation of self" and "union with God" necessitate a spiritual transformation in which the individual regains the state before the fall. The Prophet's words, "die before you die" or cease to exist in God, speak of a tradition in which the human being annihilates the individual self and begins to see the universe through the eyes of the heart, re-creating the original equilibrium with the universe that existed before the fall (cf. Chittick 84; cf. Ceylan 31). Chittick posits that "[i]t is love, in fact, which is the means whereby man dies to self, for 'Love is an attribute of God' ["The Ascetic and His Jealous Wife," Book V: 2185]" (Chittick 73). In her poem, "Les vivants se sont tus" [The Living Keep Silent], Noailles's allusion to the Sufi concept, "die before you die," finally parallels her artistic notion of true love with the Sufis' mystic vision of union with God. Although Noailles came to believe in her life and demonstrated in her art her feeling for Barrès as true love, she knew that this feeling was unlike the divine love Rumi felt for Shamsi. Her love for Barrès could never transcend worldly limitations; therefore, it could exist solely in a conceptual domain. As a staunch atheist, Noailles could admit the notion of divinity only in her artistic realm. Thus, she used, in her art, the Sufi term, "die before you die," which refers to passing away from self to reach a perfect or universal existence in the presence of God, as a wish-fulfillment of her desire to attain, in her life, a love for Barrès as true as the one Rumi had for Shamsi.[25] In the poem, Noailles's speaker is able to communicate with the dead, though the living are unresponsive to her: "Les vivants se sont tus, mais les morts m'ont parlé" [The living keep quiet, but the dead talked to me] (1). Communicating with the dead, while still alive, before meeting her ineluctable physical end, this speaker encounters *fanā*, the "death [of her false self or individual self] before dying." By declaring the annihilation of (her false) self before dying, with the line, "Je suis morte déjà, puisque je dois mourir ..." [I am dead already, since I must die ...] (16), the speaker enacts the poet's desire to arrive at a plane on which true love between two individuals exists. Unlike the nihilistic speaker of the poem, "Ils ont inventé l'âme," or the skeptical speaker of the poem, "Mon Dieu, je ne sais rien ...," discussed earlier, the speaker of this poem finds in "death" the promise of true love instead of nothingness or self-love; thus, she invites death: "Venez, chère mort, je vous aime" [Come, dear death, I love you] ("J'espère de mourir ..." [I Hope to Die ...] 5). The speaker embraces faith in true love. Obviously, this kind of love is possible only for a supreme being.

---

[25] Although I do not intend to explore Noailles's artistic creativity with a psychoanalytic perspective, Sigmund Freud's theory of wish-fulfillment sheds light on her reason for implementing this tenet of Sufi philosophy in her art. According to Freud, "the motive forces of phantasies are unsatisfied wishes, and every single phantasy is the fulfillment of a wish, a correction of unsatisfying reality" (146).

Hence, in the light of Sufi philosophy, in Noailles's life and art, death should not appear to her readers to be a dreadful end. In her art, whatever or whoever the object of her yearning may be, her expression edges on an existentialist vision. This characteristic brings her desire for actualization of ideal love close to the Sufis' divine longing to be one with God here and now: "Whereas Islam and other religions advocate returning to God or coming into the presence of God *after death*, the Sufis aspire to union with God *in this life*" (Moyne 23). In *Le livre de ma vie*, she writes that, invited by the blue waters of Lake Léman, she felt "chanceler avec une préférence égale entre la vie et la mort" [staggered by an equal preference between life and death] (6). Admittedly, early in her life, she had an instinct to search for true love. According to Arasteh and Sheikh, the mystics sense the existence of love through intuition (42). In 1900, after giving birth to her son, Anne-Jules, the writer told her close friend Mme Bulteau that, "elle se sent 'vide de vie,' elle n'a qu'un désir: 'recevoir la bonne ténèbre de la mort'... elle se sent étrangère à cet univers" [she feels "empty of life," she has no desire except to "receive the benevolent darkness of death"... she feels an outsider to this universe] (Broche 157). Noticeably, the death wish came upon her in the emptiness of worldly desires. Subconsciously, she hoped for the death of her self, which hankered after false desires, for she knew that only by the death of this false self would it be possible for her to achieve the kind of love to which she aspired. The coexistence of love and death in some of her writing seems to imply the interchangeability of the two:

> Je suis l'impétueux et douloureux effort
> Qui toujours désespère et toujours recommence,
> Qui connaît les sanglants regards de la démence,
> Qui croit chercher l'amour et ne veut que la mort.
>
> [I am the impetuous and sore effort
> Who always despairs and always begins again,
> Who knows the bloody look of madness,
> Who thinks she searches for love and wants nothing but death.
> ("Invocation" 9–12)

In the last line of the stanza, it appears as though, for the speaker, death and love have equal puissance. A closer look at this line, however, reveals that it is the placement of death in the emotive sphere and love in the cerebral sphere of the psyche that distinguishes the speaker's true preference. A Sufi at heart, Noailles valued the feeling in her "heart" more than the reasoning in her "mind." In the poem, death represents the true love that the speaker feels in her heart. The love that she "searches for" signifies the "think[ing]" in her mind. Unlike the speaker of the poem, "Le vallon de Lamartine," this speaker refrains from speculating in her mind about love, which would turn only upon itself as self-love. Instead, she desires "to die," like a Sufi, and attain the wisdom of true love and timeless existence.

In 1908, Léon Blum wrote in *La Revue de Paris*: "Elle écrit qu'elle ne mourra pas tout entière, que sa puissance d'amour continuera sa route sous le ciel" [She writes that she will not be totally dead, that her power of love will continue under the sky] (225–47; qtd. in Broche 246). Apparently, Noailles was familiar with the Sufis' path symbolized by "a ladder set up against the sky" (Moyne 50). Blum's statement epitomizes the culmination of the impact of Sufi philosophy on Anna de Noailles. Having idealized the truth of love rather than that of God, she was sure that in death love would sustain her eternal existence.

Works Cited

Aflaki, Shamsuddin Ahmad. *Manaqib ul-Arefin*. 2 vols. Tehran: Donya-I Ketab, 1983–1984.

Allard, Harry G., Jr. "Anna de Noailles, Nun of Passion: A Study of the Novels of Anna de Noailles." Diss. Yale U, 1973.

Arasteh, Riza A., and Enis A. Sheikh. "Sufizm: Evrensel Benliğe Giden Yol." Trans. Seval Yılmaz. *Sufi Psikolojisi: Bilgeliğin Ruhu, Ruhun Bilgeliği*. Ed. Kemal Sayar. Istanbul: İnsan, 2004. 41–76.

Arberry, A.J. *Sufism: An Account of the Mystics of Islam*. London: Allen & Unwin, 1956.

Barks, Coleman. "On Rumi." *The Essential Rumi*. Trans. Coleman Barks with Reynold Nicholson, A.J. Arberry, John Moyne. New Expanded Edition. New York: Harper, 2004. xix–xxi.

Barrès, Maurice. *Correspondance 1901–1923*. Ed. Claude Mignot-Ogliastri. Paris: L'Inventaire, 1994.

_____. *Mes cahiers*. Ed. Phillipe Barrès. 14 vols. Paris: Plon, 1929–1957.

_____. *Un jardin sur l'Oronte*. Ed. Émilien Carassus. Paris: Gallimard, 1990.

Blum, Léon. "L'œuvre poétique de Mme de Noailles." *La Revue de Paris* (Janvier–Février 1908): 225–47.

Broche, François. *Anna de Noailles: Un mystère en pleine lumière*. Paris: Laffont, 1989.

Ceylan, Ömür. *Böyle Buyurdu Sûfî: Tasavvuf ve Şerh Edebiyatı Araştırmaları*. Istanbul: Kapı, 2005.

Chittick, William C. *The Sufi Doctrine of Rumi*. Bloomington: World Wisdom, 2005.

Cixous, Hélène. "Le Rire de la Méduse." *L'Arc* 61 (1975): 39–54.

Cocteau, Jean. *My Contemporaries*. Ed. Margaret Crosland. Philadelphia: Chilton, 1968.

Engelking, Tama Lea. "Anna de Noailles Oui et Non: The Countess, the Critics and la poésie féminine." *Women's Studies* 23 (1994): 95–110.

Epictetus. *Discourses*. Trans. W.A. Oldfather. Cambridge: Harvard UP, 2000.

Freud, Sigmund. "Creative Writers and Day-Dreaming (1908 [1907])." *The Standard Edition of the Complete Psychological Works of Sigmund Freud*. Ed. James Strachey. Vol. 9. London: Hogarth P. and Institute of Psycho-Analysis, 1959. 141–53.

Friedlander, Ira, and Nezih Uzel. *The Whirling Dervishes: Being an Account of the Sufi Order Known as the Mevlevis and Its Founder the Poet and Mystic Mevlana Jalalu'ddin Rumi*. New York: Macmillan, 1975.

Gölpınarlı, Abdülbâki. *Tasavvuf*. Istanbul: Milenyum, 2004.

Groff, Peter S. "Al Kindī and Nietzsche on the Stoic Art of Banishing Sorrow." *Journal of Nietzsche Studies* 28 (2004): 139–73.

Higonnet-Dugua, Elisabeth. *Anna de Noailles, cœur innombrable: Biographie-Correspondance*. Paris: Maule, 1989.

Holmes, Diana. *French Women's Writing 1848–1994*. London: Athlone, 1996.

Jammes, Francis. "L'évolution spirituelle de Mme la comtesse de Noailles." *Revue Hebdomadaire* 27 Sept. 1913. *Oeuvres*. Vol. 5. Geneva: Slatkine Reprints, 1978. 203–77.

Mauriac, François. *Les Nouvelles Littéraires*. 6 May 1933.1.

Mignot-Ogliastri, Claude. *Anna de Noailles: Une amie de la Princesse Edmond de Polignac*. Paris: Méridiens-Klincksieck, 1987.

Milligan, Jennifer E. *The Forgotten Generation: French Women Writers of the Inter-war Period*. Oxford: Berg, 1996.

Moyne, John A. *Rumi and the Sufi Tradition: Essays on the Mowlavi Order and Mysticism*. Binghamton: Global, Binghamton UP, 1998.

Mugnier, Abbé (Arthur). *Journal*. Ed. Marcel Billot. Paris: Mercure de France, 1985.

Nasr, Seyyed Hossein. "The Influence of Sufism on Traditional Persian Music." *Studies in Comparative Religion* 6 (1972): 225–34.

Nicholson, Reynold A. *The Mystics of Islam*. London: Routledge, 1963.

Nietzsche, Friedrich. *Ecce Homo*: *On the Genealogy of Morals and Ecce Homo*. Ed. and trans. Walter Kaufmann and R.J. Hollingdale. New York: Random, 1967.

Noailles, Anna de. "Azur." *Les éblouissements*. Paris: Calmann-Lévy, 1925. 162.

_____. "Constantinople." *Les éblouissements*. Paris: Calmann-Lévy, 1925. 33–37.

_____. *La domination*. Paris: Calman-Lévi, n.d.

_____. "L'Exhortation." *Les innocentes ou la sagesse des femmes*. Paris: Fayard, 1923. 191–200.

_____. "Idylle: La Muse et l'Enfant." *Anna de Noailles: Une amie de la Princesse Edmond de Polignac*. By Mignot-Ogliastri, Claude. Paris: Méridiens-Klincksieck, 1987. 54–55.

_____. VI. "Ils ont inventé l'âme." *L'honneur de souffrir*. Paris: Grasset, 1927. 18–19.

_____. "Invocation." *Les éblouissements*. Paris: Calmann-Lévy, 1925. 328–30.

_____. XCI. "J'ai bien servi le dieu." *L'honneur de souffrir*. Paris: Grasset, 1927. 141.

_____. "J'espère de mourir …" *Les vivants et les morts*. Paris: Fayard, 1913. 20–22.

_____. *Le livre de ma vie*. Paris: Mercure de France, 1976.

_____. "Mon Dieu, je ne sais rien …" *Les vivants et les morts*. Paris: Fayard, 1913. 267–71.

_____. "Nature que je sers …" *Les éblouissements*. Paris: Calmann-Lévy, 1925. 398–400.

_____. "Notre amour." *Derniers vers et poèmes d'enfance*. Paris: Grasset, 1934. 182–84.

_____. *La nouvelle espérance*. Paris: Calmann-Lévy, n.d.

_____. "Les nuits de Turquie." *Exactitudes*. Paris: Grasset, 1930. 105–09; *De la Rive d'Europe à la Rive d'Asie*. Paris: Dorbon-Ainé, n.d. 7–11.

_____. "O Dieu mystérieux …" *Les vivants et les morts*. Paris: Fayard, 1913. 310–14.

_____. "Paysage Persane." *Les éblouissements*. Paris: Calmann-Lévy, 1925. 46–47

_____. Preface. *Le jardin de roses*. By Saâdi. Trans. Franz Toussaint. Paris: Art Piazza, 1912; rev ed. Paris: Stock, 1923. 1–24.

_____. "Saâdi et le jardin des roses." *De la rive d'Europe à la rive d'Asie*. Paris: Dorbon-Ainé, n.d. 79–103.

_____. "Si vous parliez, Siegneur …" *Les vivants et les morts*. Paris: Fayard, 1913. 273–75.

_____. "Le vallon de Lamartine." *Les éblouissements*. Paris: Calmann-Lévy, 1925. 219–24.

_____. *Le visage émerveillé*. Paris: Rocher, 2004.

_____. "Les vivants se sont tus." *Les vivants et les morts*. Paris: Fayard, 1913. 330.

O'Brien, Mari H. "Passion, Power, Will, Desire: Gender Trespassing in the Poetry of Anna de Noailles." *Cincinnati Romance Review* 15 (1996): 97–105.

Ortega y Gasset, José. "La poesía de Anna de Noailles." *Revista de occidente,* 1 July 1923. *Obras completas*. Vol. 3. Madrid: Revista de Occidente, 1963. 429–35.

_____. "El rostro maravillado." *El imparcial*. 25 July 1904. *Obras completas*. Vol 1. Madrid: Revista de Occidente, 1963. 33–36.

Osmanoğlu, Ayşe. *Babam Abdülhamid*. Istanbul: Güven, 1960.

Palmer, G.E.H. Foreword. *Gnosis: Divine Wisdom*. By Frithjof Schuon. Trans. G.E.H. Palmer. London: Murray, 1959. 7–8.

Perche, Louis. *Anna de Noailles: Une étude de Louis Perche avec un choix de poèmes, soixante illustrations, une chronologie bibliographique, Anna de Noailles et son temps*. Paris: Seghers, 1969.

Perry, Catherine. "In the Wake of Decadence: Anna de Noailles' Revaluation of Nature and the Feminine." *L'Esprit Créateur* 37.4 (Winter 1997): 94–105.

_____. *Persephone Unbound: Dionysian Aesthetics in the Works of Anna de Noailles*. Lewisburg: Bucknell UP, 2003.

Peyre, Henri. *The Contemporary French Novel*. New York: Oxford UP, 1955.

Proust, Marcel. "Le côté de Guermantes." *À la recherche du temps perdu: Le côté de Guermantes*, *Sadome et Gomorrhe*. Paris: Laffont, 1987. 7–482.

Quinn, Patrick J., and Steven Trout, eds. *The Literature of the Great War Reconsidered: Beyond Modern Memory*. New York: Palgrave, 2001.

Rochefoucauld, Édmée de la. *Anna de Noailles*. Paris: Universitaires, 1956.

Rumi, Maulana Jalaluddin. "The Ascetic and His Jealous Wife." *The Mathnawí of Jalálu'ddín Rúmí*. Book V. Vol. VI. Trans. Reynold A. Nicholson. London: Luzac, 1977. 130–33.

_____. "The Devoted Lover." *The Mathnawí of Jalálu'ddín Rúmí*. Book V. Vol. VI. Trans. Reynold A. Nicholson. London: Luzac, 1977. 76–77.

_____. *Discourses of Rūmī*. Trans. A. J. Arberry. London: Murray, 1961.

_____. XVII. "I was on that day." *Selected Poems from the Dīvāni Shamsi Tabrīz*. Ed. and trans. Reynold A. Nicholson. Richmond, UK: Curzon P, 1999. 70–73.

_____. XXVII. "If a tree might move." *Selected Poems from the Dīvāni Shamsi Tabrīz*. Ed. and trans. Reynold A. Nicholson. Richmond, UK: Curzon P, 1999. 108–11.

_____. "The Mouse and the Frog." *The Mathnawí of Jalálu'ddín Rúmí*. Book VI. Vol. VI. Trans. Reynold A. Nicholson. London: Luzac, 1977. 403–14.

_____. "The Sage and the Peacock." *The Mathnawí of Jalálu'ddín Rúmí*. Book V. Vol. VI. Trans. Reynold A. Nicholson. London: Luzac, 1977. 34–37.

_____. XXXI. "What Is to Be Done." *Selected Poems from the Dīvāni Shamsi Tabrīz*. Ed. and trans. Reynold A. Nicholson. Richmond, UK: Curzon P, 1999. 124–27.

Sayar, Kemal. "Geçmişin Bilgeliği Bugünün Psikoterapileriyle Buluşabilir mi? Sufi Psikolojisi Örneği" Ed. Kemal Sayar. *Sufi Psikolojisi: Bilgelğiin Ruhu, Ruhun Bilgeliği*. Istanbul: İnsan, 2004. 11–40.

Schimmel, Annemarie. *As Through a Veil*: *Mystical Poety in Islam*. New York: Columbia UP, 1982.

_____. *Rumi's World: The Life and Work of the Great Sufi Poet*. Boston: Shambhala, 2001.

_____. *Sufi Literature*: *Special Paper*. New York: The Afghanistan Council of the Asia Society, Fall 1975.

_____. *The Triumphal Sun: A Study of the Works of Jalāloddin Rumi*. Albany: SUNY, 1993.

Ségur, Nicolas. "Madame de Noailles." *Le génie européen*. Paris: Fasquelle, 1926. 145–76.

Shabistari, Sa'd ud din Mahmud. Rule IV. "Thoughts on Souls." *Gulshan I Raz: The Mystic Rose Garden*. Trans. E.H. Whinfield. London: Trübner, 1880. 26–29.

Shafii, Muhammed. "Varoluşsal Vuslat: Benlikten Kurtuluş." Trans. Nadir Denizli. *Sufî Psikolojisi: Bilgeliğin Ruhu, Ruhun Bilgeliği*. Ed. Kemal Sayar. Istanbul: İnsan, 2004. 93–119.

Suleiman, Susan Rubin. *Subversive Intent: Gender, Politics, and the Avant-Garde*. Cambridge: Harvard UP, 1990.

Yakıt, İsmail. *Bati Düşüncesive ve Mevlâna*. Istanbul: Ötüken, 2000.

Before They Were Famous:
Tristan Tzara, Nationhood, and Poetry

Stephen Forcer
University of Birmingham

Even in synopsis, it is clear that the life of Tristan Tzara offers particularly rich opportunities for the investigation of identity, cultural hybridity, nationhood, and an array of further issues to do with Tzara as a Romanian national who spent the vast bulk of his career writing in French. Born to Jewish parents on 16 April 1896 in the then-rural town of Moineşti (Bacău), the man now remembered by cultural history as the monocle-wearing Father of Dada was known until late adolescence by his original name of Samuel Rosenstock: Tristan Tzara was a pseudonym not adopted until October 1915. It officially became his name in 1925 (Béhar 12).[1] Tzara was educated in French in Bucharest (he also studied English and German, and scored well in all languages [Béhar 13]), had a voracious appetite for reading—with a particular taste for French Symbolist poetry—and indeed managed to publish a few Romanian poems in a magazine founded by his close friend Ion Vinea (Béhar 20). In 1915 Tzara's parents sent him to college in German-speaking Switzerland, where he met and became friends with an eclectic group of individuals—themselves from diverse national and ethnic backgrounds—who formed the nexus of Dada: in 1916 Jean (Hans) Arp, Emmy Hennings, Hugo Ball (Hennings's husband) and Richard Huelsenbeck joined with Tzara at the Cabaret Voltaire in Zurich, where their raucous performances included verbal abuse directed at the audience in various European languages (plus some that were invented), "simultaneous poetry" (multi-lingual verse delivered at the same time by more than one performer [*OC* 1: 491–500]), and kazoos and other percussive instruments. Drawn by the pull of André Breton and the coalescence of Surrealism, Tzara moved to Paris in 1920. In fact, he lived in France for the rest of his life, including during the Second World War. After the

---

[1] Béhar's edition appears as part of a series of monographs, *Les Roumains de Paris*, published by Oxus.

war, Tzara returned to Paris and operated from an apartment that housed work by an international collection of artists (Picasso, Arp, de Chirico, Giacometti, and Miró) as well as unique collections of African masks and artifacts (Béhar 5). His Paris apartment was situated in the rue de Lille, in one of the *beaux quartiers* of the French capital: Romanian-born Tzara died there in 1963, just a few hundred meters from the Musée d'Orsay, the Pont Royal, and a host of other sites that constitute Paris as a powerfully mythical cultural "playground" (Hayward 26) at the epicenter of French culture and history.

From this overview, let us draw out the main issues addressed in this chapter in respect of Tzara as one of the most well-known Francophone Romanians in twentieth-century European culture. Firstly, and in contrast to the reliance on authorial and historical essences that tends to characterize writing about Tzara's poetry, I want here to test his Francophonia in relation to the content and textuality of his literary work, and to look at the ways in which his diverse relationships to nation, language, identity, and selfhood may or may not play out at the level of the poems themselves. I will focus on the French translations of Tzara's very first published poems, which represent the first and last body of work that he published in Romanian. By reading these poems closely and in terms that they themselves set out in situ, I hope to establish a productive tension between, on the one hand, the textual mediation of self and nationhood in Tzara's verse and, on the other, the more low-resolution personal and historical issues for which he is more commonly remembered, such as his departure from Romania, the Dadaists' rejection of national identity, his support of the Republicans during the Spanish Civil War, and his French naturalization.

One of my more general aims in this chapter is to offer some sense of the sheer diversity and quantity of Tzara's literary output. For this is a writer whose six-volume complete works contain over thirty separate collections of poetry, and who continued to write in verse, prose, and *prose poétique* for nearly forty years after the totemic *Sept manifestes Dada* [Seven Dada Manifestos] (*OC* 1: 355–90). As such, Tzara's published output represents an extremely dense if unexploited case study for those interested in Romanian nationals writing in French. To conclude, I will return to the biographical sketch with which this chapter began. For, in some ways bizarrely, it is only recently that some of the most basic facts about Tzara's background and career have become available in published biographies or monographs in which Tzara is the central focus (the first book-length biography of Tzara was published by François Buot in 2002). Curiously, too, Tzara has also been neglected by literary criticism (my 2006 monograph on Tzara is the first book-length attempt to read in extended detail poetry written by Tzara across his whole career). It is my feeling that some of this neglect stems, precisely, from Tzara's status as an ethno-national hybrid, and that his Franco–Romanian status brings into instructive relief a set of fundamental issues to do with cultural belonging, collective memory, and the curation (or not) of literary legacies. As a final point of delimitation, I should emphasize that, though I will refer to Romanian cultural history, I am not a specialist in Eastern European literature per se and will not attempt to read the French versions of Tzara's texts next to the Romanian originals (though there remains considerable scope for an updated, detailed analysis of Tzara's Romanian work in its original form).

Let us then consider Tzara's first experiments with poetry and outline the creative decisions and possibilities these involved. At the time of Tzara's move to Zurich in 1915, he had published only a handful of poems, all written in Romanian (*OC* 1: 631). For Tzara, the geographical move to France seems to have brought with it a definitive decision to reject Romanian and to adopt French as the language of his poetic expression. Undoubtedly, French offered Tzara a way of connecting with Jules Laforgue (1860–1887, born considerably farther from France than Tzara, in Uruguay), Stéphane Mallarmé (1842–1898), Guillaume Apollinaire (1880–1918, also born outside of France, but in Rome) and the currents of experimentation that he so admired in late nineteenth- and early twentieth-century French poetry (Béhar 15, 69). It is in turn likely that, compared to Romanian, French offered Tzara greater potential for cultural visibility and perceived credibility. As Dennis Deletant notes, over the course of the eighteenth century, "French literature was translated into Modern Greek and Romanian and read by a number of the landed [Romanian] aristocracy, and the French language acquired greater prestige amongst educated Romanians" (144). Writing in a second language also allowed Tzara to reinvent himself beyond the embarrassments of family life in a relative cultural backwater (*OC* 1: 266–70).[2]

---

[2] Tzara's original manuscripts contain tantalizing signs that, long after he had left Romania, he nonetheless continued to read, and possibly write, in Romanian, and to take an interest in the country's affairs. For example, five letters written to him by his

In due course, his use of an adopted language revealed itself to be exceedingly well suited to the energies of Dada. As with Eugène Ionesco (1909–1994) and Samuel Beckett (1906–1989), there is a fundamental sense in which Tzara's use of French as a second language is inherently connected to the avant-garde appetite for linguistic play, for the malleability of linguistic expression, and for the disrespect of language as a set of rules and as an institution. In turn, linguistic mistakes can be feigned or exploited for comic or performative effect. The linguistic fragmentation of Tzara's bizarre and alienating pseudo-French also conveys something of the Dadaists' belief in the fundamental detachment that characterizes anyone's relationship to language, be the writer native or non-native. Thus opens "Pélamide" from Tzara's first published collection of verse, *Vingt-cinq poèmes* [Twenty-Five Poems] (*OC* 1: 85–119), in which the voice of the speaking subject frequently disintegrates into phonemes, graphemes, and the raw elements of language amidst clausal statements that fulfill certain rules of syntax but of which the content makes little immediate sense:

> a e ou youyouyou i e ou o
> youyouyou
> drrrrrdrrrrdrrrrgrrrrgrrrr
> morceaux de durée verte voltigent dans ma chambre
>
> [a e ou youyouyou i e ou o
> youyouyou
> drrrrrdrrrrdrrrrgrrrrgrrrr
> pieces of green duration fly around my room] (*OC* 1: 102)[3]

At the same time—and in contrast to the popular idea of Dada as aleatory anarchy—the Tzara archives, held in Paris at the Bibliothèque littéraire Jacques Doucet, reveal real care in Tzara's preparation of his French-language Dada poems for publication. It is clear that Tzara worked over his manuscripts, and in particular that he cor-

---

parents in 1925 are all written in Romanian, addressed to "Samica," a diminutive version of Samuel (TZR.C. 3484–89). Also notable is a letter from the late 1930s written by Tzara in French to a publisher on the back of a document about the development of methane gas production in Romania (TZR.C. 4033).

[3] Translations from French to English are my own. I have elsewhere looked at Tzara's non-standard verbal compounds as a form of glossolalia that can be read in Freudian terms as a psycho-poetic condensation (Forcer 10–28).

rected his French spelling in a number of Dada poems (TZR.MS 1–2, for example). Henri Béhar has said that when Tzara switched to writing French he had mastered it, and that his learning of the language was essentially complete (*OC* 1: 632). Certainly, from one end of his career to the other—and across his verse, prose, and correspondence—Tzara writes beautiful and sophisticated French, using a fully native range of registers and styles and deploying personalized flourishes of lexis and structure. But the corrections to his early manuscripts—on missed accents and verb endings as well as orthography—point to a fundamentally unfixed quality in Tzara's relationship to French at this stage, which seems to feed into his openness to linguistic expression and drive his curiosity for new words and forms in French. Indeed, original manuscripts from across Tzara's career feature lists of French nouns and verbs, many of which make their way together into published poems: at times Tzara composes his poetry in the style of a learner or collector of French vocabulary (TZR.MS 37, 46, 37, 70, 57, 31, 152, 7). Laura Ceia-Minjares also cites evidence that contradicts Béhar's talk of Tzara's "mastering" of French: according to Germaine Everling, at the time of Tzara's 1920 move to Paris his spoken French was still poor, and "his Romanian accent 'rendered him ridiculous'" (Ceia-Minjares "Opting In, Opting Out" 6, qtd. in Sanouillet 73).

In terms of both composition and performance, I would, therefore, suggest a fundamental connection between Tzara's non-French origins and the genesis of his Dada production and persona. Granted, by 1916 Tzara is a sufficiently advanced speaker of French to conduct personal and cultural affairs in the language, but Ceia-Minjares's point about his level of French underscores a crucial aspect of Tzara's early manuscripts and published poems: in the Dada period, Tzara continues to approach the French language as an unfinished field of learning, exploration, and testing, all of which provide a natural context for the linguistic experiments of Dada. Meanwhile, Tzara's inherently non-native connection to French—acquired over a period of years but not hard-wired from birth—lends itself to the ludic, flippant, and unstable postures he displayed in relation to language as performance.

So if Tzara's Romanian background is of general importance to the performative and poetic aspects of his emergence as a Dadaist, what further insights are afforded by the specific form and content of

the poetry he wrote in Romanian before his move to Zurich? In order
to answer this question fully and in context, the publication history of
these poems first requires some commentary and clarification. Thanks
to the efforts of Saşa Pană, Tzara's early Romanian poetry was first
made available in collected form in 1934 by a Bucharest-based publishing house named Unu, under the title *Primele poeme*. According
to UK-based sellers of rare books Heart Fine Art, 230 copies were
made of *Primele poeme* (in 2007 one of these copies was listed for
sale by Heart for £500). Originally written in the period 1912–1915,
some of these poems had appeared in Romanian journals before their
publication in Pană's edition; many others had never previously been
published. Two years after Tzara's death, there appeared an expanded
version of *Primele poeme* in French. It is clear that Claude Sernet,
who compiled the poems and translated them into French, had been
working on the collection for some years previous to their appearance
as *Premiers poèmes* in 1965: many of the poems had been rediscovered by Sernet as manuscripts in the personal collections of Tzara and
Ion Vinea (*OC* 1: 631). Of Tzara's Romanian poems, seven were published before he moved to Zurich in late 1915. Sernet's *Premiers
poèmes*, however, brings together French translations of thirty-six
Romanian-language poems written by Tzara in the period 1912–1915
(an English translation was published by Michael Impey and Brian
Swann in 1976). As an appendix to the *Premiers poèmes* in Tzara's
complete works, Henri Béhar offers Claude Voronca's translations of
four other poems disowned by Tzara at the time of Pană's *Primele
poeme* (all originally published in the Romanian review *Simboul* in
1912, these four poems are "Sur la rivière de la vie" [On the River of
Life], "Chanson" [Song], "Conte" [Tale], and "Danse de fée" [Fairy
Dance] [*OC* 1: 427–36]).

Clearly, then, Tzara's early, pre-Dada poems represent a considerable body of primary source material. There remains, however, little
critical work that deals in detail with these numerous early pieces. Are
there as yet undiscovered connections to be made between Tzara's
pre-1916 output, which has been more or less forgotten by cultural
memory, and the Dada period for which Tzara remains an emblem
and a spokesperson? Or is the point, precisely, that the pre-Dada poems stand on their own, contradicting or confusing the rest of his out-

put, and representing a troublesome obstacle to the continuity that Tzara saw in his own work as a poet, including his very first pieces?[4]

What is clear about the *Premiers poèmes*, even on a first reading, are the links that are traceable between the poems themselves and Tzara's own life growing up in rural Romania. For example, we might read the 1915 poem "Viens à la campagne avec moi" [Come to the Countryside with Me] as an imagined or fantasized episode of companionship addressed to Tzara's friend Ion Vinea, with whom he vacationed in the summer of 1915:

> Nous irons à cheval des journées entières,
> Nous ferons haltes dans des auberges grises,
> Là on lie beaucoup d'amitiés
> Et la nuit on couche avec la fille de l'aubergiste.
>
> [We will travel whole days on horseback,
> We will rest in grey hostels,
> Where friendship strengthens
> And at night we sleep with the innkeeper's daughter.] (33)[5]

In the next poem in the collection, "Chant de guerre" [War Song], Tzara returns to the figure of the hostel owner's daughter. This time, however, her evocation is accompanied not by the hearty homosocial images of companions on horseback but by a strange, semi-pagan petition:

> Vieux peuplier dressé au bord du fossé
> Ouvre ton ventre, répand tes entrailles
> Qu'elle est blonde la fille de l'aubergiste de Hirsoveni
> Combien d'heures en avons-nous encore?
>
> [Old poplar standing on the edge of the ditch
> Open your belly, spread out your guts
> How blond is the innkeeper's daughter in Hirsoveni
> How many hours do we have left?] (36)

---

[4] In discussions with Saşa Pană, for example, Tzara describes how, during the preparation of *Primele poeme*, he had explicitly rejected the suggested title *Poèmes d'avant Dada* [Poems from Before Dada], as it would have implied a break in his poetic persona, in which he has always seen a form of continuity (Béhar in *OC* I: 632).

[5] All French-language quotations from *Premiers poèmes* are from Tzara, *Œuvres complètes* I: 25–74.

Aside from pre-echoes of Tzara's singular poetic engagement with the natural world, which is particularly strong in *L'Homme approximatif* [The Approximate Man] (*OC* 2: 77–171), this extract is notable for its evocation of the spatial context of its own production. The vast majority of Tzara's poems from across his career retain a stubbornly oblique relationship to the geo-historical world, with explicit references to actual places, events, and people few and far between. In "l'aubergiste de Hirsoveni" [The Innkeeper of Hirsoveni], however, Tzara alludes both to a specific village in the rural space of Northeast Romania and to the time he spent there as a teenager. Indeed, Hirsoveni is only a few miles from the town of Girceni (forty to fifty miles northeast of Tzara's hometown of Moineşti), in which Tzara wrote the poem "Viens à la campagne avec moi" and that is also evoked by Vinea in one of his poems (Buot 24). So Tzara gives an indication of the country and region in which "Chant de guerre" is being sung, thereby making a basic connection between the content of the poem and his personal history living in a specified region of Romania. Indeed, the reference to war by a Romanian in the period 1914–1915 raises a historical event of major significance to Romania at that time that tends to be forgotten in discussions of Tzara's subsequent attitude as a Dadaist towards conflict: the Second Balkan War of 1913. Traditionally, Dada is seen as a gesture of disgust expressed in response to the failure of Europe-wide human systems and structures, and that finds for Tzara and the Dadaists its catastrophic embodiment in World War I. In *Premiers poèmes*, however, Tzara articulates war but at a pre-Dada moment when World War I was in its early stages, and indeed when Romania was a neutral state not actively engaged in conflict (it joined the Allies in 1916). In addition to the 1915 piece "Chant de guerre," war is a central theme in "L'Orage et le chant du déserteur" [The Storm and the Deserter's Song] (30–32) written by Tzara in 1914. While such poems can certainly be read in relation to "war" as an ubiquitous human phenomenon, the time of their composition also connects with a fundamentally national context specific to Romania as a belligerent recently victorious over Bulgaria and Turkey.

The idea that "Chant de guerre" and "L'Orage" are set in and articulate the Romania of Tzara's adolescence is strengthened by the spatial references made therein, which convey exactly the sort of pastoral and sylvan landscape through which Tzara and Vinea move in

"Viens à la campagne avec moi." The first stanza of "Chant de guerre," for instance, contains multiple abstractions of what François Buot calls "un monde de sentiers, de ruisseaux et de soleil, une enfance champêtre et bucolique" [a world of tracks, streams and sunshine, a rural and bucolic childhood] (17), and that was the milieu for Tzara's upbringing in a house "perdue au fond des bois" [lost at the ends of the woods] (17):

> Des épouvantails d'oiseaux ont poussé sur les champs
> Là où se nouent les sillons d'airain.
> Qu'as-tu à traîner dans les étables
> En écoutant le cor des gardes forestiers?
>
> [Scarecrows of birds have grown out over the fields
> Where furrows of bronze knot together.
> Why do you loiter in stables
> Listening to the horn of the forest guards?] (35)

The final two lines in particular might almost be a continuation of Tzara's poetic dialogue with Vinea, what with their allusion to horses and forest wardens as part of an informal second-person address. The rural topography of "Chant de guerre" is extended by Tzara's diction throughout the poem, as in "l'herbe" [grass] "ruisseau" [stream] (×2), "blé" [wheat], "la fôret" [forest] and "étang" [lake] (35–36). In "L'Orage" the speaking subject ranges over a wider terrain, this time passing though "la montagne éventrée" [the eviscerated mountain], "les collines lépreuses" [leprous hills], and "la fôret broyée" [the crushed forest].[6] Again, these topographical descriptions could well be read in relation to aspects of World War I, such as the infamous disemboweling—literal and figurative—of human beings and nature respectively, particularly in the massacred landscapes of the Western front. But there remains a strong topographical match between "Viens avec moi," "Chant de guerre," and "L'Orage" that provides a commonality of space for teenage journeys of friendship and war as themes treated within the various poems. In turn, the articulation of war in Tzara's early poems can be differentiated from the military allusions—markedly rare, moreover—made in his Dada poems, such

---

[6] A leprous, malignant natural world is a central and eponymous part of Tzara's 1917 Dada poem "Le Géant blanc lépreux du paysage" [The Great White Leper of the Countryside] (*OC* I: 87–88).

as in "La Grande complainte de mon obscurité deux" [The Great Lament Over My Obscurity Two]: "le soldat / dans les régions boueuses où les oiseaux se collent en silence" [the soldier / in muddy regions where birds stick together in silence] (OC 1: 92). By contrast with poems like "Chant de guerre" and "L'Orage," this sort of utterance is explicitly evocative of the mud and mess associated with the trench warfare of WW I, suggesting a region in which the infamous gunk of the front has stuck even birds together.

So while the *Premiers poèmes* by no means offers a full cartography of Tzara's life in Romania, the collection does articulate definite traces of the spaces through which he moved growing up in the country. Other parts of the collection add their voices to the distinctly biographical context of Tzara's early work. In "Mamie, amie" [Grandmother, Friend], for instance, the poet proclaims:

> Je t'achèterai sans conditions des boucles d'oreilles
> Chez des bijoutiers juifs
>
> [Unconditionally I will buy you earrings
> At Jewish jewelers] (65)

As I mentioned previously in respect of Hirsoveni, in Tzara's post-Romanian Francophone texts it is highly unusual for him to name specific, unambiguous markers of identity or place, including those that relate to his own history and background. In "Mamie, amie," however, Jews are referred to as part of an utterance explicitly connected to Tzara as the "Je" of the poem. So, too, in "Viens à la campagne" we read

> Le cimetière juif a poussé parmi les pierres;
> Au-delà de la ville, sur la colline
>
> [The Jewish cemetery has grown among the stones
> Beyond the town, on the hill] (33)

In both "Mamie, amie" and "Viens à la champagne," the references to Jews evoke key issues to do with the status of Tzara's family in Romania. Firstly, there is in "bijoutiers juifs" the suggestion of Jews as wealthy, or at least involved in the trade of potentially lucrative materials. At the same time, the extract from "Viens à la campagne" figures the Jewish community as outsiders in a doubly determined spatial dislocation: the cemetery is situated both outside the bounds of the town ("Au-delà de la ville") and on a different level to it ("sur la colline"). The notion of a Jewish community that works with profitable natural resources, but that is also in some sense displaced or alienated, makes for a compelling point of reference to Tzara's own family. Tzara's grandfather, as François Buot points out, managed a lumber company but, as a Jew, was not allowed to actually own such an enterprise himself (17). The confluence of industrial productivity and anti-Semitism is also to be found in the figure of Tzara's father, who was both a director of an oil company and—as all Jews at the time—denied Romanian citizenship (by the same turn, Tzara's school-leaving certificate is delivered to "Samuel Rosenstock, de nationalité israélite" [Béhar 12]). In "Mamie, amie" and "Viens à la campagne," however, Tzara names Jews in a time and place in which they are not officially nameable. The localized detail of the poems also contains brief but strong references to Tzara's own family as Jews living in a country that did not recognize them as full national citizens.

The clear biographical resonances of *Premiers poèmes* make for an important point of reference with Tzara's later work and cultural status. Traditionally, for instance, Tzara and his fellow Dadaists are remembered for their rejection of national identity: "nationhood" is attacked by Dada as an othering logic of stupidity fundamental to the deranged mass murder of WW I, and is viewed as part of an absurd but ubiquitous chain of meaning that begins with "community," travels through regional and ethnic identities, and ends with an (inter)national dynamic of difference that allows ruling classes to range whole armies against each other on the basis of arbitrary or constructed forms of otherness. As a Dadaist, Tzara refuses to define himself in ethnic or national terms, and he promotes Dada as a space in which identity is a matter of personal choice and performance rather than imposed or unavoidably collective. As he writes in the "Manifeste Dada 1918," "Ainsi naquit DADA d'un besoin d'indépendance, de méfiance envers la communauté. Ceux qui appartiennent à nous gardent leur liberté" [Thus Dada is born out of a need for independence and out of mistrust towards the community. Those who belong to us retain their freedom] (*OC* 1: 361). Laura Ceia-Minjares has stressed the additional connotations of Dada's relation to community, noting "Tzara's refusal to function within the borders of a traditional communal realm, be it a community of thought or a concrete territory" ("Trans-national Avant-Garde" 6).[7] It might thus be said that Tzara's resistance to nationhood is part of a wider rejection of any concept or signifier that seeks to describe or order human experience within over-arching, collective structures, be its basis physical (such as geo-national terrain) or abstract (such as ideology).

And yet what one finds in the *Premiers poèmes* is, precisely, a poetic voice that openly and frequently refers to its own national and personal space—taking us through the forests, hostels, and religious and educational architecture among which it has grown up—and which is unmistakably attributable to Tzara as an uncertain young poet from a Jewish family in rural Romania. Certainly, it would be surprising if a poet's work did not contain at least some trace of the scenes, events, and personal issues that have shaped his or her person-al life. But in the case of Tzara, the *Premiers poèmes* brings textual substance to the common-sense supposition that existing in an ethno-national vacuum is impossible, however attractive such an idea may be to avant-garde orators or scholars of their rhetoric. At the same time, for all these echoes and resonances, it is important to note that Tzara does not articulate his biographical references too easily or ac-cessibly: one of the most effective and pleasing general aspects of *Premiers poèmes* is that it already carries some of the uniquely strange but natural style that one finds from *Vingt-cinq poèmes* to *Miennes* [Mine] (*OC* 4: 209–28), and that is fundamental to the en-joyment of Tzara as a poet who—in the tradition of Mallarmé and "difficult" poetry—reveals himself not straightforwardly in the linear narratives of conventional verse or prose, but elliptically, across read-ings and re-readings. At one point in the poem "Tristesse domestique" [Domestic Unhappiness], the poet refers to "de tristes fragments de biographie" [sad biographical fragments] (44). It is a typically Tzarian meta-reference: the line points to the oblique way in which *Premiers poèmes* articulates its authorial references, functioning as a clausal statement that speaks back to ideas and representations that are dis-parate or that only emerge after a first reading. Here, as throughout Tzara's poetic output, it is as if he has pre-loaded his poems in a way

---

[7] For a published version of Ceia-Minjares's important account of Tzara as a trans-national avant-garde figure, see Ceia-Minjares (2006).

that anticipates the arrival of the critic, suggesting a sharp awareness of the themes and content of his own poetry.

However fragmented and abstracted, the biographical discourse of Tzara's early poems, therefore, leave a sense that it is surely unhelpful to conceive of him already writing in the guise of the a-national, a-ethnic outsider who is part of the caricatured picture that often emerges in accounts of Tzara's time in Zurich. Ceia-Minjares has written elegantly of two major tendencies in Tzara's performance of identity. The first tendency, connected to his desire to escape from his upbringing and reinvent himself, "pushes him to transform into something different, in a new shape, amorphous, unfixed, unstable, dynamic and anarchic" (Trans-national Avant-Garde 8); the second, which could be read as a product of the inevitable tension produced by the first attempt to transform into a wholly new identity, is "locked in a specific cultural memory by which it is forever haunted" (8). I have elsewhere argued that this tension—between a transformed sense of self and a residual memory of Romania as homeland—is fundamental to some of Tzara's later poetry, in which he performs a highly charged and complex mourning for his country of birth. This mourning seeps into the very phonemes of Tzara's French verse, producing a stuttering around *roumain*, and leaving an individual collection of poems with a phonetic watermark of national identity (Forcer 77–102). To borrow from Ceia-Minjares, what *Premiers poèmes* makes clear is that Romania is inscribed as a "specific cultural memory" from Tzara's very first poems, themselves written in Romanian as the language of his first country though it did not recognize him as one of its own citizens.

Not that biography is the only level on which Tzara's early poems are of interest. In particular, we should not pass over their fundamentally poetic qualities, which invite links with poetry as an ancient, technical, and cultural practice. In "L'Orage," for example, the eponymous song-man/deserter introduces a formula that is then rearticulated in variations both in the middle and at the end of his song. The formula first appears as a stand-alone stanza that follows the first stanza:

> Le froid: il effrite les os, ronge la chair
> Nous laissons le cœur pleurer

> [The cold: it crumbles bones, eats away at flesh
> We let our hearts weep] (30)

Parts of the formula recur in the first stanza of the second part of the poem:

> L'écume du froid durci s'agglomère en rameaux de sel,
> Effrite les os, ronge la chair
>
> [The foam of hardened cold piles up in rafts of salt
> Crumbles bones, eats away at flesh] (31)

The formula then closes the piece, the cold of which it speaks not only interrupting the deserter's song ("interrompue") but terminating it:

> Le chant – pensée interrompue
> Le froid effrite les os, ronge la chair,
> Laisse le cœur pleurer.
>
> [The song – interrupted thought
> The cold crumbles bones, eats away at flesh,
> Lets the heart weep.] (32)

A second formula in "L'Orage" is based around the solitude of the deserter: "Pour moi seul la nuit n'est pas belle" [Only for me is the night not beautiful] first appears in the middle of the second section. Four further versions are to be found subsequently, appearing as paired lines. Thus, in each of these cases, the second instance of "Pour moi seul" reads as an anaphora: "Pour moi seul la nuit n'est pas belle / Pour moi seul."

As I have argued in relation to Tzara's extraordinary epic *L'Homme approximatif* (Forcer 46–76), the style of "L'Orage" and other poems from *Premiers poèmes* suggests an affinity with the improvisation and oral inflection of much older poetic genres. For example, Rita Lejeune writes, "la chanson de geste des jongleurs ne procède pas de la littérature écrite mais de la littérature orale. Elle aussi touche à un temps où le poète improvise, sur des thèmes bien connus, à l'aide des formules" [the minstrel's *chanson de geste* derives not from written literature but from oral literature, and from a period in which poets improvised around familiar subjects with the help of formulas] (328–29). Scholars of medieval literature also stress the importance of repeated phrases as a performative safety device:

formulas would have served as structural *points de repères* upon
which the poet-singer could fall back in times of creative drought
(Aspland 4). As throughout Tzara's poetry, "L'Orage" carries traces
of these techniques and characteristics: common to poetry as a rhetorical and performative practice, the refrains and anaphoras provide
markers around which Tzara develops the themes of desertion and
solitude. Aesthetically, the refrains also bring to the deserter's song a
lyric quality, concentrating the poem's ambient sense of plangent elegy into memorable moments of intensity. All of which lyricism makes
for a crucial point of reference to Tzara's subsequent career, as Marc
Alyn observed compellingly in a review of *Premier poèmes* in 1965:

> [On] croit généralement que la poésie de Tzara s'est dé-
> ployée selon un itinéraire allant de la destruction au ly-
> risme…. Or les *Premiers Poèmes* me paraissent prouver
> précisément le contraire: Tzara à ses débuts était déjà un
> élégiaque de grand souffle, aimant sans doute les rappro-
> chements insolites ("La lumière met des gants") et
> s'exprimant pour ainsi dire d'emblée en vers libre mais an-
> nonçant beaucoup plus, en définitive, le lyrisme souverain
> de la maturité que le dynamiteur du langage de la brève—
> mais éclatante—période dadaïste.

> [It is generally thought that Tzara's poetry followed a line
> that moved from destruction to lyricism…. His *Premiers
> poèmes*, however, seem to me to prove precisely the oppo-
> site. That is, from the start Tzara was already a full-blooded
> elegiac poet, one who was fond of strange pairings ("The
> light puts on its gloves") and who expressed himself from
> the outset in free verse—but who anticipated more the sov-
> ereign lyricism of his later years than the linguistic detona-
> tions of the brief but explosive Dada period.]
>   (qtd. by Béhar *OC* 1: 633–34)

At the same time, the *Premiers poèmes* do inevitably contain
pleasingly poetic anticipations of the persona for which Tzara would
achieve his place in cultural infamy. For instance, in the opening stanza of the first poem Tzara provides a direct reference to linguistic violence and meaninglessness, writing to his eponymous "Cousine,
interne au pensionnat …" [Cousin, boarder at school …]: "… tu dé-
chires des lettres / qui n'ont pas de sens" [… you tear up letters / that
have no meaning] (27). The double meaning of "lettres" creates the
image of a destroyer not only of written texts but also of verbiage it-

self, joining with "qui n'ont pas de sens" to anticipate the cultural memory of Tzara Dadaistically feeding "meaning" into the mangle of his own poetic invention. Meanwhile, in "Viens à la campagne," there are flashes of Dada and its quintessential spirit of joy, irreverence, and reckless optimism:

> Nous nous mettrons tout nus sur la colline
> Pour que le prêtre se scandalise et que les filles se réjouissent
>
> [We will strip ourselves naked on the hill
> To scandalize the priest and thrill the girls] (34)

The notion of communal outrage—evocative of Zurich, Berlin, and other spheres of operation for Dada—returns in "Le Jour décline" [The Day Draws Down], where there is talk of a town in scandal (39). The *Premiers poèmes* also contains striking moments of intertextuality with some of Tzara's later and better-known poems. In "Chant de guerre," for instance, we read

> Le vent nous enfonce ses ongles dans les yeux
> Pour nous faire éclater les prunelles comme des grenades
>
> [The wind digs its nails into our eyes
> Bursting our pupils like grenades]

Itself evoking a distinctly Oedipal immolation that may on some level relate to Tzara's open remarks about incest,[8] this extract contains the grenades, fingers, and ocular violence spoken of in the 1916 Dada poem "Le Marin" [The Seaman]:

> les excursionnistes assis dentelle au bord de l'eau
> enfonce les doigts dans les orbites que la lumière crève grenades
>
> [the seated trippers lace at the water's edge
> thrust your fingers into the eye sockets exploded by
>   light grenades] (*OC* 1: 210)

---

[8] See *Faites vos jeux* [Place Your Bets] (1923–1934): "Quel est le garçon qui n'a pas senti des courants suspects ondoyer dans sa sensualité quand, pleurant, sa mère lui serrait la figure contre son sein, et prolongé cette sensation pour se venger de la dureté du père?" [What sobbing boy has not felt his senses ripple with dubious currents when his mother holds his face tightly to her breast, and what boy has not prolonged this sensation as revenge against paternal severity?] (*OC* I: 267).

So while the *Premiers poèmes* are lyrical in a way that Tzara's Dada poems are not, they nevertheless represent an extended opportunity for Tzara to rehearse and test some of the scenes, metaphors, objects, and voices that make up *Vingt-cinq poèmes* and *De nos oiseaux*. Some of these experiments are brilliantly and memorably odd. In "Dimanche" [Sunday], for instance, Tzara writes, "Ton histoire s'endort ainsi qu'un enfant qui berce un éléphant de laine" [Your story drifts off to sleep like a child rocking a woolen elephant] (40). Capable of more than simply combining things that do not belong together, part of Tzara's literary personality consists in articulating unusual and original unions between objects and parts of speech but without over-stressing strangeness into hysterical zaniness. The sleeping story and woolen elephant from "Dimanche" is a case in point: as the reader's mind dwells on the line and works through the strange mechanics of the simile, Tzara follows it up with a perfectly standard poetic description of rural tranquility: "Chez nous tout est calme lorsque les chevaux boivent à la fontaine" [At ours, all is calm when the horses drink at the fountain] (40). "Dimanche" closes with a further suggestion of the wry, self-referential, and playfully lugubrious persona Tzara develops as a Dadaist: "Je m'en vais rencontrer un poète triste et sans talent" [I am off to meet a sad and talentless poet] (41).

Is there, however, a more serious point in Tzara's joke about inferior poets? Why, that is to say, has there arisen such a discrepancy between Tzara's general visibility within twentieth-century European culture (his name is very well known) and familiarity with his poetry (his verse tends to be read only by specialists, and even then with heavy concentration on the period 1916–1924)? To my mind, the full response to this question involves a complex set of issues to do with the preservation of Tzara's status as Dada anarchist, dominant tendencies in traditional avant-garde criticism, Tzara's own self-image, and print runs, all of which I have attempted to set out elsewhere (Forcer 126–29). But the focus on Tzara as a Romanian-born writer working predominantly in French does bring into relief a further factor that I have not previously given sufficient thought to and that seems endemic to the ways in which Tzara is remembered, forgotten, written about, and not written about. For one cannot help feeling that Tzara's ethnonational characteristics—his status as a Jew living within Romania but outside the bounds of national citizenship, his switch from one language to another and movement between countries—are also symptomatic of Tzara's treatment by cultural history. In other words, Tzara does not "belong" to any one national heritage, and his case suggests that a conventionally clear and unproblematic national identity—one of the very ideas attacked by the Dadaists as arbitrary and malignant—is fundamental to the chances of an author's body of work being protected within a national patronage. Certainly, epic efforts to investigate Tzara's literary output have been made by individual researchers. One thinks in particular of Henri Béhar, the editor of Tzara's complete works with Flammarion, or of Mary Ann Caws as an Anglophone critic promoting Tzara within the canon of modern French poetry. As regards academic and cultural communities as a whole, however, Tzara occupies a position of limbo, neither wholly excluded nor wholly integrated. One thinks, for instance, of the distribution of Tzara's manuscripts after his death: now housed in the Jacques Doucet Library, Tzara's original material was first offered by his estate as a "Fonds Tzara" to the Bibliothèque Nationale in France, but the offer was declined (Béhar 7). Also revealing is the fact that Tzara's complete works have yet to be published on the Bible paper of the prestigious Collection Pléiade, the Gold Members' Area of French literary history (Pléiade editions exist for a number of Tzara's French-born avant-garde peers, including Louis Aragon, André Breton, René Char, and Paul Eluard). Arguably, there remains both recognition of Tzara as a major figure within Modernist culture—as in the 2005–2006 international Dada exhibition in Paris, New York, and Washington, DC—as well as a certain reluctance to take full ownership of his contribution to French and European culture.

For Ceia-Minjares, this ambiguous, checked attraction towards Tzara is fundamentally rooted in a set of problematic assumptions that characterize his treatment in cultural and literary history, and that derive in part from a basic failure to acknowledge Tzara's background as an (im)migrant Romanian Jew:

> Taken by Tzara's later mastery of French language and his semi-canonical status within the French Dada experiment, few critics or biographers have attended to the fact that the writer was an immigrant in Paris, a dislocated author writing in a borrowed language which he both revered and rejected. Oblivious to the relocation issue, contemporary critics often refer to Tzara as a *French writer*, for France, in the words of sociologist Gérard Noiriel, is a cultural cru-

cible whose central tenet is (and has been for at least two
centuries) the idea of "assimilation."
("Opting In, Opting Out" 5)[9]

By drawing attention to the ways in which the memory of Tzara is
constructed and perpetuated, Ceia-Minjares raises the important point
that traditional criticism of Tzara—which concentrates overwhelm-
ingly on the French-language poems of the seductive Dada period—
performs a naturalizing effect on Tzara, effectively writing him out of
his ethnic, national, and cultural past and into a French-based
memory. In her specific comments about "mastery" and her general
call for us to think critically about critical language, Ceia-Minjares
also takes us back to Béhar's suggestion that the Tzara of Zurich
wrote in a French of which he had complete command. The critical
downplaying and omission of Tzara's Romanian background may
retrospectively make safe anxieties circulating at the time to do with
"Tzara the refugee" ("Opting In, Opting Out" 21)—an unsettlingly
"foreign" figure who generated unease among Modernist luminaries
such as Apollinaire and Soupault in his "worrisome eclecticism" and
"dubious national associations" (6, 20, drawing on Soupault 3). If so,
then, it might also be asked whether Béhar's unequivocal conviction
about Tzara's level of French does not carry an understandable but
instructive trace of anxiety. After all, the claim for an author's literary
achievements is unlikely to be helped by the revelation that he had
trouble with spelling and conjugation.

In fairness to the critical tendency to think of Tzara as a "French"
writer, "Frenchness" is one of the principal characteristics that emerges across Tzara's literary output, considered apart from the authorial
and biographical essence of the person who produced it. From his Dada works, which account for only the first of six volumes in his complete works, to his last prose poems and short verse produced in the
1950s, there arises a striking series of connections to a quintessential-
ly French literary tradition as the reader is reminded variously of
French epic and lyric poetry, the *chanson de geste*, Nerval (1808–
1855), Mallarmé (1942–1898), Rimbaud (1854–1891), and Laforgue
(1860–1887) among others. Tzara was not naturalized French until
1947 (the same year he joined the French Communist Party), but one

---

[9] The emphasis and parentheses are the author's. On "assimilation," Ceia-
Minjares cites Noiriel, 1988.

could argue that he was writing himself into a French tradition from his earliest Romanian poems. As for Tzara's formal adoption of French identity, this must be placed in the immediate context of WW II, during which Tzara was sought by the Gestapo under multiple markers of identity—Jew, Communist, foreigner, cultural agitator—and forced into hiding in Souillac for the years 1942–1944 (Buot 350–54). To an extent, what Andrew Hussey says about Isidore Isou and a younger group of writers and artists born in Romania applies to Tzara as an older Romanian Jew: "Like Gellu Naum, Victor Brauner, Jacques Hérold and Ghérasim Luca, Isou was […] obliged, through the experience of war and Occupation, to renounce Romanian specificity for an imagined cultural and linguistic country which had Paris as its capital" (133).[10] Had Tzara returned to live in Romania between the end of WW II and his death in 1963 as a Francophile man of letters, he might also have been a target for the totalitarian regime led by Gheorghe Gheorghiu-Dej (Deletant 143).

The idea that Tzara in various ways "renounces" Romania, or at least ignores it, appears to gain further weight through Claude Sernet, translator of Tzara's *Primele poeme*, who detected no influence therein from Romanian writers (Browning 39). Given the apparent dominance of French literature in Romania in the nineteenth century—and what Dennis Deletant calls Romanian "gallomania" (144)—this is not particularly surprising. As we have seen, however, Tzara may take many of his cues from French literature and language; yet, this does not preclude the importance of Tzara's background as an (im)migrant Romanian Jew, either as an influence within his poetry or as a marker of his cultural identity that informs his reception by others. On the contrary, consideration of Romania—as an historical entity with its own cultural traditions and practices, and as a series of topographies articulated in individual poems—is fundamental to a developed understanding of Tzara and, crucially, of the Dada activity with which he is so intrinsically associated. In particular, Vasile Măruţă has offered considerable evidence that nineteenth-century Romanian culture

---

[10] In "Jean Isidore Isou," Ioan-Isidor Goldstein also took on a moniker that—like the pseudonym "Tristan Tzara" chosen by Samuel Rosenstock in 1915—cloaks the Jewish origins of its owner at a time when, as Hussey says, "Romania, and in particular the heavily pro-German provincial towns of Iaşi and Sibiu, [was] one of the most dangerous places in Europe to be a Jew outside the immediate influence of the Third Reich" (134).

(particularly literature) played a fundamental part in the formation of aesthetic and performative qualities traditionally seen as the hallmarks of Tzara's persona within Dada and the Franco-centric avant-garde.

For on top of his diet of heavyweight French Symbolists and *poètes maudits*, Tzara's literary beginnings were supplemented by an active and experimental poetic scene in Romanian poetry. Prominent among Romanian poets of the time was Ion Minulescu, in whom Măruţă describes "un goût du scandale dont va profiter son très jeune disciple Tristan Tzara" [a taste for scandal that Tristan Tzara, his very young disciple, would make the most of] (120). Măruţă identifies in other Romanian poets of the late nineteenth century further principles and characteristics that are intrinsic both to Tzara's development as a poet and to Dada, such as Alexandru Macedonski's (1854–1920) idea of an inherent absurdity in poetry (Măruţă specifically describes Macedonski as an influential figure around whom Tzara and other young Romanian poets would have gathered [119]). It could certainly be said that for Dada all human activity, not just poetry, is in some way ridiculous, but Macedonski's view of poetry as "illogique, donc absurde" [illogical, and therefore absurd] (qtd. in Măruţă, 119) does anticipate a specific principle underlying Dada's bewildering free verse: by definition, all poems disrupt the content, structure, and logic of prose into "illogical" forms, and Dada poetry can be thought of as an extreme form of the grammatical "rule breaking" that is common to poetry as a centuries-old cultural practice (Forcer 40–41). In turn, by willfully showcasing the illogical constructedness both of themselves and of poetry more generally, Dada poems implicitly make a notable, paradoxical claim: they are a more "authentic" verbal phenomenon than conventional poetry, for the latter enters into the "illogic" of the poem only to disavow its absurd potential with punctuation, syntax, beautifully metered lines, crafted metaphors, and so on. Măruţă notes that Tzara's early poems share with Urmuz (Demetru Demetrescu-Buzău, 1883–1923) a concurrent desire to explode language as part of "[une] révolte [...] contre l'impossibilité du langage à signifier quelque chose de cohérent" [[a] revolt [...] against the impossibility of language signifying anything coherent] (124). At the same time, the fetishized memory of Dada as "revolt" should not blind us to the more positive aspirations that run alongside the Dadaists' rattling of linguistic convention, such as the insistence on the sharing of playfulness, laughter, self-satire, and other life-affirming human energies beyond arbitrary divisions such as class and nationality. In respect of Tzara, Romanian literature, and Dada's appeal not to nationalities but to the whole of the human cosmos, we can see a poignant point of reference in Ovide Densuşianu (1873–1938), for whom "le devoir du poète est d'être en liaison avec les esprits humains de partout" [the duty of the poet is to be in contact with human spirits from all places] (qtd. in Măruţă 119).

So it is possible to locate in nineteenth-century Romanian culture numerous points of reference for the spirit and tone of Tzara's early poetry: scandal, violent verbal reaction against linguistic and literary convention, the sharing of human experience, and the straightforward desire to do something new. Măruţă adds that Tzara's fellow Dadaists would have been unaware of the collected resonances from Romania that were part of the "expérience roumaine du poète" (124). Indeed, Măruţă goes so far as to say that, "Ces premiers poèmes roumains, fortement imagés et fortement authentiques, sont les seuls en mesure d'expliquer la véritable révolution littéraire entreprise par l'inventeur du [sic] 'dada'" [Loaded with imagery and powerfully authentic, these first Romanian poems are the only texts capable of explaining the true literary revolution undertaken by the inventor of "Dada"] (125). At the same time, it is important not to become beholden to the necessarily broad and speculative links between writers and periods that can be produced by exercises in cultural comparison. As Magda Radu notes in an instructive parody of the seductive but potentially dangerous syllogisms involved in the cross-mapping of cultural histories, "if the vaudeville and cabaret tradition was an important precedent for Hennings and Ball, and if this tradition also influenced [Ion Luca] Caragiale [1853–1912], then there is the obvious link between Tzara, Janco and Caragiale."

Cultural history can take us so far, and the recent growth of published interest in Eastern Europe and Modernism is to be welcomed. But there remains a considerable body of work to be written regarding the fine detail of the relationship between different types of texts. Indeed, it may ultimately be the case that the full account of European avant-gardists will treat the detail of individual poems not only as supporting evidence but as the prime driver of research questions and results. In other words, beyond establishing that Tzara began writing poetry in a particular cultural climate—a necessary but also limited stage of research that keeps us bound to biography, cultural narratives, and a rhetoric along the lines of "trends that probably had a general influence on Tzara's work"—critics should also work from the internal world of Tzara's textuality and take their agenda from his poems themselves. Individual poems, by driving and introducing the prevailing critical interest in manifestos, who said what to whom, and who was influenced by whom—rather than finding themselves framed or simply occluded by bio-historical context—can bring some much-needed high resolution to the inevitably complex question of "influence." Noting that we cannot be sure of the extent to which Tzara had already detached himself from Romanian Symbolist currents on leaving the country in 1915, Radu quotes a helpfully direct reminder from Ion Pop that we can at least be sure of one aspect of Tzara's aesthetic ambition at the time: "on his way to Zurich Tzara already knew what *not* to do next" (44). Tzara's poems themselves, in all their singular detail, are still waiting to be asked for their full response as to what Tzara *did* do next.

Works Cited

Aspland, C.W. *A Syntactical Study of Epic Formulaic Expressions Containing the –ant Forms in 12th Century French Verse*. St. Lucia, Queensland: U of Queensland P, 1970.

Béhar, Henri. *Tristan Tzara*. Paris: Oxus, 2005.

Browning, Gordon Frederick. *Tristan Tzara: The Genesis of the Dada Poem or from Dada to Aa*. Stuttgart: Heinz, 1979.

Buot, François. Tristan Tzara*: L'homme qui inventa la révolution Dada*. Paris: Grasset, 2002.

Ceia-Minjares, Laura. "Opting-in, Opting Out: The Radical Melancholy of the Modernist Margin or, Tristan Tzara Places a Double Bet." *The Avant-Garde and the Margin: New Territories of Modernism*. Eds. Sanja Bahun-Radunovíc and Marinos Pourgouris. Newcastle: Cambridge Scholars P, 2006. 1–25.

_____. "Trans-national Avant-Garde: The Case of Tristan Tzara." *Between a Melancholic History, and an Urgent Revolution: Performance, Identity, Francophonie in the Early Works of Tristan Tzara*. Diss. U of California, Davis, 2005. ebook.

Deletant, Dennis. "The Image of France in the Romanian People's Republic, 1948–1965." *Forum for Modern Language Studies* 36.2 (2000): 143–52.

Forcer, Stephen. *Modernist Song: The Poetry of Tristan Tzara*. Oxford: Legenda, 2006.

Hayward, Susan. "The City as Narrative: Corporeal Paris in Contemporary French Cinema (1950s–1990s)." Ed. Myrto Konstantarakos, *Spaces in European Cinema*. Exeter: Intellect, 2000. 23–34.

Heart Fine Art (books, print, documents, sound and object multiples related to the international avant-gardes and contemporary art) <http://www.heartfineart.com/Total.html> [accessed 16 July 2007].

Hussey, Andrew. ""La Divinité d'Isou": The Making of a Name and a Messiah." *Forum for Modern Language Studies* 36.2 (2000): 132–42.

Lejeune, Rita. "Technique formulaire et chansons de geste." *Le Moyen Age: revue d'histoire et de philologie* 60 (1954): 311–34.

Măruţă, Vasile. ""L'Esprit de révolte" dans l'art à Paris et à Bucharest." *Forum for Modern Language Studies* 36.2 (2000): 118–31.

Noiriel, Gérard. *Le Creuset français. Histoire de l'immigration: XIXe et XXe siècles*. Paris: Seuil, 1988.

Pop, Ion. *Avangarda în literatura română*. Bucharest: Atlas, 2000.

Radu, Magda. Rev. of Tom Sandqvist, *Dada East: The Romanians of the Cabaret Voltaire*. Cambridge, Mass., & London: MIT, 2006. *Art Margins: Contemporary Central and Eastern European Visual Culture* 18 October 2007 <http://www.artmargins.com/index.php/archive/132–dada-east> [accessed 26 July 2010].

Sanouillet, Michel. *Dada à Paris*. Paris: Flammarion, 1993.

Soupault, Philippe. "Souvenir de Tristan Tzara." *Europe*, numéro spécial, 555–56 (July–August 1975): 3–7.

Tzara, Tristan. *Œuvres complètes*. 6 vols. Ed. Henri Béhar. Paris: Flammarion, 1975–1991. (*OC*)

_____. *Primele Poeme/First Poems*. Trans. Michael Impey and Brian Swann. New York: New Rivers P, 1976.

_____. *Primele poeme, urmate de Insurecţia de la Zurich*. Ed. Saşa Pană. Bucharest: Unu, 1934.

TZR.C. Correspondence sent and received by Tristan Tzara. Bibliothèque Littéraire Jacques Doucet, Paris.

TZR.MS. Numbered original manuscripts of Tristan Tzara. Bibliothèque Littéraire Jacques Doucet, Paris.

The Surrealist Group of Bucharest: Collective Works, 1945–1947

Monique Yaari
Pennsylvania State University

The surrealist group of Bucharest, active—mostly clandestinely—during the 1940s and dissolved in the early 1950s, consisted of five men born between 1910 and 1916: Virgil Teodorescu, Gellu Naum, Ghérasim Luca, Paul Paon (Păun at the time), and D[olfi] Trost.[1] Their collective work is searching, experimental, at times intensely theoretical, written primarily in French, and, in the case of the last three, ranging across word and image. As a cohesive entity best known through a series of texts and a related exhibition known as the "Infra-Noir," squeezed into a narrow window of post-war cultural liberalism between a fascist and a communist regime (1945–1947),

---

[1] Virgil Teodorescu was born in 1909. Also known as the founder, in 1932, of the youthful avant-garde journal, *Liceu*, he published under several pseudonyms, including Virgil Rareş (see Pană, ed., 433 and Pop, ed., 601; however, the pseudonym that Pană mentioned Teodorescu as using in his "collaborative writings with Ghérasim Luca" does not appear in any of the known published works). He signed Teodoresc*ou* to all his French-language texts. Ghérasim Luca was born Salman Locker in 1913. He chose to transform in 1947 the pseudonym he had adopted during his adolescence into his official last name, Gherasim Luca, although he has come to be known as Luca, and his work is referenced under Luca, Ghérasim (or Gherasim). In my text here, I will be using interchangeably Ghérasim Luca and Luca. Gellu Naum was born in 1915. Also born in 1915, Zaharia Herşcovici, who officially changed his name to Zaharia Zaharia in 1945, had taken on since the 1930s the pseudonym Paul Păun, become, during the 1950s–early 1960s, Paul Paon, and later Paul Paon Zaharia. But, to hide his identity while still in communist Romania, he sometimes signed Yvenez (an inversion of the French "venez-y"). I will be referring to him as Paon. Dolfi Trost was born in 1916. He preferred to be known as D. Trost, or simply, Trost, to avoid (according to private testimonies) a first name reminiscent of Hitler. In my list of primary sources, I have faithfully reproduced the form of each name as it appears on each of the respective publications.

this group is infinitely more somber than an earlier avant-garde group to which some of its members had belonged.[2] Yet, by way of introduction, the connection deserves to be mentioned.

The earlier, 1930s group, known through its iconoclastic journal *Alge*, "algae" in Romanian, published from 1930 to 1933, was closer in its spirit to Dada. Youthfully defiant, the "Algists" (Ghérasim Luca, Paul Paon, Sesto Pals, Jules [Puiu or S.] Perahim, Aurel Baranga)[3] are often remembered for a not-so-innocent prank, which in turn echoes a similar, earlier exploit by one of their older friends, the poet Geo Bogza, but which in their case brought about the cessation of their journal's publication. A particularly provocative issue of their journal having been mailed to several prominent personalities of the time, including a foremost cultural and political figure, Nicolae Iorga, a series of police searches instigated by the latter yielded even more insolent material of the Algists' making, particularly an *hors-série* whose title was the Romanian slang word for the male sexual organ, humorously dubbed in the subtitle "universal organ." Arrested "for pornography" together with their publisher, and their mischief featured on the front page of a particularly inimical press, they were imprisoned and served nine days of the initial thirty-day sentence.[4] This

---

[2] The small number of participants in this group may seem surprising. Not only was their selection made on the basis of strict elective affinities, but those who, we might surmise, might have potentially joined them, had already left or would soon leave the country—Jacques Hérold and Victor Brauner for France, Jules Perahim for the USSR. Back in Bucharest after the war, Perahim had become a staunch supporter of the communist regime and its socialist realist aesthetics (until his escape to Paris in 1969 and return to a surrealist vein), an attitude that triggered a definitive break with his 1930s friends.

[3] Aurel Baranga was the journal's editor. Occasional contributors to *Alge* included (famously) a five-year-old boy, Freddy Goldstein, but also Man Ray, Jean David, B. Fondane, Mattis Teutsch. The journal knew two iterations. The subtitle used in its second iteration, *Revistă ditirambică* [Dithyrambic Journal], reflects more accurately than its initial subtitle, *Revistă de artă modernă* [Journal of Modern Art], the nature of its avant-garde spirit, which is precisely what distinguished it from earlier or fully contemporary journals.

[4] See Pană 417–22. A first-hand account of this incident was provided by Sesto Pals in a letter to Paon's widow, late in life.

experience of freedom curtailed, together with the encounter, in prison, with representatives of the workers' movement, reinforced their
political sensibilities, which were already anti-establishment and
markedly to the Left. In some sense, this experience is also a fitting
prelude to the subsequent ethos and fate of the mature surrealist group
of the 1940s.

The broader interwar cultural climate in the Romanian capital—
where a thriving, cosmopolitan avant-garde activity had flourished
beyond such mid-1920s journals as *75HP* and *Contimporanul*—also
merits attention as part of the group's background. Pre-surrealist manifestations in 1930s Bucharest included, aside from *Alge*, the earlier
periodical, *Unu* (1928–1932). *Unu* resurrected in its pages the Romanian writer Urmuz as a purely autochthonous ancestor of surrealism,
while at the same time exposing its readers to the revolutionary mentality and aesthetics of French surrealists, their rival group Le Grand
Jeu, and their precursors. Even a cursory glance at the Table of Contents of various *Unu* issues will testify to the presence in its pages of
Rimbaud, Reverdy, Cocteau, Breton, Éluard, Aragon, Vitrac, Daumal,
Audard, Tanguy, and the like. The memoir of *Unu*'s editor, the poet
Saşa Pană, titled *Născut în '02* [Born in '02], remains a vivid account
of both the avant-garde spirit of the time and the obvious awareness,
within local artistic circles, of French developments in literature and
the arts. More concretely, in the domain of the visual arts, besides
Perahim's regular contributions to *Unu* and *Alge* in a surrealist vein,
and aside from Marcel Janco and Tristan Tzara, temporarily back in
Bucharest from their shared adventure in Zurich (the founding of the
Dada movement), a web of connections was being woven westward,
throughout the 1920s and 1930s. A major presence was that of Victor
Brauner, who straddled Bucharest and Paris before settling in France
definitively. Jacques Hérold, who moved to Paris at age twenty, remained a reference for his Bucharest friends. And the Paris-educated
Jean David was active during the 1930s in the Romanian capital. It is
not surprising, therefore, that upon the return of Ghérasim Luca and
Gellu Naum, in late 1939, from a trip to Paris begun in 1938, the surrealist group of Bucharest was constituted as such, some of its mem-

bers having adopted a surrealist idiom even earlier on. But although the affinities between the already famous and the emerging group were substantial and affirmed, this belated Eastern European surrealist group was not to be simply a carbon copy of its Parisian counterpart.[5] Much to the contrary, as we shall see below.

A Brief History

Founded, therefore, some fifteen years after the birth of Breton's Parisian group, the Bucharest surrealist group came into being at a particularly unpropitious historical moment. Given the onset of WW II, it was immediately forced underground, its public activity curtailed. Moreover, three of its members were Jewish—Luca, Trost, and Paon. As Mihail Sebastian's memoir, *Journal*, recounts, and as expressed by Eugène Ionesco's *Rhinocéros*, the atmosphere of the years 1935–1944 was one of gradual indoctrination and betrayal. But there was worse, as amply testified today.[6] While the pogrom that took place in Bucharest in January 1941 (on the heels of a terrifying earthquake only a few months earlier) left the three unscathed, they experienced throughout the war, in addition to the war's miseries endured by all, various forms of uncertainty, discrimination, and forced labor—albeit not of the worst sort that befell so many. Another member of the group, Gellu Naum, was drafted, and profoundly traumatized by the experience of the war seen up close from another angle. And, as evidenced by published post-war letters from Luca to Brauner, there was extreme anxiety about the fate of their friends in France (Brauner, Hérold), who, as both Jewish and avant-garde artists, were imperiled under Pétain's fascist regime. Yet in spite or perhaps because of these experiences, in a kind of parallel life that provided both a shield and a form of resistance, the group managed to engage in a

---

[5] I have opted to refer to Romania as an Eastern European country because in the historical context discussed here, this term's political connotations are appropriate. But Romania's geographical location, its basically Romance language, and some of the earlier chapters of its history would qualify it as Southeastern or Central European.

[6] See Moscovici, Solomon, Carp. See also studies by Iancu and Laignel-Levastine.

feverish covert activity during this period, judging from drawings and literary works that came to light immediately after the war and some that are still awaiting attention. Deeply marked by the darkness of the political events but also sustained by their own group's effervescence during the war years, they resurfaced for the fleeting period of liberty mentioned above, under a still somewhat permissive regime. But with increased Stalinization, they soon were forced once again to cease all public activities since these so markedly deviated from the Party's Zhdanovist line,[7] and eventually dispersed.[8]

The period 1947–1952 was one of prolonged and agonized transition, during which desperate attempts were made to maintain the connection among those who departed and those who stayed behind, on the one hand, and on the other to establish or renew connections with Parisian friends and with André Breton and his group. But isolation ensued and, as Paon writes late in life in a private autobiographical note, the "élan associatif" [the associative momentum] came to an end.

Two of the group's members remained in Bucharest for the rest of their lives and reverted of course to the native language. Remaining also meant—if not following to the letter at the very least not fully

---

[7] Post-war communist Romania adopted Stalinist cultural policies: Socialist realism, inflected and hardened since 1946 by Andrei Zhdanov's doctrine, known as Zhdanovism. The resulting diktats forbade formal experimentalism as well as any thematic deviation from the ruling party's ideology. Ignoring the party line was a seriously punishable offense.

[8] These data are culled from a variety of sources, in addition to those individually cited: the holdings of the Doucet Library in Paris; the private archives of Paul Paon and his wife, Rahel Zaharia; interviews and correspondence with Paul Paon, Rahel Zaharia, Antonia Rasicovici (Luca's first wife, a primary witness to his youth); biographical information in Dominique Carlat's thoroughly researched essay on Ghérasim Luca; Victor Brauner's correspondence published by the Centre Pompidou; and Rémy Laville's biographical study of Gellu Naum (based largely on interviews with Naum). The latter, however, with respect to other members of the group and in correlation with multiple other sources, contains numerous inaccuracies, some of which are noted in Petre Răileanu's study of Ghérasim Luca's Bucharest years. They may be due, at least in part, either to the nature of the information received or to the difficulties of transmission across languages.

transgressing in their art the regime's diktats, which were eased
somewhat at the end of the 1960s. Gellu Naum resorted for a long
time to publishing mainly children's literature and translations, and
for twenty-five years was forbidden to travel outside the borders of
his native country. Regaining some freedom after 1968, he in time
became a celebrated poet and much-admired personality. Virgil
Teodorescu managed to walk a thin line between autonomy versus
conformity in his artistic production, after 1968 becoming, first, vice-
president (see Dragomir), and then president of the Writers' Union. In
this capacity, private testimonies (notably Paon's) indicate that he
endeavored to discreetly help rather than control his friends and fellow writers, which in those days was not generally the rule for those
in power.

The other three (referred to as "la trinité" [sic] in Biro and
Passeron's *Dictionnaire du surréalisme*)[9] were able to leave Romania
legally between 1950 and 1961, after a failed illegal attempt in 1947.
Trost and Ghérasim Luca left via Israel in 1950, and reached Paris in
1952. A few years later and with two important volumes published at
the Éditions Arcanes in 1953 and 1955, Trost moved on to the US
(New York and Chicago). Subsequently, as far as present research can
ascertain, he was barely heard from again. Ghérasim Luca stayed in
Paris definitively, dedicating himself to his poetry and art. Published
first by Soleil Noir, later by Corti, and finally by Gallimard, he has
been considered by no other than Gilles Deleuze "one of the greatest
of French poets and of all times" (*Superpositions* 108). He also continued creating in a range of other media (works on paper; objects,
including *livres-objets*; and poetry recitals). Today, sixteen years after
his suicide, he has acquired the status of a somewhat legendary figure,
at least in French-speaking Europe, his work circulating not only in
print but also through exhibitions, recordings, and film. Paul Paon,
who in 1941 obtained his diploma in medicine and surgery, becoming
therefore a much-needed practitioner, could not easily be granted an

---

[9] The expression is found in the article dedicated to surrealism in Romania, signed
V.I., i.e., Virgil Ierunca (370). See also *La Planète affolée*.

exit permit from Romania and left last, in 1961. In the interim he had kept his artistic activities secret, with rare veiled manifestations abroad. Settled in Haifa, Israel, he was finally able to resume his artistic activity openly without renouncing his medical profession, which for him was a guarantor of artistic autonomy. He marked this turning point by signing his work Paul Paon Zaharia, adding his real surname to his pseudonym. But he remained a discreet presence on the art scene, seemingly relishing this posture of relative retreat.

Thus, each of the five group members continued their literary and artistic activity after 1947 independently and under radically different conditions, yet all marked, for shorter or longer periods, by some form of at least internal exile. By the mid-1990s all the group's members had died: Trost very early, in 1966; Teodorescu in 1987; Luca and Paon, who had remained very close, at a few months from each other in 1994; and Naum in 2001. But their youthful bonding, common experiments, and lasting friendships—albeit increasingly challenged by distance, disagreements, and even estrangement—appear through the prism of their work and correspondence (a correspondence either intense, like that between Luca and Paon, or more sparse with friends of the 1930s—Brauner in Paris, Sesto Pals in Tel-Aviv, Bogza in Bucharest)—as a unique and precious moment.

The Choice of French

From 1945 onward, in the majority of its collective production, the group chose French as its main vehicle of expression. Since then, three of its members held on to this idiom in their individual works. Why French? Was it a case of snobbism or a result of France's hegemonic presence in Eastern Europe? The answer, I argue, is infinitely more complex, and specific to this group's historical context.

Granted, for centuries French had been the language of the local intellectual elites, at least in the capital, and a venue through which a more marginal culture could aim to reach a wider audience and participate in international debates. But French, for this particular group, was also the idiom in which could best be kept alive those passionate friendships and intellectual exchanges with far-away friends from the past and from a potential future, such as Brauner and Breton, respectively. Most importantly, I presume, it was the language of cultural and political affinities, namely with the main surrealist group based in Paris, which criticized vehemently all forms of totalitarianism, from the extreme Right to the extreme Left, as well as all forms of nationalism and rootedness. In the political context of the time, trapped between fascism on the one hand and Stalinism on the other, and subjected to dogmatic and discriminatory forms of nationalism, it is likely that they elected to express themselves in French because it was a language untainted, *in their own personal experience*, by either of these ideologies, and therefore available to them as a vehicle of affirmation and of resistance to impositions and censorship. French was also the language in which was written (by Breton with Trotsky under the signature of Diego Rivera) a manifesto to which they could subscribe, *Pour un art révolutionnaire indépendant* (1938), which argued for the freedom and autonomy of art against the diktats of Stalinist socialist realism, and led to the creation of the Fédération Internationale des Artistes Révolutionnaires Indépendants (FIARI). Moreover, it is plausible to surmise that, underlying these linguistic, cultural, political, and existential reasons, was a deep psychological imperative. French allowed these individuals and the group as a whole to "shift," at least in spirit, to an alternative, broader cultural space while keeping their autonomy intact, that is, without completely adhering to it. A space other than the one that constrained them, and one that they were free, from afar, to *make* into their own: neither here nor there, both here and there.[10] Finally, in time, Paris would become also (or again) a concrete geographical reality, a place to physically be in, for each of them to differing degrees: for Trost during a few years in the

---

[10] I stress "personal experience," "internal," "psychological," and "existential" to indicate that I do not claim they attributed any essence or purity to the French language (which, from a certain point onward, would have hardly been possible, given France's collaborationist government during WW II). Rather, I suggest that French was both a venue of escape from the narrower and hostile home context and a means of connecting with a group that displayed a kindred sensibility and political stance. This connection became during the war strictly virtual, since all concrete forms of communication were severed.

1950s; for Ghérasim Luca since 1952 for the rest of his life; for Paul Paon since the 1960s through short visits and exhibitions; and even for Teodorescu and Naum who were occasionally allowed to travel to the West. But the five who resurfaced as a group between 1945 and 1947 had already inhabited that city *in absentia*, while at the same time molding its surrealist culture to their own conceptual frame.

From this perspective, it would be improper to consider the group's choice of language as a form of cultural exile. Instead, the use of French appears to have been a tool to recompose one's cultural or at least artistic identity, in a however de-centered way, an identity that conditions in the homeland were aiming to colonize, or stifle and suppress. This is the hypothesis I wish to suggest through the use of the terms "surrealist group of Bucharest" and "of French expression" rather than "Romanian surrealist group." It is the predominant language of their most substantial collective works together with the urban environment in which this activity occurred that are thus foregrounded as the dual "site" of their activity, rather than an adverse and consistently countered national context.

Yet, it would be equally mistaken to essentialize the group's use of French, as I hope results from the above statements. Nor would it be accurate to assume that the French option held the same status for all five individuals, for the situation was in fact more nuanced and complicated. Gellu Naum was profoundly conflicted about the abandonment of the native language. Although he signed all of the published group's collective texts, meant to represent their common positions and written in French, he did not contribute to the set of individual texts by each of the other group members gathered in the collection Infra-Noir. Nor did he sign the programmatic statements the other four addressed to Breton in 1947. Virgil Teodorescu, consistently present in all the group's publications and declarations formulated in French, never used French, to my knowledge, in his other works. Yet it is interesting to note that he composed in 1940 a poem "în leopardă," that is, in "Leopardian," an invented language.[11] By contrast, Ghérasim Luca published exclusively in French since 1945,[12] and Trost and Paon switched definitively to French in 1945 and 1946, respectively. Perhaps, in addition to the reasons for this choice discussed above, Luca, Trost, and Paon were also already engaging, through language, in their migration away from a homeland hostile not only to their philosophy of life and art (as was equally the case for Naum and Teodorescu) but in addition hostile to their ethnicity.[13]

The Group's Collective Activity

By "collective activity" I mean, first of all, literary texts, manifestos, and theoretical statements co-authored or at least signed or illustrated by a total of two, three, or all five of the group's members; or else sets of individually authored texts (*plaquettes*) published together as one collective unit. I also include under this term exhibitions and their attendant publications: one exhibition by two of the group's members, Trost and Ghérasim Luca, accompanied by a text signed by the two (while Paon was exhibiting separately at about the same time without any parallel written statement); a second exhibition that brought together Luca, Trost, and Paon, accompanied by a text signed by all five protagonists. Some, but not all of these texts were likely produced according to the surrealist technique of *cadavre exquis* [exquisite corpse]. Certain programmatic statements communicated in

---

[11] According to Saşa Pană's anthology, this text was accompanied by *stilamancies* by Trost; see the entry for Virgil Teodorescu (433).

[12] He actually had written *Le Vampire passif* directly in French already in 1941, although it was published in 1945 (Bucharest, Éditions de l'Oubli). The selected bibliography I provide here does not include individual works produced by each. The majority of these are mentioned, however, in the body of the text.

[13] The linguistic choice away from the native tongue, however, should not in any way be directly associated with one's ethnic roots. Jewish writers such as Petre Solomon opted for the Romanian language, however trying the conditions in Romania may have been; Celan chose the language in which the atrocities that killed his parents were perpetrated (German) even though he settled in France; while writers such as Cioran, who in the 1930s had been one of the voices of the nationalist anti-Semitic ideology, eventually opted for France and the French language, partly to leave communism behind.

epistolary form to André Breton and some unpublished texts belong to this category as well, as do other types of activities—experimental *jeux* [games] performed in the 1940s, or attempts at non-verbal, telepathic communication following the group's dispersal, in the early 1950s.[14] I limit my focus here to co-authored materials published between 1945 and 1947 and, more briefly, to the artistic endeavors they theorized.[15]

Friendship and Dissent: 1945

That some of these activities reflect oppositions between subgroups formed fleetingly then quickly dissolved, is overshadowed by the overall close ties and collaborations among all five group members (as results from publications and correspondence ranging from 1945 to 1947). In fact, friendship and collective identity were paramount within the group during the 1940s. Yet a sharp intellectual divergence rocked the group for the first few months of 1945, the first year of their public resurfacing, sparked partly by the question of choice of language, and indeed expressed *through* this choice. Ghérasim Luca and Trost published *Dialectique de la dialectique: message adressé au movement surréaliste international* (discussed further below) in the guise of a manifesto claiming the group's specificity: positioned as much in the wake of French surrealism as in dialogue with it and ultimately surpassing it. Naturally, for European surrealists to take note, the language of the friendly but markedly distinct group had to be French. The same holds true for the *Présentation de graphies colorées, de cubomanies et d'objets*, the text that accompanied Luca and Trost's January 1945 joint exhibition and outlined

---

[14] Paul Paon's *La Rose parallèle* [The Parallel Rose], published privately in 1975, documents some of these activities.

[15] Throughout the discussion that follows, all translations into English are my own. For all works mentioned, I have included their titles in the original language, to avoid the confusion that reigns in many, especially electronic, sources. All italics and underscores are the authors' as quoted, unless otherwise specified.

the processes they had invented to create new forms of art (Figures 4.1, 4.2, 4.3, and 4.4).[16]

For their part, Naum, Paon, and Teodorescu published *Critica mizeriei* [The Misery of Critique] in Romanian as a manifesto against homegrown literary criticism, while at the same time voicing opposition in a footnote to some of the theoretical positions put forth in the above two texts by their peers (an opposition further expanded in that same year by Naum in "Inventatorii banderolei" [The Inventors of Banners], a particularly aggressive appendix to his *Teribilul interzis* [The Terrible Interdiction]).[17] If one steps outside of the rift per se, however, a cumulative meaning emerges from the double gesture that consists of the parallel publication of *Dialectique de la dialectique* and *Critica mizeriei*: the endeavor to stake out a space for the group, away from everything that was despised at home, but also distinct-from that which was admired abroad—in short, unique. That it is the

---

[16] Reproduced by permission, as well as the documents shown in Figures 4.5, 4.7, and 4.8 (private archives Paul Paon).

[17] Does the title *Critica mizeriei* echo Breton's *Misère de la poésie* (which in turn resonates with Marx's *Misère de la philosophie*, directed against Proudhon's *Philosophie de la misère*)? It is this possible echo that has inspired my translation, while the content of the work might have warranted the translation "miserable critique." Is the title *Teribilul interzis* an oblique allusion to "le terrible interdit," which "la seule imagination" [imagination alone] can possibly break through and vanquish, according to Breton's 1924 *Manifeste*? And if so, might "The Inventors of Banners" refer to what was perceived as too assertive and prescriptive in Luca and Trost's pronouncements? Given the terms in which Naum's attack was formulated, the most important of which is the accusation of "idealism," later softened by a jocular allusion to Hegel in Naum's 1945 letter to Brauner discussed below, this is a plausible hypothesis but one I have not yet fully verified. A minor page in the history of this avant-garde, as there are so many in the histories of all avant-gardes, its core can find elucidation in Dominique Carlat's study of Luca. Without delving into the Romanian side of the conflict because of a language barrier, Carlat offers a superb analysis of the pull between idealism and materialism and their dialectical surpassing through poetry in *Dialectique de la dialectique* and in Luca's other works from the same period—an analysis that should put to rest any misinterpretations of Luca's and Trost's positions on this axis at the time (see his chapter "Autour du renversement: une lecture intempestive de Hegel," in *Ghérasim Luca l'intempestif* (subsequently referred to as *L'Intempestif*).

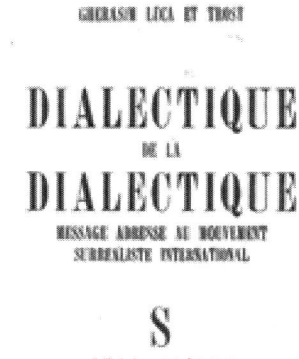

Figure 4.1. Gherasim Luca and Trost, "Dialectique de la dialectique." Cover.

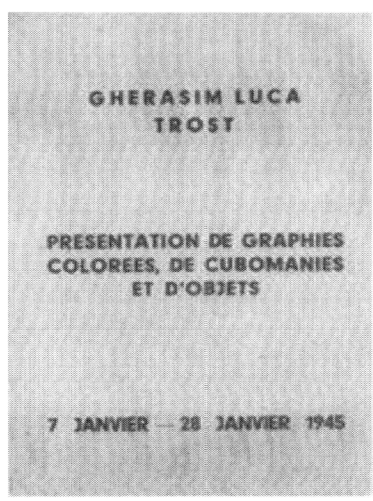

Figure 4.2. Gherasim Luca and Trost, "Présentation de graphies colorées, de cubomanies et d'objets." Cover.

Monique Yaari

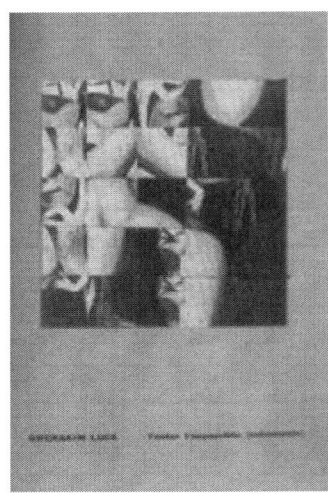

Figure 4.3. Gherasim Luca, "Tenter l'impossible" (cubomanie).
"Présentation de graphies colorées, de cubomanies et d'objets." Illustration.

Figure 4.4. Trost, "Mouvement relatif-absolu" (vaporisation).
"Présentation de graphies colorées, de cubomanies et d'objets." Illustration.

first of these texts that has remained in the annals of international surrealism is not surprising, given—beyond the linguistic choice—its
daring substance and theoretical tenor.

To follow up on the questions of language and the ethos of friendship, Trost, Luca, and from this point onward Paon as well never
reverted to the native tongue, while Teodorescu joined Naum in a
common 1946 volume that included Teodorescu's *Spectrul longevității* and Naum's *122 de cadavre*. Paon, although he provided illustrations to works by the dissenting two, including a frontispiece to
Naum's *Teribilul interzis*, seems to have been more invested in maintaining the group's cohesion. His mixed-media work termed "lovaj"
that illustrates Naum and Teodorescu's 1946 volume mentioned
above, and the four "lovaje" that illustrate Teodorescu's 1945 *Butelia
de Leyda*, are accompanied by a short insert in the latter publication,
which he humorously titled "Brevet de lovaj" [Lovage patent]. The
"Brevet" can be read as a gentle, even "lov[ing]" reply to the entire
group, one that minimizes the divisive issues and supports collective
authorship, alluding to Lautréamont's "La poésie doit être faite par
tous. Non par un" [Poetry must be made by all. Not by one]. In describing a new technique he had devised, named *lovaj*, Paon provides
a modest pendant to the multiple new techniques detailed by Trost
and Luca in their co-authored text, *Présentation*, but refuses to call it
an "invention," as they had done.[18] In some sense, however, it is
Paon's 1945 individual exhibition of drawings, *Expozitia de desene
Paul Păun*, devoid of any accompanying theoretical statements, that
was his actual intervention in the visual dimension of the discussion.
Using a more traditional medium and support, pen-and-ink on paper
with a surrealist thematic ranging from the nightmarish to the humor-

---

[18] "Lovaj" *may* be the transcription, in Romanian, of the English "lovage," in Romanian "leuștean," a flavorful cooking herb much used in local popular cuisine. But it
also happens to include the root of the word "love." One way of interpreting this
denomination is that Paon wished to cast in a friendly light the disagreement his "brevet" (which was in fact an anti-patent, so to speak) ironically expressed. The technique in question is described as follows: "Place three images on a white paper and
establish among them the first formal relation that comes to mind."

ous, he lets some of the figures and their settings dissolve to a point approaching abstraction (Figures 4.5 and 4.6).

Finally, in March 1945, Naum's poignant letter to Brauner, which received from the painter a warm response studded with linguistic code switching (between Romanian and French) brushes away the earlier conflict and describes his friends in the group as "admirable," in particular in light of the ordeal of the war.[19] Luca's sustained, illuminating correspondence with Brauner in 1946 (before censorship altered its tone and pace), while fully maintaining the *distinguo*, confirms, "Nous restons cinq, les mêmes" [We remain five, the same] (21 April, 218).[20]

Yet he nuances this insight: "there are, perhaps, three or four" factions within the group of five, and if they have "renounced, for the moment, any divisiveness," it is partly to test the possibility of establishing among themselves a "rapport plus exact (séparation nettement qualitative ou, au contraire, une collaboration plus serrée" [a more precise rapport (clear qualitative separation or, on the contrary, a closer collaboration)] (218). Some thirty years later (in 1977), Paon, reminiscing in an interview with the poet Stefan Baciu, a witness of their

---

[19] "Admirable Zola [Luca to his Bucharest intimates], Dolfi, Paul, and especially Virgil, enormously changed from the way you knew them. Ceaselessly ravaged, the violence with which we rattled each other may only be attributed perhaps to the gravity of the moment and the impossibility of allowing the slightest point of vulnerability" ("Două scrisori" [Two letters], *Athanor* 1: 55, in Romanian in the text). This about-face recalls Breton's own retractions in the "Avertissement" [Foreword] to the second, 1946, edition of the *Second Surrealist Manifesto*, originally published in 1930. To explain the violence of the polemics that permeated it, including some of his own past attacks against close friends and partners, Breton incriminates not only the example of revolutionary literature's tone, but above all the high exigencies and high stakes involved in a context marked by "le malaise des temps" [the troubled times], i.e., the awareness of the "ineluctable return of a worldwide disaster" (*Manifestes* 65, 63).

[20] I refer (by date of letter and page of publication) to the selection of fourteen out of thirty-seven letters from Luca to Brauner spanning the years 1946–1947, published and annotated in *Victor Brauner: écrits et correspondances 1938–1948* (subsequently referred to as *Brauner*).

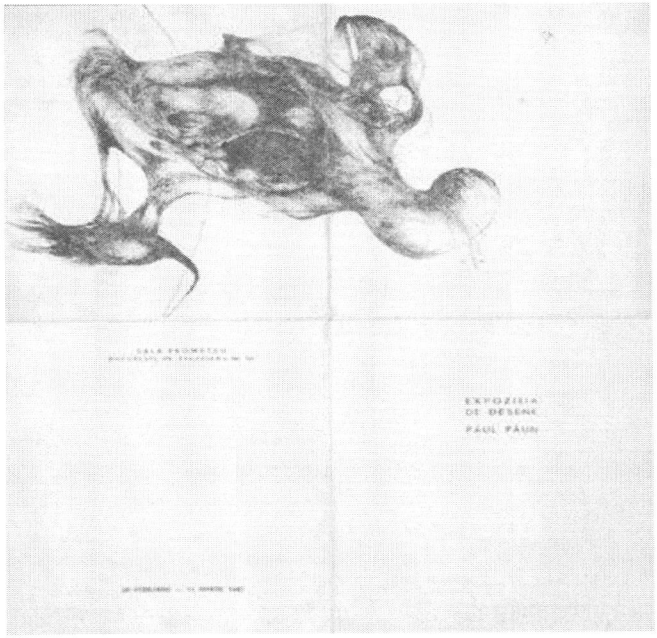

Figure 4.5. "Expoziția de desene Paul Păun." Flier.

youth, stresses the other side of the coin: "[F]orgetting and decanting, what remains for me as essential from that period, is the collective character, I'd even say the anonymity, within the group, of our activity at the time. [...] Collective work was introducing chance within individual automatism, the artist become modest was admiring the great art of the encounter, of instigated chance."[21]

---

[21] The interview was published in the Gautemalan newspaper, *El Impartial*, under the title "Surrealismo en Bucarest: Salida Super-Anárquica Hacia la Poesía Total: El poeta Paul Paun contesta a Stefan Baciu," March 23, 1977 (Xeroxed copy, n.pag., private archives Paul Paon); subsequently "Salida."

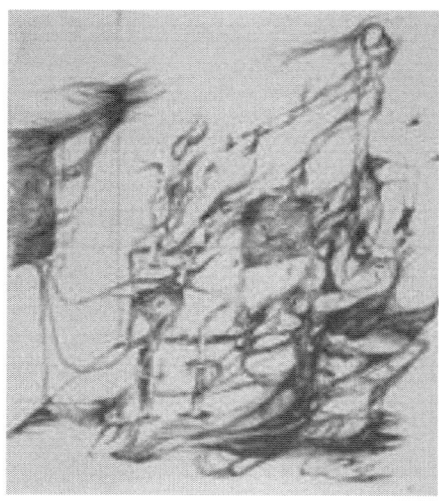

Figure 4.6. Paul Paon, pen-and-ink drawing, untitled, 1943,
signed PP 43. Private collection. Reproduced by permission.

The Flurry: 1946–1947

The year 1945 saw the publication of several individually authored books by each of the group's members, aside from those mentioned above—in French by Trost and Luca. But it is the period of the
next two years that finds the group united again in a surge of activities, the core of which is set under the sign of the concept of "infra-
noir" [infra-black]. *L'Infra-Noir: préliminaires à une intervention*
sur-thaumaturgique dans la conquête du désirable is the collective
poetic text, signed by all five (published in the same S Surréalisme
collection as *Dialectique de la dialectique*), that accompanied Paon,
Trost, and Luca's joint exhibition in the fall of 1946 (Figures 4.7 and
4.8).[22]

---

[22] *Expoziţia Gherasim Luca, Paul Păun, Trost* is the title of the invitation card.

Figure 4.7. Gherasim Luca, Gellu Naum, Paul Păun, Virgil Teodorescou, Trost, "L'Infra-Noir: préliminaires [...]." Cover.

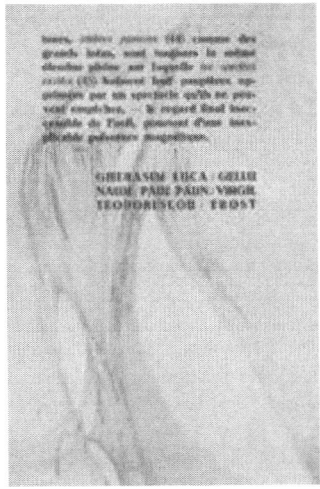

Figure 4.8. Gherasim Luca, Gellu Naum, Paul Păun, Virgil Teodorescou, Trost, "L'Infra Noir: préliminaires [...]." Signature page.

Produced, most likely, through the surrealist technique of *cadavre exquis* [exquisite corpse], except for the closing text titled "Une
Question," this publication also served as the exhibition's catalogue.
Italicized and numbered in the body of the text are those words that,
in an aleatory manner, gave their titles to the pieces on display. As far
as can be gathered from testimonies and the catalogue, these included
objects, works illustrating the techniques theorized by Luca and Trost,
and abstract (or semi-abstract) pencil drawings by Paon. The latter
also provided, palimpsest-like, the background to the catalogue's text
(see Figure 4.8). That the five had hoped for a moment to give this
exhibition if not quite an "international character" (due to insurmountable practical difficulties), then at least something broader than
a strictly "national character," by including surrealist art of French
provenance, is an attempt that remained unfulfilled, as expressed in
Luca's letters to Brauner (21 April, 217; n.d., 219). Only the open
invitation to join the quest for new ways of being in the world, formulated interrogatively on the last page of the catalogue-brochure ("Une
Question"), retains a trace of the international vocation of this event.

The year 1947 represents the apex of the group's collective activity, with an explosion of publications. Best known are the two sets of
four "Infra-Noir" *plaquettes* authored by each except Naum and dated
respectively 15 February and 10 April, in a series they named Collection Surréaliste Infra-Noir (discussed below).[23] *Éloge de Malombra:*

---

[23] Let us note that in these group publications, a variant of some of the authors' names
was used: Trost (no first name) and Virgil Teodores*cou* (to accommodate French
phonetics). Păun had not yet started using the French version of his pseudonym, Paon.
The eight *plaquettes* were reproduced half a century later together with the text of the
1946 exhibition catalogue, in a striking black jacket bearing the title *Infra-Noir* (Paris: La Maison de verre, 1996). However, the facsimiles as well as the publisher's
introductory statement contain several inaccuracies. The original publication date on
the back cover of each *plaquette* was altered on four of them, to read uniformly February 15, 1947. Secondly, the background images that appear on the pages of the
1946 catalogue (reproductions of Paon's drawings) were left out; and, strangely, the
numbers that in the original referred to the actual works displayed were expurgated
from the text. Granted, this gesture encourages the reading of this text as poetic rather
than just a catalogue, which is one way of approaching it. Finally and most surpris-

cerne de l'amour absolu, signed by all five and published in the S Surréalisme collection, expresses their fascination with the 1942 Italian film, *Malombra*, Mario Soldati's haunting cinematic adaptation of Antonio Fogazzaro's 1881 eponymous novel. Replete with some of their favorite themes—uncompromising love, occultism, and revolt against authoritarianism and the grip of social conventions, Soldati's film may also have appealed to them for its *calligraphisme*, a formalist aesthetics considered to have harbored a "secret hostility" to fascism and to the aesthetics imposed by it.[24] Lastly, "Le Sable nocturne," a text echoing one of the group's experimental games thus titled, was their contribution to the volume edited by Breton and Duchamp on the occasion of the 1947 international surrealist exhibition in Paris, *Le Surréalisme en 1947: exposition internationale du surréalisme*.[25]

This salvo was, however, also their swan song, since from that point onward they could no longer act publicly as surrealists or as a group. Continuing would have meant imprisonment, or worse. "Discreet messengers informed us of the treatment that was awaiting us, in short: imprisonment, of one sort or another, others said death, pure and simple death" (Paon, "Salida"). Weakened, their adventure did not entirely cease; it continued for a few years longer, until the departure of Luca and Trost. Some collective texts remain unpublished, and correspondence bears testimony to enduring ties, new experiments, and also powerful new rifts that eventually left intact only the bond between Luca and Paon. But that is another story.

---

ingly, in the editors' introduction, *Dialectique de la dialectique* is said to have appeared in the catalogue of the 1947 Paris international surrealist exhibition.

[24] See the article "Malombra," in Jacques Lourcelles, *Dictionnaire du cinéma: les films* 891.

[25] Correspondence suggests that Victor Brauner played a role in making this contribution possible.

The Texts

This is not the place to present in equal detail all the texts identified above as "collective." By privileging the 1945 *Dialectique de la dialectique* (subsequently *DdlD*) and the 1947 "Infra-Noir" *plaquettes*, I focus on that which is generally best known from this selection, albeit known mostly from secondary sources or in a strictly French-speaking context. What follows is to a great extent descriptive, given that the texts are, for most of the public, unavailable or extremely rare; and given also that the challenges they present have made their deciphering, at a first reading, arduous at best.

"Dialectique de la dialectique" (1945)

> Nous nous adressons à nos amis surréalistes, dispersés dans le monde entier et comme dans les grands naufrages, nous leur indiquons notre position exacte, à 44°5' de latitude nord, et 26° de longitude est.

> [We address ourselves to our surrealist friends scattered the world over and, like in great shipwrecks, we indicate to them our precise position, at 44°5' north latitude, and 26° east longitude.] (*DdlD* n.pag.)

It is this motto that opens Ghérasim Luca and Trost's 1945 message addressed to the international surrealist movement and "in particular to André Breton" (8). Referring at least as much to friends already departed as to members of Breton's group, the message continues in the same vein: "Séparés de nos amis, depuis le début de la guerre impérialiste mondiale, nous ne savons plus rien d'eux" [Separated from our friends, since the beginning of the imperialist world war, we know nothing more of them] (7). Yet, from the pit of this isolation, surrounded by "means of cretinization" and "oceans of blood," they launch both a critique of the impasse reached by surrealism globally and programmatic suggestions for surpassing it.

For the first point, namely their critique, they argue that a simple aesthetization of the "discoveries" of surrealism, turning surrealist artistic practices into mere technical devices (such as so-called "surrealist landscapes"), or the appropriation of these practices by any "politique culturelle" [cultural politics] (including the compilation of surrealist texts in specialized anthologies), betray the truly "revolutionary," "objective necessity" of these practices, and endanger the real quest for the development of thought and action, which are the movement's true goals (8–13).[26] Surrealism should not be allowed to succumb to such a fate, as was the case with many other revolts (13).

Before developing the second point, i.e., the specific theoretical conclusions they had themselves reached, Luca and Trost put forth a set of "fundamental viewpoints" underlying surrealism generally, as they understood it (13–16):

- "The need to maintain surrealism in a constant revolutionary state, capable of bringing about synthetic solutions (Hegelian, materialist, utterly new) as yet unattained" (14) and potentially "immediate" (15).

- This can only be achieved through an all-encompassing "dialectical position of negation and negation of negation" (14), in a "continual opposition to the world as a whole and to itself" (15).

- Surrealism cannot be confined to any definition or any delimitation, neither as heir to other tendencies (14), nor through any future "heritage" of its own (15).

- This is because surrealism is about "the expression of all our desires" or, further still, about an unlimited "desire to desire" (14).

---

[26] It is not entirely clear if Luca and Trost's critiques reflect only developments up to 1939, the year from which "date [their] last informations," or they extend beyond, to the surrealism of "these last years" (9, 12), pertaining to materials they may somehow have received more recently. In fact, Breton had already warned of such dangers in his first surrealist manifesto of 1924.

- Such perpetual self-surpassing, of and within surrealism, requires infinite, spiraling series of new discoveries, including
  the discovery of new desires, that is, not only those repressed
  and buried in the unconscious, but also desires actively and
  constantly reinvented (16).

Having established this dialectical, expansive, assertive foundation, Luca and Trost proceed to deploying their own findings, through
which they aim to connect in a new way certain forms of individual
freedom with the implosion of class divisions. To begin with, grounded in the "materialist (Leninist) position of the *relatif-absolu*," they
take the *hasard objectif* to be not only the "encounter of human finali-
ty with universal causality" (16), but also a way of revealing the "*contradictions* of a class-based society," and the key to considering "*love*
[in all its guises] as the general revolutionary method characteristic of
surrealism." "[E]rotic magnetism" becomes "[the] most valid insur-
rectional support" (17), and, therefore, "the boundless erotization of
the proletariat" constitutes in their view "the most precious" way of
access of this class to a "real revolutionary development" (19). "Nous
proclamons l'amour, délivré de ses contraintes, […] comme notre
principale méthode de connaissance et d'action" [We proclaim love,
free of its constraints, […] as our primary method of knowledge and
action] (18).

It is worth noting that this position, which claims that individual
freedom, particularly sexual freedom, can or should precede and even
lead to a revolutionary change on the socio-economic plane, goes
much further than that articulated by Breton in an important footnote
(fn. 1) to the Second Surrealist Manifesto. For Breton, the resolution
of class divisions could only precede, rather than follow, the proletariat's access to surrealist ways of thinking and being. It is this deviation, away from a classical reading of materialist (Marxist–Leninist)
positions, that had triggered the accusation of idealism voiced by
Naum against Luca and Trost. Yet, for the latter two, it is *their* views
that were truly objective and materialist: "cet amour dialecticisé et

matérialisé" [this love made dialectical, and materialized], "*l'amour objectif*" [objective love] (18).

From this point onward, the specific modalities of thought, action, and visual artistic production their text proposes are divided into three major sections, the themes of which are explicitly attributed to one or the other of the two authors via references to their respective pertinent individual works published or forthcoming;[27] yet, the subject pronoun remains plural throughout. Many of these themes are also found in some of their other collective works.

For Ghérasim Luca, the quest for radical liberation, primarily through love, involves a revolt against "nature" itself (especially the psychological, biological, and cosmological limitations related to love as well as to questions of life and death). This revolt consists in the negation and hence the surpassing of the two major factors claimed by psychologists to be at the root of anxiety and repression in human behavior: the trauma of birth and the Oedipal complex. Ghérasim Luca wants to extend this freeing, inventive, transgressive, *non-Oedipal* stand to the proletariat in such a way as to bring about the very obsolescence of this (and by extension all) class label(s), arguing that any class struggle—or even victory—devoid of such inner freedom can only amount to a simple symmetrical negation of the bourgeoisie, and therefore can be only "illusory" (rather than dialectical and concrete). Daringly criticizing, moreover, "humanitarian internationalism," Luca calls for "une position anti-nationaliste à outrance, concrètement de classe et outrageusement cosmopolite" [an extreme anti-nationalist position, concretely class-based and outrageously cosmopolitan] (19–24).

In a similarly contesting vein, Trost deflates the psychoanalytic valorization of dreams, by taking a critical stance toward the "regressive" elements harbored in some of those "restes diurnes" [diurnal

---

[27] Among already published works, specifically referenced are Ghérasim Luca's *L'Inventeur de l'amour* (which in fact at the time existed only in the original Romanian version, *Inventatorul iubirii*) and Trost's *Vision dans le cristal* and *Le Profil navigable*. Not all the works announced as forthcoming have subsequently seen the light (at least not under the stated title) or are currently known even in manuscript form.

residues] of which dreams are not necessarily freed. In so doing, while he endorses the notion of "fonctionnement réel de la pensée" [the true mechanisms of thought] (which was Breton's very definition of surrealism in art and daily life through its affinities with dreams and madness), Trost carries it beyond any "mechanical" reduction of the former (surrealism) to the latter two (dreams and madness). But at the same time he also (dialectically) negates the symmetrical, "artificial separation" between "diurnal life" and "nocturnal life," citing "somnambulism, automatism and several other exceptional states" as the "first degrees" of the fusion of the diurnal and nocturnal realms. For him, "oneiric functioning within diurnal life" carries "explosive consequences" and hence, presumably, the promise of revolutionary renewal (24–26).

Lastly, Ghérasim Luca and Trost approach "the problem of knowledge through the image" by positing a clear distinction between "images produced through artistic means and images produced through scientific procedures strictly applied, such as the action of chance and of automatism" (26). Opposed to painterly techniques, they argue that access to the "unknown that surrounds us" is best achieved through "procédés a-plastiques, objectifs et entièrement non-artistiques" [objective procedures, neither painterly nor artistic]. Their experimental methods continue, they claim, in the spirit of surrealism, but by surpassing the very modalities of surrealist painting known to them at the time, which were figurative (27).[28] There follow succinct presentations of the techniques they advance (such as *surautomatisme, graphomanie entoptique, vaporisation, mouvements hypnagogiques, objectanalyse, cubomanie*), all of which aim at "capturing" chance, actively provoking it, as it were, through automatism or mechanical operations, as opposed to simply registering instances of *hasard objectif* as they occur. Through these procedures they attempt to "snatch away new areas from the objective world," aiming to "surmount the coldness [i.e., indifference] of universal causality" (28). Thus, in this realm as well, they wish to shake off any and all deter-

---

[28] These methods do in fact present some affinities with those of earlier avant-gardes.

minism, while remaining grounded in a materialist, objective frame-work. A more detailed development of these notions had already been provided a few months earlier by Ghérasim Luca and Trost in *Présen-tation de graphies colorées, de cubomanies et d'objets*, the catalogue that accompanied their eponymous exhibition of January 1945, and more extensively still by Trost alone in *Le Profil navigable: négation de la peinture* [The Navigable Profile: A Negation of Painting] (1945).

It is worth noting that, while Paon did not engage at the time in any comparable theoretical and technical pronouncements, it is clear that visually he increasingly adopted, since at least 1945, a mode of drawing that is a form of abstract automatism, as confirmed by later exhibitions and a life-long subsequent production in this vein.[29]

The closing paragraphs of *Dialectique de la dialectique* take one additional—and substantial—step further, suggesting affinities (in-deed, "correspondences [...] cosmologiques") between their own "at-titude" in the world and certain scientific discoveries, ranging from quanta theory to homeopathic medicine, potentially leading to a rap-prochement between the research conducted in each of the two domains:

> D'accord avec la science dans ses aspects attractifs et cryp-testhésiques, le mouvement surréaliste bouleverse, en même temps, sa rigidité mathématique, avec l'assurance qui rappelle les voyages des somnambules vers l'intérieur de leur propre mystère, identifié un instant au destin secret de l'humanité.

---

[29] An early example of this approach is Paon's participation, alongside Ernst Martin and Scottie Wilson, in an exhibition titled *3 Types of Automatism* (London 1948), the catalogue of which opens with an excerpt from a text by Breton on automatic writing. Likewise, at the 1951 Tel-Aviv exhibition with Ghérasim Luca and Mirabelle Dors, where Paon exhibited "Un Signe" (under the pseudonym Yvenez) and Luca and Dors "Un Objet," the bilingual texts (French and Hebrew) of the exhibition flier evoked both the concept of Infra-Noir and Breton's automatism (the latter through quotes from the First and Second Surrealist Manifestos). How his participation in these post-1947 exhibitions abroad was made possible is a story that has yet to be written.

> [The surrealist movement, while in agreement with the sciences in their attractive and prophetic aspects, disrupts their mathematical rigidity with an assuredness reminiscent of the sleepwalkers' incursions into the core of their own mystery, a mystery fleetingly identified with the secret destiny of humanity.] (30)

In this respect as well, Luca and Trost stretch further and beyond the intuitions and line of thought proper to the French surrealist movement and, we might add, also suggested (although in a different spirit) in Apollinaire's 1918 manifesto, *L'Esprit nouveau et les poètes*. However, the intensity, excess, and urgency of tone of their somewhat protean attempt to harness nature, befriend science, connect to the cosmos, reinvent love, fundamentally revise visual art, and achieve ultimate liberation both on the individual and social plane, may be viewed, at least in part, as a response to what Paon would call "la pestilence de ce monde" [the stench of this world], "la conspiration de l'asphyxie" [the suffocation conspiracy] [*Les Esprits animaux* 6, see below]). In this interpretation, the meaning of their search and assertions is that of a philosophical, existential, and artistic resistance and affirmation within a particularly somber historical context.

The Infra-Noir Plaquettes (1947)

The identically formatted *plaquettes* (seven-page, uncut, folded-and-gathered, 8.5" × 11" sheets) printed in a mere 500 copies, are in fact vastly different from one another in content, style, even graphic presentation, although, as already noted, some common threads traverse all eight of them.

Illustrated by an *échographie* titled "Nécessairement belle" [Necessarily Beautiful], Ghérasim Luca's *Le Secret du vide et du plein* [The Secret of Void and Matter] transposes in poetic terms some of *Dialectique de la Dialectique*'s essential points, using a staccato voice that plays on repetition and personifies concepts with tragicomic theatricality:

> Désir et Pensée. Blessure projette Désir et Pensée, Pensée et Désir se jettent sur Blessure. […] Volonté et Action font

éclater Pensée et Désir dans leur Signe. Mais Signe est depuis longtemps vidé de son Plein. L'automatisme mental est une précieuse divinatoire conduisant aux sources du plein et du vide.

[Desire and Thought. Wound projects Desire and Thought, Thought and Desire throw themselves at Desire. […] Will and Action cause Thought and Desire to explode in their Sign. But Sign has long been emptied of its Matter. Mental automatism is a precious divination leading to the sources of the matter and the void.] (2)

There follows a poem in which alliteration, word play, and free association evolve into an unraveling of semantic meaning, and which, in closing, evokes a key figure of surrealist mythology: "desade desassassade / sade desassassade desassassa sade" (7).

With his distinct brand of wry humor, Luca imagines in *Amphitrite: mouvements sur-thaumaturgiques et non-oedipiens* (at least in my reading) the staging and resulting spectacle of a sort of magic stunt meant to illustrate what love is, in the new acceptation given to it by *Inventatorul iubirii* [The Inventor of Love],[30] and a fleeting allusion, perhaps, to Rimbaud's "dérèglement des sens" [disordering of the senses]:

La femme aimée, jusqu'aujourd'hui simple objet perdu et vainement trouvé, est devenue dans notre manière d'aimer, la perpétuelle *boîte à surprise* du monde à changer, l'inépuisable agent du dérèglement de l'esprit et de la matière désirante.

[The beloved, who until now was a simple object lost and vainly found, has become, in our way of loving, the perpetual *box of surprises* of a world in need of change, the inexhaustible agent of the disordering of the spirit and of desiring matter.] (2; my italics)

---

[30] This work, already mentioned (see my note 27), appeared posthumously, with some revisions, in a translation by the author: *L'Inventeur de l'amour* suivi de *La Mort morte* [*The Inventor of Love* followed by *The Dead Death*] (Paris: Corti, 1994).

Amphitrite ends with (or opens up into) what would later become Ghérasim Luca's perhaps best-known poem, "Passionnément," a recurring piece until the very end of his life in his poetry recitals and recordings.[31]

Trost's *Le Plaisir de flotter: rêves et délires* [The Pleasure of Floating: Dreams and Delirium] consists of a series of dream sequences interspersed with scenes of hypnosis meant to be read as embedded in a dream. Often erotic in nature, these sequences evolve into one another through a process of fluid scenario transformations. Reverting in *Le Même du même* [The Same of Same] to expository writing, Trost expounds on his critique of psychoanalytic theory. If psychoanalysis posited a hidden real meaning to the manifest meaning of dreams, he argues instead that manifest meaning is in fact the dreams' one and only real, i.e., literal meaning. Through dramatization, dreams express desire, but a desire not only for human beings; rather, for any and all objects in the universe (for example, the moon's rays). Dreams, therefore, perform an "erotization of the universe" (3), incorporating the regressive aspects of diurnal life only under the sign of humor. Thus the dream should be considered "poetic[ally]," but not in the literary, painterly, or metaphorical sense of the word. Rather, Trost stresses, in a "dialectically tautological" manner, through an "eternal return on itself"; autotelically, one might say. "Le rêve est le rêve" [A dream is a dream] (6) he writes as if echoing Gertrude Stein's 1913 "A rose is a rose is a rose." Trost's 1945 *Vision dans le cristal* [Vision in the Crystal], accompanied by his own illustrations, would further expand the material and the approach developed in these two pieces.

In turn, Paul Paon's *Les Esprits animaux* [The Animal Spirits] and *La Conspiration du silence* [The Conspiracy of Silence], in addition to echoing several of the group's common themes, are traversed by a series of interconnected topics that would become central to his later work: the warmth of friendship; the nauseating surrounding society; the few, unique forms of resistance still imaginable; and, most

---

[31] For an analysis of these texts in a broader philosophical context, see Carlat.

importantly, the call to refuse the generally accepted "dichotomy of means" (*Esprits* 3). The latter term refers to the differentiation between means of concrete action and means of making art (or praxis versus poësis), akin to the "choix des outils" of which Breton was still a proponent in his *Prolégomènes à un troisième manifeste du surréalisme ou non* (1942).[32] In a manner that would become a trademark of his writing, he expresses these concerns and concepts in a lyrical (personal and impassioned) poetic form, punctuated by the autobiographic "je," the collective "nous," and an occasional "vous." "C'est une lettre, un discours" [Here is a letter, a speech]; thus opens *Les Esprits animaux*. "Je pense à mes amis, à leur place dans le monde" [I think of my friends, of their place in the world]. "Car tout nous est pris et volé" [Since everything is taken away and stolen from us] in this "boorish society," in the midst of "general destruction" (2), in this "conspiration anti-poétique mondiale" [worldwide anti-poetic conspiracy] (3). "Tel est ce moment, la nuit de ce midi, tel est ce gouffre" [Such is this moment, the night of this midday, such is this abyss] (2), against which the only weapon is not simply to retreat into imposed or benign silence, but rather to create a form of silence that "*conspires* in our favor" (4).

It is this "conspiracy," meant to counteract the nefarious effects of the "conspiration de l'asphyxie" (6), that lends its title to *La Conspiration du silence*. Here Paon once again includes his comrades: "Je ne pense pas être le seul, en ces derniers temps, qui"... [I do not believe being the only one, lately, who] (2), "je connais quelques hommes qui" ... [I know a few men who] (5). But the overall import of this piece is essentially twofold. First, it puts forth the notion of

---

[32] My interpretation of this "dichotomie de nos moyens," in which resides "tout le mal" [all the evil], and of assertions such as "Je ne crois pas que nous devions chercher complémentairement une autre politique que celle du hasard objectif" (*Esprits* 6) [I do not think that we should seek any other complementary politics than that of objective chance], was reinforced by my reading of *La Rose parallèle*. But see also, in *La Conspiration du silence*, the invitation Paon addresses to those poets whose "genius" shines so far solely through "the strength of the[ir] opposition to oppression" to seek reaching, in addition, for the "langage objectif du silence universel" [objective language of universal silence] (6).

"présence à distance" [presence from afar], exemplified in this text through experimental treatments of hysteria in the 1880s. This notion found actual forms of expression later on, in some of the group members' experimentation with telepathic communication via selected objects, meticulously documented elsewhere in their writing. Second, it further elaborates on "automatic action," as well as on the difficulty of achieving "le contact permanent de la chimère" [permanent contact with the chimera] (5) while always groping for it "with eyes like the outstretched arms of the blind" (5). The text closes with an invocation of a metonymic form of this quest: "le sable nocturne" [nocturnal sand], one of the games actually practiced by the group, in which desire, chance, silence, and darkness converged (see above).

Virgil Teodorescu's free-verse poem, *Au Lobe du sel* [To the Lobe of Salt] and his prose poem, *La Provocation* [Provocation] are both hymns to the beloved. Somewhat reminiscent of Breton's "L'Union libre" (also known as "Ma Femme"), *Au Lobe du sel* is driven by the endless repetition of the word "comme," in a cascade of unlikely comparisons. Here, as well as in *La Provocation*, images, acts, and settings, intensely lyrical and erotic, morph into one another, signifiers no longer corresponding to expected codes: "Oh ta main, je rêve d'elle je la mange" [Oh your hand, I dream of it I eat it]; "Tu es le bruit du sel jeté dans l'eau" [You are the sound of salt thrown into the water]; "Devant moi tu t'arrêtes / comme un golfe paisible / où les requins dévorent les papillons" [Before me you stop still / like a peaceful gulf / where sharks devour butterflies] (*Lobe* 6, 7, 2). Dominated by a sense of passionate urgency, these texts are also traversed by flashes of violence, doom ("le délire néfaste de notre amour" [our love's nefarious delirium] thrice repeated on one page [*La Provocation* 6]), and humor: "je te mange, je te bois, je te couvre de blessures, je te guéris, je t'arrache les oreilles plusieurs fois et je voudrais dormir maintenant dans ton oreille pour que tu puisses entendre mon amour" [I eat you, I drink you, I cover you with wounds, I heal you, I tear out your ears several times over and I wish I could sleep now inside your ear so that you may hear my love] (5). The author's imprint figures *en abyme*: his name ("tu peux dire virgil" [you may say virgil] 3); an embedded allusion ("longévité spectrale" [spectral longevity] to his 1946 text, *Spectrul longevității* [The Specter of Longevity]); and a long paragraph in a nonsensical idiom, his invented "Leopardian" language: "Anod thoy hypathetic aspetoe ermetualy cerrood ion oo balenaos" (*Provocation* 3, 4, 5). Much more recessive than in the other "Infra-Noir" texts, two of the group's main themes are nevertheless present: the rapport between love and chance, "L'amour force le hasard / le hasard ouvre l'amour" [Love forces chance / chance opens up love] (*Lobe* 2); and an inhuman humanity, "les hommes que je rencontre revêtent leur ancien costume de scaphandre préparant leur venin pour la promenade dans le vent" [the men I encounter don again their diving suits while preparing their venom for the stroll into the wind] (*Provocation* 3).

The Problematization of Language

To return now to the question of language, beyond the actual idiom used, it is worth noting that Ghérasim Luca, Paon, and Trost share a certain problematization of language that goes sometimes as far as a denial of language. Throughout their lives, this uneasy rapport took vastly different forms in each of their cases.[33]

Trost's evolution is marked by silence in the most radical way. He stopped all activity after the mid-1950s, and because his life on the other shore of the Atlantic was brief and as yet undocumented, not much can be speculated, so far, about this silence. However, ever since his *Profil navigable*, one can sense in his theorization of automatism in painting, a desire and claim to supersede language, because words for him necessarily carried unwanted "traces mnésiques" [memory traces].

Paul Paon started his truly surrealist literary production with two rather hermetic lengthy poems in Romanian separated by total silence, each published in individual booklets. They bear the deeply meaning-

---

[33] Given that Teodorescu's "Leopardian" invention is, to the best of my knowledge, a one-time occurrence in his work, I am not inclined to consider it of a similar nature. To comment on it any further, access to the poem in its entirety and to its complementary materials would be needed.

ful historic dates of 1939 and 1945, and can be read as respectively
foreshadowing and recalling the cataclysmic nature of the war:
Plămânul sălbatec [The Wild Lung] and *Marea palidă* [The Pallid
Sea]. In 1947, regarding the strategy of silence discussed above, Paon
wrote, "Car ce n'est que de l'intérieur de la flamme du silence, noire
et conspiratrice, que tout devient le *jamais-vu* universel, toujours at-
tractif et à séduire" [Because it is only from the black and conspiring
flame of silence's core that everything becomes the universal *yet-
unseen*, always attractive and awaiting seduction] (*Esprits* 4). Here,
silence should not be taken literally, but rather as referring to a type of
literary activity that, being both challenging and hidden, is marked by
a kind of secrecy that resists appropriation.[34] Yet eventually, he too
stopped writing almost entirely, after having completed, in 1975, a
200-page prose poem in French that evokes the group's friendship and
activities, its subsequent dissolution, Paon's solitude, and the ensuing
grief (*La Rose parallèle*, see my note 14). Thereafter, he "spoke" almost exclusively in a silent manner, through abstract pen-and-ink
drawings, which he related to handwriting by naming them "graphisme illettré" [illiterate writing]—"graphisme" in French meaning
handwriting as well as drawing.[35] "Illiterate," the hand draws in an
automatic, non-mimetic fashion, devoid of any anterior model, nor
even any "interior" one, as Breton would have it.[36] The "model," for
Paon, is thus strictly "ulterior," and in this sense his approach con-

---

[34] Jean-François Lyotard's "Une ligne de résistance" expounds on this type of writing
(*Traverses* 33–34 [Jan. 1985]: 60–68).

[35] A presentation of Paon in the journal *Pleine Marge* 36 (Dec. 2002) was titled by
the editors "Entre deux langues" ("Paul Paon 'Entre deux langues' présenté par
Monique Yaari," 87–110). The allusion can apply not only to Paon's statement to the
effect that he had "only two languages," one verbal, one visual, which constantly
interrogate each other, as Jacqueline Chénieux-Gendron remarks in her introduction
to the volume (5), but also beyond it, to Kristeva's description in those very terms, of
the condition of *étranger* [stranger/foreigner] (see *Étrangers à nous-mêmes* 27). Taking this a step further, one can be a stranger (without being a foreigner) in one's own
birthplace and language.

[36] See Breton's *Le Surréalisme et la peinture* (1928, repeatedly revised and enhanced,
starting in 1945).

verges with some of the theories expounded by Trost and Luca. Although this mode of non-figurative visual expression goes back to the 1940s in Paon's work, its scant theorization, as far as is currently known, appears only decades later, in some unpublished statements.[37]

Ghérasim Luca entertained since the outset and consistently over the years, a critical, somewhat strained relation to language (or indeed no doubt to any conventional mode of communication), while being the only artist in the group who spent the majority of his life in France—and in French—continuing to live and write in that language until his disappearance in 1994. Yet this tension is one of the distinguishing and most engaging qualities of his art. His is a poetry whose oral and aural dimensions are paramount, given its characteristic "bégaiement poétique" [poetic stammering], as his most subtle critic, Dominique Carlat, has put it:

> il est né de la né
> de la néga ga de la néga
> de la négation passion gra cra
> crachez cra crachez sur vos nations cra
> ....
> il est né de la né de la néga
> néga ga cra crachez de la né
> de la ga pas néga négation passion
> passionné nez passionném je
> je t'ai je t'aime je
> je te jet je t'ai jetez
> je t'aime passionném t'aime […]
>   ("Passionnément," *Amphitrite* 7)

Turning on its head any theory of origin that might explain away this peculiarity of Luca's poetry through bilingualism, Gilles Deleuze writes, "He certainly does not owe this to his Romanian origin, but he is making use of this origin to make the French [language] stammer,

---

[37] Paon's and Trost's respective positions on writing and painting are both similar and different, in ways that require further investigation. Tentatively, however: even though Trost stated, "I say *painting* as if I said *writing*" (*Profil navigable* 29 fn. 1), it seems he meant something substantially different by this phrase than the sensual analogy Paon appeared to establish between the two *graphismes*.

in itself and with itself, to bring stammer into the language itself, not just in speech." To Luca's French, just as to Beckett's, Deleuze refers as "*one's own*" (*Superpositions* 108–109).[38]

But Luca also communicated through objects, which he fashioned from *objets trouvés* [found objects], in a more elaborate manner and with a different intent than, but still somewhat akin to, Duchamp's "aided" ready-mades. From the "objets objectivement offerts" [objects objectively offered] amply discussed and exemplified in his early text, *Le Vampire passif*, to the objects he displayed in the group's exhibitions, and finally to those conceived later on (among them *livres-objets*), by himself or in collaboration with other artists (notably Piotr Kowalski), this non-verbal activity—complemented by his syncopated *cubomanies* and ink drawings "aux petits points" [with tiny dots]—followed through on the theories expounded in his youth.

It would be too easy, although not erroneous, to subsume the peculiarities of these three artists' relation to language under an all-encompassing crisis of language, in turn inscribed in a larger twentieth-century crisis of representation. I argue that within this framework they display a shared specificity, partly via ties to their surrealist group and partly through their personal trajectories, a specificity that would be worth examining more closely. In a nutshell: in their collective experience there had been an early shift away from the native language and from any monolithic, univocal identity; moreover, their group shared an overall mistrust of History, with roots in the multiple treasons of History they had experienced and witnessed over the years. This unsettling and this hybridity would eventually be further compounded, for Trost and Paon respectively, by the addition of one more leg to their journey beyond Luca's Paris, together with an additional linguistic and cultural layer. Yet on the other hand, and importantly, there was also for the latter three, unlike for the two poets who stayed in Romania and reverted to their native language, the enduring and arguably comforting presence of French,

---

[38] See Carlat's analysis of Ghérasim Luca's relation to language (*L'Intempestif* 104–105), including his reference (fn. 113) to yet another text by Deleuze than the one just mentioned, which also engages with this question (*Critique et clinique* 138–39).

linking their youth to their maturity, and each of them to a larger community.

"Another" *Francophonie*

At this point in our narrative and analysis, several aspects of the materials discussed so far deserve to be restated, while further avenues of research suggest themselves to our attention.[39] To begin with, it appears that a particularly tight rapport exists between word and image in this group's work. The image (including the object) is consistently present in their work, in several guises: through ekphrasis; as illustration of text; collected into books composed exclusively of visuals;[40] transmitted through acts and gestures; or in its own right, displayed in exhibitions. To what effect? Beyond its own intrinsic interest, the visual element plays a role as a theoretical tool, as a stand-in for words, and as a vehicle for negotiating affinities and disagreements within the group; as such, it is a constant, multi-tasking companion to verbal expression. This rapport requires further examination, as does its comparison to equivalent situations in other avant-garde movements of French expression.

Secondly, while I've noted only in passing the names the members of this group invented for the series in which their collective and individual works appeared, a careful overview of the meaning of these names might be in order, because they reflect the protagonists' underlying philosophy (for example: Éditions de l'Oubli [The Oblivion Press] or Negația Negației [The Negation of Negation]). Likewise, from perspectives informed by book history or cultural history, piecing together the story of the production of these publications as well as of strategies of display might yield interesting results, as would a detailed examination of the reception that this particular avant-garde group encountered at the time, domestically and internationally.

---

[39] For a careful reading of this entire chapter and suggestions for its conclusion, my thanks to Denis Moscovici and to Gabriel Yaari.

[40] Examples include Trost's *Le Profil navigable: négation concrète de la peinture* (1945) and Ghérasim Luca's *Les Orgies des quanta: trente-trois cubomanies non-oedipiennes* (1946).

Notably, we may wish to determine with greater precision the nature of the echoes this group elicited within other surrealist groups of French expression. Clear leads are available concerning its rapport with the Paris and Brussels groups. Paris was receptive to some extent. But their radical brand of existential revolt, which I suggested reading as a response to the somber surrounding conditions in Romania at the time, did not resonate well in Brussels. The mutual rejection that ensued, of and by especially Magritte and his circle, is emblematic: a surrealism "en plein soleil" [in full sun] could only clash with what might be called a surrealism of trauma, albeit suffused, as we have seen, with both humor and poetry.[41]

Finally, given the group's predominant linguistic choice in its most substantial body of collective works, given also its transnational vocation and its political sensibility versus the ideological context in which it operated, I opted for the designation "surrealist group of Bucharest" in conjunction with the mention "of French expression." To contextualize, this type of denomination is not unique in Europe, if we think for instance of the "surréalisme de/en Belgique" [from/in Belgium] rather than "belge" [Belgian], where "surrealism" sometimes takes the plural "s" to designate the groups of Brussels and the Hainaut.[42] Moreover, art history often associates modernist and avant-garde phenomena with the urban environments in which they sprouted rather than with national frameworks—see, for example, the Centre Pompidou's landmark exhibitions on the distinct modernity of Paris, Berlin, Moscow, and Vienna (1977–1986) and the transnational axes that connected them. Lastly and importantly, in a key document addressed by Trost to Breton in the early 1950s, which outlined the

---

[41] See Ghérasim Luca's letters to Brauner, stating the group's position and recounting their epistolary exchanges with Magritte; see also in the same volume the editorial reference to Magritte's 1946 manifesto, *Le Surréalisme en plein soleil* (letters of 28 September 1946 and 20 March 1947 and fn. 62, in *Brauner* 224, 228).

[42] See for example Marcel Mariën, ed., *L'Activité surréaliste en Belgique*.

nature of the group's activities, the expression used is "le groupe sur-réaliste de Bucarest."[43]

These nuances gently counterbalance the understandable though not fully founded tendency of some national and diasporic discourses to reclaim—within a (re)discovered, long-hidden trove of avant-garde production—those authors born on Romanian soil but who chose to position themselves in a cultural francophone space and express themselves in French, often from afar.[44] With respect to the hybrid production of the 1940s group discussed here, such appropriations beg the question. As they do with respect to the full span of the individual careers of three of its actors, which resists (and who have resisted) appropriation.[45] Hence, the complexities of cultural translation, so to speak, that arise when taking these considerations into account.

That said, what does the group's inclusion in "'another' *francophonie*" mean? Another form of appropriation? Perhaps, to some extent. But it may be more fruitful to envisage this inclusion as a re-balancing, away from troubled origins, which places the group in a broader, hybrid space. To recap, French was, for much of the group's collective work in the 1940s, and for three of its members beyond

---

[43] Titled "Activité du groupe surréaliste de Bucarest (1940–1950)," this hand-written document, slipped inside the covers of Trost's *La Connaissance des temps* (1946), is now in the private archive of Denis Moscovici. My thanks to him for making it available to me.

[44] Understandable because, as Paul Ilie writes in *Literature and Inner Exile*, "Excision is a reciprocal relationship; to cut off one segment of a population from the rest is also to leave the larger segment cut off from the smaller one" (2).

[45] There is a certain sense of disconnect, for instance, between Ghérasim Luca's life and stance and the fact that Petre Răileanu's pioneering study of the poet's early years appeared in a by now very rich collection titled "Les étrangers de Paris: les Roumains de Paris" [The Foreigners/Strangers of Paris: The Romanians of Paris]. Upon losing his citizenship, like all those who left Romania in the 1950s and 1960s, Luca chose to embrace his statelessness: "[J]e ne suis pas roumain—avec ou sans majuscule—mais apatride" [I am not Romanian—with or without an article—but stateless], writes, and underscores, Ghérasim Luca in 1963 to an editor who committed the "regrettable error" of labeling him "Romanian" (see the back cover of *Le Cahier du Refuge* 172, dedicated to the artist on the occasion of his exhibition at the Centre International de Poésie Marseille, July 2008). But neither was he a stranger in Paris, or in French.

1947 when the group's public activity came to an end, a space *within* and *from* which they could speak freely, even if not necessarily *in* the physical location called France (or any other French-speaking environment for that matter). It is in such a way that the story of this little-known avant-garde group, together with the subsequent trajectories of some of its protagonists, can be understood as partaking of "another" *francophonie*, unrelated to postcolonial contexts. And, it is in these terms that it can contribute to the expansion and modification of the currently predominant meaning of *francophonie*, challenged as it is already by the notion of *littérature-monde*.

Selected Bibliography

Primary Sources (authors' names follow their original spelling; see note 1)

Collective or multiple-authored works (in chronological order)
Gherasim Luca and Trost. *Dialectique de la dialectique: message adressé au mouvement surréaliste international*. [Collection] S Surréalisme. Bucharest: Imprimerie "Slova," 1945.
_____. *Présentation de graphies colorées, de cubomanies et d'objets*. Bucharest: Imprimeriile "Independenţa," 1945.
Naum, Gellu, Paul Păun, and Virgil Teodorescu. *Critica mizeriei*. Colecţia Suprarealistă. Bucharest: Tipografia "Editura Modernă," 1945.
Naum, Gellu. *Teribilul interzis*. Frontispiece by Paul Păun. Colecţia Suprarealistă. Bucharest: Tipografia IC Văcărescu, 1945.
Teodorescu, Virgil. *Butelia de Leyda*. With a "Brevet de lovaj" and 4 *lovaje* by Paul Păun. Colecţia Suprarealistă. Bucharest: Tipografia "Bucovina," 1945.
Naum, Gellu, and Virgil Teodorescu. *Spectrul longevităţii* and *122 de cadavre*. Colecţia Suprarealistă. Bucharest: Tipografia "Bucovina," 1946.
Gherasim Luca, Gellu Naum, Paul Păun, Virgil Teodorescou, and Trost. *L'Infra-Noir: préliminaires à une intervention sur-thaumaturgique dans la conquête du désirable*. [Collection] S Surréalisme. Bucharest, 1946.
_____. *Éloge de Malombra: cerne de l'amour absolu*. [Collection] S Surréalisme. Bucharest: [Imprimerie] Socec, 1947.

_____. "Le Sable nocturne." André Breton and Marcel Duchamp, eds. *Le Surréalisme en 1947: exposition internationale du surréalisme*. Paris: Editions Pierre à Feu, 1947.

Single-authored works in the Infra-Noir series (a group publication)
Gherasim Luca. *Amphitrite: mouvements sur-thaumaturgiques et non-oedipiens*. [Collection Surréaliste] Infra-Noir. Bucharest: Imprimerie Socec, 1947.
_____. *Le Secret du vide et du plein*. [Collection Surréaliste] Infra-Noir. Bucharest: Imprimerie Socec, 1947.
Păun, Paul. *La Conspiration du silence*. [Collection Surréaliste] Infra-Noir. Bucharest: Imprimerie Socec, 1947.
_____. *Les Esprits animaux*. [Collection Surréaliste] Infra-Noir. Bucharest: Imprimerie Socec, 1947.
Teodorescou, Virgil. *Au Lobe du sel*. [Collection Surréaliste] Infra-Noir. Bucharest: Imprimerie Socec, 1947.
_____. *La Provocation*. [Collection Surréaliste] Infra-Noir. Bucharest: Imprimerie Socec, 1947.
Trost. *Le Même du même*. [Collection Surréaliste] Infra-Noir. Bucharest: Imprimerie Socec, 1947.
_____. *Le Plaisir de flotter: rêves et délires*. [Collection Surréaliste] Infra-Noir. Bucharest: Imprimerie Socec, 1947.

Selected Secondary Sources
Athanor: Caietele Fundaţiei Gellu Naum 2 (January 2004).
Biro, Adam, and René Passeron, eds. *Dictionnaire général du surréalisme et ses environs*. Paris: PUF, 1982.
Breton, André. *Manifestes du surréalisme*. [1962]. Rpt. Paris: Folio Gallimard, 2001.
_____. *Le Surréalisme et la peinture*. Paris: NRF, 1928. Rpt. revised and enhanced. New York: Brentano, 1945, and Paris: Gallimard, 1965.
Carlat, Dominique. *Ghérasim Luca l'intempestif*. Paris: José Corti, 1998.
Carp, Matatias. *Cartea neagră: le livre noir de la destruction des Juifs de Roumanie (1940–1944)*. Trans. Alexandra Laignel-Lavastine. Paris: Denoël, 2009.
Deleuze, Gilles. "Un Manifeste de moins." Carmelo Bene and Gilles Deleuze, *Superpositions*. Paris: Minuit, 1978. 85–131.
Dragomir, Lucia. *L'Union des Écrivains, une institution littéraire transnationale à l'Est: l'exemple roumain*. Paris: Belin, 2007.

Iancu, Carol. *Les Juifs en Roumanie, 1919–1938: de l'exclusion à la marginalisation*. Leuven, Belgium: Peeters, 1996.

Ilie, Paul. *Literature and Inner Exile: Authoritarian Spain, 1939–1975*. Baltimore and London: Johns Hopkins UP, 1980.

Kristeva, Julia. *Étrangers à nous-mêmes*. Paris: Fayard, 1988.

Laignel-Levastine, Alexandra. *Cioran, Eliade, Ionesco, l'oubli du fascisme: trois intellectuels roumains dans la tourmente du siècle*. Paris: PUF, 2002.

Laville, Rémy. *Gellu Naum, poète roumain prisonnier au château des aveugles*. Paris: L'Harmattan, 1994.

Lourcelles, Jacques. *Dictionnaire du cinéma*. Vol. 3. *Les films*. Paris: Robert Laffont, 1992.

Lyotard, Jean-François. "Une ligne de résistance." *Traverses* 33–34 (Jan. 1985): 60–68.

Mariën, Marcel, ed. *L'activité surréaliste en Belgique (1924–1950)*. Brussels: Éditions Lebeer Hassmann, 1979.

Moscovici, Serge. *Chronique des années égarées*. Paris: Stock, 1997.

Pană, Saşa. *Născut în '02*. Bucharest: Editura Minerva, 1973.

_____, ed. *Antologia literaturii române de avangardă*. Bucharest: Intreprinderea poligrafică "13 Decembrie 1918," 1969.

Paon, Paul. "Surrealismo en Bucarest: Salida Super-Anárquica Hacia la Poesía Total: El poeta Paul Paun contesta a Stefan Baciu." *El Impartial*. 23 March 1977. Xeroxed copy, n.pag., private archives Paul Paon.

La Planète affolée: surréalisme, dispersion et influences, 1938–1947. Exhibition, Centre de la Vieille Charité, Marseille, 12 April–30 June, 1986. Paris and Marseilles: Flammarion and Direction des Musées de Marseille, 1986.

Pop, Ion, ed. *La Réhabilitation du rêve: une anthologie de l'avant-garde roumaine*. Paris: EST, Maurice Nadeau, and Institutul Cultural Român, 2006.

Răileanu, Petre. *Ghérasim Luca*. Paris: Oxus, 2004.

Sebastian, Mihail. *Journal: 1935–1944*. Trans. Patrick Camiller. Chicago: Ivan R. Dee, 2000.

Solomon, Petre. *"Am să povestesc cândva aceste zile…": pagini de jurnal, memorii, însemnări*. Bucharest: Editura Vinea, 2006.

Victor Brauner, écrits et correspondences, 1938–1948: les archives de Victor Brauner au Musée national d'art moderne. Eds. Camille Morando and Sylvie Patry. Paris: Centre Pompidou–INHA, 2005.

The Trans-cultural Journey
of Benjamin Fondane

Monique Jutrin
University of Tel-Aviv

"Je n'ai pas connu la littérature française comme
je peux connaître l'allemande—je l'ai vécue"

[I have not known French literature in the way
I have known German literature, which is to say, I have lived it]
— Benjamin Fondane, *Images et Livres de France*

Benjamin Fondane is an atypical writer, one who is difficult to categorize. Many critics have focused exclusively on the negativity so prevalent in his philosophy, but this focus fails to recognize an un-compromising demand that oriented his thinking—a fact that helps explains his distance from literary, philosophical, and political systems of all kinds. Forgotten by the public between 1944 and 1980, Fondane was finally rediscovered, and his most important questions remain relevant. Fondane himself did not imagine any such resurgence, as he wrote to Georges Ribemont-Dessaignes in August 1943, "nous verrons bien vers 1980 … ou ne verrons rien du tout" [we will see around 1980 … or we won't see anything at all].[1]

Fondane's œuvre is marked by a migration through cultures and languages and by a dialogue between different kinds of knowledge. It is a polymorphic body of work, expressed equally in poetic, philo-sophical, and critical texts, as well as in the theatre and the cinema. Fondane was passionate about all the innovative aspects of the philoso-phy of his time, and he was not afraid to venture into anthropology, psychoanalysis, logic, and physics. Thus, he maintained an intellectu-al commerce with the likes of Lévy-Bruhl, Caillois, Artaud, Wahl, and Maritain, to list only a few. His lucidity is still remarkable: he was one of the first to truly understand Heidegger and Céline, one of the first to recognize the importance of the works of Bachelard and

---

[1] Bibliothèque Jacques Doucet, ms 8946.

Lupasco. Indeed, numerous authors have been influenced by his work: Cioran, Lupasco, Celan, and Jean Lescure, among others.

Fondane was born Benjamin Wechsler in 1898 in Jassy, Romania, in what is now Moldova. Having grown up steeped in Romanian culture, he quickly became familiar with French literature from an early age; at the same time, he remained rooted in the Jewish world.

The Romanian Years: *Images et Livres de France* [Images and Books of France]

When, in 1923, at the age of 25, B. Fundoianu (Benjamin Fondane, né Benjamin Wechlser) permanently left Romania, he was already established as a poet and critic. He is still considered today to be an important poet of modernity, among those who did much to alter the poetic landscape. His only collection of Romanian poems was published in Bucharest in 1930, even though he had been living in Paris for seven years at that point. The collection brought together poems written or published between 1917 and 1923, entitled *Privelişti*, which can be translated as "landscapes" or "views." This poetry breaks with the lyrical, contemplative Romanian tradition of the landscape. One of these poems would fascinate the young Paul Celan. This poem begins "et un soir viendra où je partirai d'ici" [and a night will come when I will leave here].

In 1922, a year before his departure from Romania, still only 24 years old, Fundoianu published *Images et Livres de France*, a collection of critical essays that had been published in periodicals between 1920 and 1922. All articles concern French authors from the end of the century. From the very beginning, the young Fundoianu showed himself to be an original, aggressive critic. He had no fear of questioning or calling out the authors he wrote about; nor did he refrain from questioning his own readers. He could already see that certain major texts of modernity were "en état de guerre" [in a state of war], to quote Dominique Rabaté.

The major influences on his thinking are familiar giants: the shadow of Nietzsche, though the philosopher is rarely cited, hovers, omnipresent; on the margins, André Gide and Jules de Gaultier with his theory of *bovarysme*. Even though Fondane would later distance himself from them, renouncing their views only a few years later, he was nonetheless marked by an initial imprint. Their works aided in the construction of his mode of critical thinking. One of the underlying leitmotifs of the book, unsurprisingly, is a revolt against a process of logic that suffocates what is real.

Let us consider for a moment the philosophy of Jules de Gaultier, known for his theory of bovarysme. Encountering Nietzsche was, for him, decisive. Like Bergson, who was a contemporary, his work was a clear reflection of the scientific model of the nineteenth century. Gaultier defines bovarysme as an essential faculty, as "un pouvoir départi à l'homme de se concevoir autre qu'il n'est" [a lost power of man to conceive of himself other than he is].[2] He continues, "Toute activité qui prend conscience de sa propre action la déforme, dit-il, par le geste même dont elle s'en empare dans la connaissance" [Any activity that is aware of its own action becomes deformed by the very gesture it employs in its consciousness of itself].[3] But this illusion was, for Gaultier, a source of joy, a creative error, the aesthetic substance of reality. What interested the young Fondane was the rehabilitation of the original foundational power of error and illusion in the creation of reality.

The young Romanian critic displayed an unusual awareness of the essence of modernity. He quickly recognized the significance of many now-familiar French authors: Baudelaire, Flaubert, Gide, Huysmans, Mallarmé, the playwright Maeterlinck, and Proust. With regard to *À Rebours* [Against the Grain], he said, "l'histoire du symbolisme est liée à ce livre, s'est heurtée à ce livre, est partie de lui" [symbolism's history is tied to this book, is bound up with it, takes off from it]. With regard to Proust, Fondane was resistant but ultimately read him with pleasure. While many readers of the time were put off by the length of *Recherche*, Fundoianu, anticipating Spitzer and Genette, savored every element central to the Proustian style: digression, parenthesis, anecdote. "La digression, n'est-ce pas là tout l'art des romans de Proust?" [Digression, is it not the whole art of Proust's novels?] *Images et Livres de France*, 139)

Fondane proclaimed the nineteenth century the century of poetry par excellence. Baudelaire represented the "somme de la poésie du siècle" [sum of the poetry of the century] (153). Fondane expected that anthologies over the next hundred years would give notice to Hérédia and to Leconte de Lisle, would evoke the cult of Mallarmé, or

---

[2] Jules de Gaultier, *Le Bovarysme*, Mercure de France, 1902, 13.
[3] Jules de Gaultier, *Le Génie de Flaubert,* Mercure de France, 1913, 6.

esteem the art of Gautier, but it was the *Flowers of Evil*, he believed, that would emerge as the most influential. Baudelaire had marked his readers with a hot iron, "le fer rouge d'une sensibilité superposée—créatrice d'une autre pudeur, d'une autre compréhension, d'une autre perception" [the hot iron of a layered sensibility—the creator of a new sense of modesty, of a new kind of comprehension, of even a new kind of perception] (156). Fondane would even dedicate himself during the long months of the war to his final essay: *Baudelaire et l'expérience du gouffre* [Baudelaire and the Experience of the Abyss]. Even in Auschwitz, he spoke endlessly of Baudelaire's verses, arguing that they evoked "la consolation métaphysique" [the metaphysical consolation] (157) that only poetry could bring:

> Baudelaire nous a conduit en wagonnet là où la lumière prend fin, où l'air se raréfie, où le jour devient nuit […]. On peut fuir la mine et quitter Baudelaire. On ne pourra jamais l'oublier.

> [Baudelaire has brought us by cart to this place where the light is closing off, where the air is growing scarce, where the day is becoming night […]. We can flee this mine and leave Baudelaire behind us. But we can never forget him.]
>
> (157)

The question of modern lyricism is certainly at the heart of contemporary critical reflection. It was in the chapter dedicated to Mallarmé that Fundoianu diagnosed the crisis of the lyric subject; and to underline this paradox, he noted that just when a revolution in poetry was being prepared, Mallarmé "the Parnassian" became the monarch and the theorist of this very revolution. It was as if, he argued, instead of guillotining the king, the revolutionaries of 1789 had put him at the head of the Reign of Terror. Despite his admiration for Mallarmé, Fundoianu could not stop himself from condemning his poetry: "L'art de Mallarmé est stérile" [Mallarmé's art is sterile] (71). Cut off from the world, from all human communication, the poet refused to even throw a penny out the window, "de peur de s'apercevoir que l'orgue de Barbarie ne fonctionne pas tout seul" [for fear of discovering that the barrel organ didn't function by itself] (71). Though Fondane cited Verlaine on many occasions, he had uncharacteristically little to say about Rimbaud. Fondane was totally silent on Rimbaud, though he later dedicated an essay to this major poet: "Rimbaud le Voyou" [Rimbaud the Ruffian]. Did he only discover Rimbaud's range later? Presumably this must have been so, as in 1929, he exclaimed, "Avec Baudelaire et Rimbaud seuls pointait une lueur de vérité" [Only with Baudelaire and Rimbaud did there shine a glimmer of truth].[4]

The development of Fondane's dramatic aesthetic can be seen in the daily publication *Rampă* [Ramp] between 1921 and 1922. Exasperated by the "théâtre de bavardage" [theatre of chatter], fiercely opposed to the theatre of the boulevard that dominated Bucharest, he developed his ideal of a "théâtre sans paroles" [theatre without words]. Moreover, for Fondane, there was no border between theatre and poetry: "Mais où s'achève le poème et où commence le théâtre? Une pièce de théâtre qui n'est pas un poème [...] ne relève pas de l'art" [But where does poetry end and theatre begin? A play that is not a poem [...] is not art] (*Images et Livres de France* 162). This suggestion applied to Claudel, in whose works, he said, action kills tragedy, an unforgiveable move, as tragedy lies at the heart of all conflict. His attraction to the early theatre of Maeterlinck, then, is understandable. Fondane premiered some of Maeterlinck's work in his avant-garde theatre *Insula*, created in 1922, just before his departure from Romania. To the reader of Schopenhauer (whose philosophy was well known in Romania thanks to Eminescu), the universe of this little "théâtre de marionnettes" [theatre of marionettes] was immediately familiar: people in this universe are laughable puppets with fatal power, prisoners to a destiny they do not understand. Above all, he admired Maeterlinck's use of silence: "le mystère avec lequel il nous a enrichi [...] c'est le Silence" [The mystery with which he enriches us [...] is Silence]. The absence of a hero struck him especially. Similar to entities or sentiments, the characters "courent sans corps" [run without bodies];[5] he named them Fear, Presentiment, Despair, Death. A few sentences sum up the essence of this harbinger of the new theatre, this "theatre of the absurd," of the 1950s:

> Car le théâtre est sans contour et sans limite. Il y a dans la vie des instants où l'abîme est si proche que le cri même serait dissonant. L'homme en perd ses gestes et sa logique. Il ne peut parler. Il se tait.

---

[4] Preface to *Privelişti*, Paris-Méditerranée, 1996, 21.
[5] "Maeterlinck," *Rampa*, 22 January, 1920.

> [Because theatre knows no bounds and no limits. In life
> there are moments when the abyss is so close that even cry-
> ing out would seem dissonant. Man loses his gestures and
> his logic. He cannot speak. He is silent.]
>
> (*Images et Livres de France* 136)

His preface to *Images et Livres de France* caused a scandal in Romania; it outraged the critics, and some of them still have not pardoned him for his insolence. Essentially, he presented Romanian literature as a "colony" of French literature. What good would it be, then, to write in Romanian? He had never "known" French literature—as he had known German or English literature—but had "lived" it, he said. In other words, he felt at home there.

Some have questioned the reasons for his departure from Romania: Was it due to a crisis, some kind of rupture, or a voluntary exile? In fact, from Fundoianu to Fondane, there is continuity. Well before his departure, his link to French culture was profound; he translated French poems, and his poetic language was marked by syntax unique to French. In a letter from 1924 to his friend Felix Aderca, he confided that he was afflicted by the non-existence of Romanian culture, that he was convinced it would never exist, and that this was the reason he had left his country.

Another reason that could have contributed to his departure was the virulent anti-Semitism that was rampant in Romania. It seems that Fondane preferred not to mention it, however.

Works in French: 1923–1927

Fondane's first four years in Paris, from 1923 to 1927, were particularly painful. To survive, he worked at an insurance company, before being employed as a screenwriter for Paramount Studios. At the same time, he struggled to gain the language skills necessary to compose in French. One legend holds that he wrote nothing during these four years, but this silence was, in fact, only with respect to his poetic activity. A recently discovered manuscript has shown that by 1925 he had already composed his first essay in French, *Faux Traité d'esthétique* [False Treatise on Aesthetics],[6] a title he would reuse in 1938.

---

[6] For more on this subject, see Monique Jutrin's article in *Cahiers Benjamin Fondane*, no. 5.

At the time of Fondane's arrival in Paris, surrealism dominated the literary scene. Fondane had invested a lot in this movement, but he was soon disillusioned by it and subjected it to an unforgiving critique. In fact, his preference leaned toward Dada; Fondane was tied to Tzara before he was won over by Breton. Fondane never took part in any literary group, with the possible exception of *Discontinuité*, founded by Claude Sernet and Arthur Adamov, but this group's existence was brief. His sympathies also lay with surrealism's dissidents: authors like Artaud, Desnos, and members of *Le Grand Jeu* [The Great Game].

Fondane criticized Breton's surrealism for its rational exploration of the unconscious, its appropriation of Rimbaud, its dogma of automatic writing, its political engagement, and its allegiance to communism. Instead, Fondane gave his allegiance to surrealist cinema. He saw in silent film "l'appareil à lyrisme par excellence" [the means to lyricism par excellence]. The only surrealist texts that Fondane ever wrote were his *Ciné-Poèmes*, published in 1928. These scripts, which were never intended to be produced, show just how popular this genre was at the time.

Meeting Léon Chestov

The most important meeting of these Paris years was with Léon Chestov, as Fondane's work would be influenced by Chestov's philosophy of tragedy. This meeting would influence Fondane's life and his work. He first met Chestov in 1924 at Jules de Gaultier's salon. (The previous year, before leaving Romania, he had discovered Chestov's *Les Révélations de la Mort* [Revelations of Death] and had written a long article about him, knowing nothing about the author.) It was not until 1927 that the two men made any kind of real connection. They became friends, and Fondane became Chestov's only disciple.

Lev Itzhak Schwarzman was born Léon Chestov in Kiev on February 13, 1866. Fed on Nietzsche and Dostoevsky, Chestov developed an unsystematic existentialist philosophy that denied evil and necessity. His philosophy, of course, was always struggling against institutionalized philosophy, and remained on the margins of larger philosophical debate. Chestov strongly opposed the theory of knowledge: he fought against what reason takes to be obvious, or better, against the supremacy of reason. He was inspired by Shakespeare and Nietzsche, as well as Dostoevsky, and, for him, peace is impossible between reason and faith, between Athens and Jerusalem. Existentialist thought begins where rational thought ends, at the place where despair rises up against evil, as evil, Chestov believed, must not be accepted as a necessity. "La liberté ne consiste pas dans la possibilité de choisir entre le bien et le mal" [Freedom does not exist in the possibility of choosing between good and evil].[7] It exists in the strength and power of not accepting the idea of evil. Though Chestov was neither a believer nor a churchgoer, his philosophy required an all-powerful creator God. As with Fondane, it was not about obedience but about a spiritual demand.

Fondane wrote down the most important parts of his interviews with Chestov after each of their meetings from 1929 until Chestov's death in 1938. These notes constitute a sort of chronicle of many aspects of intellectual life in the 1930s. The two men were not indifferent to political events, and they testified lucidly with regard to the Nazi and Communist dangers. At a time when French intellectuals were generally aligned with either the Right or the Left, Fondane set himself apart with his intellectual independence. Where did his lucidity come from? He rejected conventional modes of political thought and customary logic. He attempted to see beyond and diagnose a spiritual failing.

In his preface to *La Conscience Malheureuse* [The Unhappy Conscience], he defines philosophy as

> l'acte par lequel l'existant pose sa propre existence, cherchant en lui et hors de lui, avec ou contre les évidences, les possibilités mêmes du vivre, [et conclut que l'homme] continuera à témoigner de son irrésignation tant que la réalité sera telle qu'elle est, par tous les moyens mis à sa disposition : par le poème, par le cri, par la foi ou par le suicide.

> [the act through which a being interrogates its own existence, searching within and without itself, with or despite obvious facts related to the possibilities of living, [and concludes that man] will continue to show his own irresignation as long as reality remains what it has been, through every means at his disposal: through poetry, through screaming, through faith, or through suicide.] (11)

---

[7] See Lev Shestov and Yves Bonnefoy, *Athènes et Jérusalem: un essai de philosophie religieuse* (Paris: Flammarion, 1967), 238.

Readers will note the neologism: *irresignation*. Fondane felt compelled to create a new term for distinguishing a particular form of revolt, a revolt against the philosophy of philosophers. This was due to his following in the footsteps of Chestov and Nietzsche, going to war against a philosophy where resignation held a privileged position. He proposed another philosophy, existentialist, living, in actuality.

1933–1945: Literary and Philosophical Essays

1933: *Rimbaud le Voyou*

1936: *La Conscience Malheureuse*

1938: *Faux Traité d'Esthétique*

1945: *Le Lundi Existentiel et le Dimanche de l'Histoire,* published in the collection of Jean Grenier: *L'Existence* published by Gallimard

1947: *Baudelaire et l'expérience du gouffre*, published posthumously by Seghers (the unfinished text was composed during the years 1941–1944)

All these essays center around the same questions: those of man torn between reason and existence, between thought and life. *Rimbaud le Voyou*, his first essay in French, established his name in the world of French letters. Dedicated to Chestov, this book analyzed Rimbaud's life and work through Chestov's philosophy of tragedy. It applied an existentialist hermeneutics to Rimbaud, attempting to discover, under the text, the experience of a particular existence torn apart by an irresolvable conflict.

At the beginning of the 1930s, Rimbaud was at the center of many discussions: the surrealists saw in him the precursor to automatic writing; on the other hand, Rolland de Renéville had just published *Rimbaud le Voyant* (1929). In a letter from February 1930 to his friend Claude Sernet, Fondane wrote, "je sors Rimbaud de sa théorie du voyant, je porte plainte en escroquerie contre les surréalistes, contre Breton et le commerce au miracle" [I'm taking Rimbaud out of his theory of the clairvoyant, I'm pressing charges against the surrealists for swindling, and against Breton for being in the business of the supernatural].[8]

"C'est un livre dirigé contre moi" [It's a book aimed at me], Breton would say to the English poet David Gascoyne. Fondane introduced a tragic Rimbaud, the one in *Une Saison en Enfer* [A Season in Hell], a hoodlum Rimbaud, a poet who cheated by having sought to eliminate the Unknown through rational means, with the aide of a rational method. For Fondane, the poetic act was incompatible with a goal of consciousness. In order to bypass conceptual thinking, he advocated a poetics where the method is the scream. For Fondane, however, the poem is not the scream itself; it is merely witness to the scream. And this presents the question of the essence of lyricism and of its limits. Fondane never stopped seeking the limits of poetry, questioning his own power to transgress them in an attempt to modify reality.

Five years later, in 1938, the publication of the *Faux Traité d'esthétique* spurred debate about poetry and poetic experience among critics like Albert Béguin, Marcel Raymond, Marcel De Corte, Jean Cassou, the Maritains, and others. It was a debate on the nature of poetry, on its existential or mystical stakes. It was a debate about poetry as a living or mystical existence, as consciousness, as revolution, as well as its relationship to dreams and the unconscious. Fondane asked, "Pourquoi l'art? Pourquoi justement l'art chez le seul animal raisonnable?" [Why art? Why does art exist only in the one rational animal?] (*FT*, 11[1980 edition]). With regard to this question, he developed his existentialist poetics, and the originality of this question is still striking, something unrivalled in his time.

The title of the *Faux Traité* seems inspired ironically by a work that was required reading in Romanian high schools and that served as a model for writing: *The False Treatise of the Hunt* by Odobescu, a nineteenth-century author. It is a "false treatise," because Fondane did not intend to respond to questions of aesthetics with regard to the philosophy of art. If philosophy seeks to resolve the contradictions inherent in life, poetry and art are the places where opposing forces, often obscure and arbitrary, can coexist. The only aesthetic possible, according to Fondane, must be aware of the impossibility of reconciling artistic truths with speculative truths. The meaning of the subtitle,

---

[8] Published in *Non Lieu*, 1978.

"Essay on the Crisis of Reality," is made clear by Fondane's consideration of *known* reality, that of the philosophers, as a "sérieux empêchement à la réalité *'possédée'*" [serious obstacle to *possessed* reality,] adding that reality only becomes reality *in the act of participation*. And yet, this "participation à la réalité possédée" [participation in possessed reality] (*FT* 78) must come to be through poetic experience. The notion of participation is described by Lucien Lévy-Bruhl as the way the so-called "primitives" think. Social relations are not objects of reflection for primitives: they are lived and felt less than thought; they are apprehended in an intuitive way immediately. Fondane considered Lévy-Bruhl to be a metaphysical philosopher in spite of himself, whose ideas could overwhelm the foundations of the theory of consciousness. Indeed, Lévy-Bruhl's name is often cited in support of Fondane's ideas. Lévy-Bruhl asserted, in fact, that "la pensée logique ne serait jamais l'héritière universelle de la pensée prélogique" [logical thought would never be the universal heir to pre-logical thought]. He added that "s'il est vrai que notre activité mentale est logique et pré-logique à la fois, l'histoire des dogmes religieux et des systèmes philosophiques peut s'éclairer d'un jour nouveau" [if it is true that our mental activity is logical and pre-logical at the same time, the history of religious dogmas and philosophical systems might one day become clearer].[9]

Referring to the idea of the participation of primitives, (such as Lévy-Bruhl describes them), Fondane affirms the coexistence in history of mythical and rational thought. At a certain moment in history, Fondane argues, the progressive separation of reason and mythical thought became inevitable. This moment marked the date of the birth of poetry. He conceived of poetry as "a restorative force," a power that does not permit rational thought to push man too far from this state of equilibrium that existed in the ancient past: "Il subsiste dans l'homme je ne sais quelle nostalgie de cette vérité première, une soif d'autre chose, un coefficient d'irréalité, qui n'a pu être réduit entièrement par la connaissance rationnelle" [There exists in man an unknown nostalgia for this original truth, a thirst for something else, a coefficient of irreality, which could not be entirely reduced through rational consciousness]. It is, therefore, at the end of a long process that rational thought was imposed. If it is true that poetry developed

---

[9] *Les fonctions mentales dans les sociétés inférieures*, Alcan, 1910, 33.

along this line of demarcation between the idea of participation and rational thought, each true poet is part philosopher and each of us must be part poet.

This is the explanation for Fondane's refusal to recognize poetry as an aesthetic category, with poetry as a tool for exploring the conscious mind and the unconscious. He understood the necessity of finding a modality for uniting *lived experience* and *thought*. Traditional philosophy taught him the path of reason: one must extract from a blurred reality the pure concepts and apply to them the immutable laws of logic in order to arrive at eternal truths. While, for some, poetry would be complementary to philosophy, for Fondane, it represented the escape, the way to evade rational thought: he wrote in his preface to the *Faux Traité* that poetry "peut penser bien des choses qui ont été refusées à la philosophie" [can consider ideas that have been rejected by philosophy] (16).

Thus, for Fondane, poetry was an existential function, something integral to man, something even secreted by him. Poetry was a metaphysical function, much like philosophy:

> Qu'est-ce donc pour nous que la poésie—cri, prière, acte magique? Qu'importe! Que celui pour lequel elle est un cri, crie! Qu'il prie, celui pour lequel elle est prière! Et qu'il se fasse sorcier, voyant ou prophète, celui qui y voit un acte magique! Mais avant tout, que le poète *ose*! Qu'il descende des catégories de sa pensée dans les catégories de sa propre vie.

> [What, then, is poetry to us—shout, prayer, magic? What does it matter? Let those who think it's a shout, shout! Let them pray, if they think it's a prayer! And let those who think it's magic do magic, see into the future, or prophesy! But above all, let the poet *dare*! Let him step down from categories of thinking into categories of living.] (*FT* 103)

Poetry is risky, but it's a risk worth taking. In "Considering the Struggle with Ultimate Reality" (*FT* 102), it is expressed, however, in this "object" known as the poem, an object that Fondane often treats with condescension: "artefactum, objet manufacturé par l'esprit et qui requiert toutes sortes de conditions morales et pratiques dont, épris de rigueur, des écrivains avertis ont essayé de tirer les rudiments valables d'une technique" [artifact, object manufactured by the spirit and which requires all sorts of moral conditions and practices; then, infatuated with technical rigor, some experienced writers tried to extract the valuable elements from a technique] (13). If the poetic experience is not reduced to the poem, we can hardly do without it. Fondane was only too conscious that a poem could also be the fruit of technique. How to accommodate these contradictory demands: poetic activity conceived of as ultimate freedom, and the existence of technique, however "obscure"? How can one reconcile insight with work? Serendipity and craft?

At the end of his essay *Baudelaire et l'expérience du gouffre*, Fondane formulates what he called "l'esthétique d'Ulysse" [the aesthetic of Ulysses] (358–62). A poetic art comprising two poles crystallizes around the figure of Ulysses: poetic risk and acquired craft. If the figure of Ulysses can embody this bipolar aesthetic, it must be during his adventurous wandering when he catches sight of an Ithaca to which he can, despite everything, choose not to return:

> Reculant de jour en jour cette rentrée à Ithaque qui mettra fin, une fois pour toutes, à la recherche de la trouvaille. Car la trouvaille est, par elle-même, une limite; elle est la frontière d'un univers voulu, qui ne craint pas moins de quitter la circonférence où il s'est de bonne foi enfermé.

> [Deferring day by day this return to Ithaca that will set an end, once and for all, to the quest for the find. Since the find is in and of itself the frontier of a willed universe, a universe that dreads equally as much as the quest to let go of the circumference within which, in good faith, it has enclosed itself.] (*BG* 360)

Will he renounce Ithaca, like Dante's Ulysses venturing beyond Hercules's Columns, at risk of perishing there? Will he tether himself to the rocks and stop up his ears to resist the song of the sirens? Because, as greedy as he is for his discovery,

> Tout voyage vers l'inconnu suppose la précaution prise d'une bonne quantité de cordes et d'une ample provision de cire pour le cas où, qui sait, on viendrait vraiment à rencontrer cet inconnu.

> [Every voyage toward the unknown assumes the precaution of taking a good quantity of rope and an ample supply of wax just in case, who knows, you actually meet this unknown.] (*BG* 61)

As mentioned before, this is not about reconciling conflicting tendencies, of resolving contradictions, but of living this conflict: "Le conflit, la tension, voilà qui serait plus *vrai* que la fausse unité, que la fausse paix, de la connaissance!" [The conflict, the tension, this is what will be *truer* than false unity, than false peace, of knowledge!] (*FT* 104). This leads to a poetics of risk, carrying the danger of the imperfect, of imperfection, of the incomplete. Fondane never stopped debating these questions of the "limit" in art. In one of his un-published notebooks, he brings up this question with regard to a poet of tragedy like Baudelaire. We arrive at this "frontière où commence autre chose—où il faut enfin QUITTER l'art, peut-être, pour aller de l'avant" [border where something else begins—where one must per-haps LEAVE art behind in order to go forward] (Carnet inédit de 1942, Archives Michel Carassou).

Fondane gained French citizenship in 1938. Consequently, he was drafted in 1940. As a soldier, he took part in what is known as the Debacle of 1940, after the French defeat at the battles of the Somme and Aisne, which led to an exodus of eight million people out of German-invaded territories in France and, ultimately, Pétain's signing of the armistice with Nazi Germany. He was imprisoned, but he man-aged to escape. And when recaptured, he was freed for health reasons: he was suffering from a stomach ulcer. But by the beginning of 1941, he had returned to his home at 6 Rue Rollin.

During the war years, Fondane had been working simultaneously on several books: he was preoccupied with questions of epistemology and logic, so he planned a volume, *L'Être et la Connaissance*, dedi-cated to three thinkers: Chestov, Lupasco, and Lévy-Bruhl. At the same time, he reworked his *Rimbaud*, rewrote *Ulysses*, composed *Ex-odus*, and dedicated articles to Stéphane Lupasco and to Gaston Bachelard. His essay on Baudelaire situates itself at the intersection between his thinking at the time and an extension of his earlier thought as revealed in his previous writing. Everything seemed to be leading toward this book, everything feeding it, fertilizing it. In it we can follow the leaps of an agile mind in dialogue with itself, perpetu-ally in gestation. The first version of his essay *Baudelaire et l'expérience du gouffre* was finished at the end of 1941 or the begin-ning of 1942. However, he never stopped working on it, and the book remains unfinished.

This work was a response to the polemics of the pre-war critical interpretations of Baudelaire from Valéry and Jouve to Georges Blin, Eliot, and Huxley. He also refuted the psychoanalytic interpretations of René Laforgue. In 1947, at the time of its posthumous publication, the book was hardly commented on, having been eclipsed by Sartre's *Baudelaire*, which had come out several months prior. Sartre, who collaborated on *Cahiers du Sud* [Notebooks of the South] around the same time, might have read an excerpt of Fondane's *Baudelaire* in 1943 in that journal. Upon first picking it up, the reader finds herself plunged into a dense, impenetrable work: thirty-four chapters without titles or epigraphs, where a spiraling thought process moves slowly, returning endlessly upon itself. The reader does not know which Minotaur awaits her, nor which Ariadne guides her: everything seems aimed at losing her, leading her astray, while the reader feels that she is actually being led somewhere. Certain leitmotifs are seen as signals: for example, quotations from Dante, from Baudelaire, from Kafka. These quotations are repetitive, much like the recurring motifs of the monad without doors or windows, or the allegory of the living rat, or, again, the opposition between "thinking and feeling."

Finally, I can say that the book refuses to be confined to the category called "literary criticism." Neither does it pretend to establish a new doctrine or a new mode of interpretation, but it refuses even the possibility of such a mode of interpretation (*BG* 266 *et seq.*). It refuses to impose a new way of thinking, but instead it aims to convince us that another mode of thinking is possible. It encourages the reader to leave criticism behind, to go beyond literature, to "briser le cercle enchanté de l'art pour aller au-delà" [break up the enchanted circle of art and go beyond it] (*BG* 265). Beyond? To where? This is the question that Fondane would not dream of answering. He contents himself with saying simply that "le créateur peut, à tout instant, franchir les frontières de l'art pour n'y plus revenir, éveillé à une nouvelle réalité qui ne se soucie pas d'être exprimée" [the creator, at any moment, can cross over the borders of art and never return, as he is awakened to a new reality that doesn't have to be articulated] (265).

Le Lundi Existentiel et le Dimanche de l'Histoire [The Existential Monday and the Sunday of History] was published in 1945 in the collected volume *Existence*. In 1943, Jean Grenier decided to put together a number of essays on diverse topics within the world of existentialist thinking. He aimed this collection at the representatives of institutional philosophy like Gilson and Lavelle, but also to Camus and to Fondane. The title of Fondane's essay drew on a passage from the Diaries of Kafka: "Tu es réservé pour un grand Lundi!—Bien parlé, mais le Dimanche ne finira jamais" [You're saved for a great Monday!—Nicely said, but Sunday will never be over]. This text can be considered Fondane's philosophical testament. It was handed to Grenier at the beginning of March 1944, shortly before Fondane's arrest. In it Fondane faces the new strain of existentialist thought, responding to Camus and Sartre as well as to Heidegger. For Fondane, "l'existant apprend que sa liberté est refus" [a being learns that his freedom is denied]—denied by all who hope to confine him in his own immanence and only offer him false escapes. It falls to him to break "le pouvoir magique du Dimanche de l'Histoire" [the magical power of the Sunday of History].[10]

French Language Poetry

From 1929 to the moment he began his poetic work in French, all his poetry led toward the same existential odyssey, comprising four long poems: *Ulysse* (1933), *Titanic* (1936), *L'Exode* (begun in 1932–1933 and rewritten during the war years), and *Le Mal des Fantômes* (1943–1944), which would become the title of his entire poetic work. All this poetry is rightly considered tragedy. That poetic experience and tragic experience should join up, or that only poetry could spring from witnessing tragedy, seems clear enough. But Fondane possessed the strange power to face the big questions of existence, solitude, suffering, and death. It is a harsh poetry, but not a despairing one.

Ulysse

A sea voyage to Argentina seems to have triggered the writing of *Ulysse*. Fondane had been invited in 1929 by Victoria Ocampo, the *grande dame* of Argentinean letters, to give some lectures about avant-garde cinema.

Dedicated to his brother-in-law Armand Pascal, who had just died, the poem begins with mourning and distress; it is a sort of descent to hell and a *nekyia*, an evocation of the dead. The geographical

---

[10] "Le Lundi existentiel et le Dimanche de l'Histoire" in *L'Existence*, Gallimard, 1945, 76.

journey of the ocean liner that left from Marseille and took him to Argentina is retraced in the poem: like Dante's Ulysses, he had passed over the columns of Hercules, descending next to Dakar before crossing the ocean. *Ulysse* took shape between 1929 and 1933; it was profoundly reworked during the war. In the first version, written in 1933, the poet describes himself as a divided being: "Juif, naturellement, et cependant Ulysse" [Jew, naturally, but still Ulysses]. This schism disappears in the final version: "Juif, naturellement, tu étais juif, Ulysse" [Jew, naturally, you were a Jew, Ulysses] (*MF* 25). In this moment of Ulysses's self-identification, the destiny of man, of Jew, and of poet are tied together. Closer to Dante's Ulysses (the one who appears in *Canto XXVI* of the *Inferno*) than to the wise and measured man of Odysseus, Fondane's Ulysses does not confuse himself with the first or the second. He uses the mythical structure as a foil, allowing him to emphasize, by way of contrast, how he is different. Born, not in Ithaca, but in Jassy, in a "ville de petits juifs accrochés à l'air" [city of little Jews hung on air] so that his wandering recalls an ancient exodus. The voyager revolts against a forced destiny, refusing to be simply a toy, and reclaims a sense and a place, situating himself in History, against History, beyond History: "Je pose mon poing dur sur la table du monde, je suis de ceux qui n'ont rien, qui veulent tout, je ne saurai jamais me résigner" [I place my hard fist on the table of the world, I come from those who have nothing, who want everything, I will never give up] (*MF* 45). Fondane rejected the circularity and Ulyssean wandering of the Greek vision of history for which finitude was synonymous with perfection. The biblical perspective introduces a notion of time as linear, historic, and irreversible.

Ulysses came to embody an individual and collective destiny, an existential and poetic experience. The figure of the immigrant, this exile without land or language, who confuses himself sometimes with the wandering Jew, obsessively haunts Fondane's poetry. In 1936 Fondane once again took a boat to Argentina, this time to make a film. This second trip inspired the poem *Titanic*.

Titanic

For his second journey among men, Ulysses's rowboat is changed into a deluxe ocean liner, this liner that became the emblem of a world in perdition. It evokes a world of machines, of paths that crush and humiliate men, the world of the city: the entrances to the metro, bis-

tros, the cinema, workers' gatherings…. Nevertheless, the poet en-
trusts "les leviers de commande" [the control levers] to prayer and
hope (*MF* 140). It is on the deck of Noah's ark that a pair of each species will "refaire le monde anéanti" [remake the annihilated world]
(*MF* 151). After diving into his past—that of the small village of Jews
"vêtus de prières anciennes" [dressed in ancient prayers] of peasants
"en chemise brodée" [in embroidered shirts] (*MF* 161)—the poet
climbs back to the surface to find his solitude again. And he goes
forth from then on, lampless, into his own netherworld:

> Toute l'histoire me suit, – suis-je un résidu ou un terme ?
> A la lumière du sang je redescends en moi-même,
> toutes les routes se croisent, toutes les races se toisent.
>
> [All of history follows me, – am I a remnant or an ending?
> By the light of blood I go back down into myself,
> all roads meet, all races size each other up.] (MF 187)

Titanic concludes with a final Apocalypse that borrows from Ec-
clesiastes its refrain:

> Il est un temps de mourir et un temps de ne pas mourir
> de révolte perpétuelle—Un temps de folie et de haine?
> **SANS DOUTE!**
>
> [There is a time to die and a time not to die
> of perpetual revolt—A time of madness and of hate?
> **WITHOUT A DOUBT!**] (*MF* 188)

Le Mal des Fantômes [The Evil of Ghosts]

As for *Le Mal des Fantômes* composed in 1942–1943, the "chef-
d'œuvre de ma quarante-cinquième année" [masterpiece of my forty-
fifth year] (as Fondane wrote in a letter to Léon-Gabriel Gros), it had
originally been titled "Le Mal d'Ulysse" [Ulysses's Trouble], as rec-
orded in a work notebook. This poem is shorter: written in decasyl-
labic tercets, recalling the terza rima of Dante. It is divided into 23
"Tableaux," dominated by the figure of the voyager, of the immigrant.

This is the dawning of a Jewish vision of history: the Bible, which
describes events of the past, also reveals the framework of future history: "Nous étions au bord des Fleuves. Nous y sommes" [We were
by the rivers' shores. Now we are there].

L'Exode

In the afterword to *L'Exode*, Fondane makes clear that the poem was written between *Ulysses* and *Titanic*, around 1934, at a moment when "l'auteur était fort loin de penser qu'il prophétisait" [the author was very far away from thinking that he was prophesying]. During the Occupation, Fondane reworked the text, adding the "Prose Preface" as well as the "Interlude."

If the Exodus, the flight from Egypt, is the founding event for the Jewish people, the subtitle of the poem *Super Flumina Babylonis*, borrowed from Psalm 137, recalls the bitter experience of the Babylonian exile. Thus the poet reunites, all at once, liberation and captivity, hope and anguish. The entire text is animated by this double, antinomic movement. But the Jewish man, who has so often suffered reluctantly, can here recognize, from the "Prose Preface," an existential condition:

> Oui, j'ai été un homme comme les autres hommes,
> nourri de pain, de rêve, de désespoir.
>
> [Yes, I was a man like other men,
> fed with bread, with dreams, with despair.] (*MF* 192)

Then, thinking better of it:

> Et pourtant, non!
> Je n'étais pas un homme comme vous.
> Vous n'êtes pas nés sur les routes: personne n'a jeté à l'égout vos petits
> vous n'avez pas erré de cité en cité
> traqués par les polices
> vous n'avez pas connu les désastres à l'aube,
> les wagons de bestiaux
> et le sanglot amer de l'humiliation,
> accusés d'un délit que vous n'avez pas fait,
> d'un meurtre dont il manque encore le cadavre, […]
>
> [And before, no!
> I was not a man like you.
> You were not born on the roads: no one threw your young ones in the sewer
> you've never wandered from city to city
> hounded by the police
> you haven't known disasters at the break of dawn,
> cattle cars and the bitter blood of humiliation,
> accused of a crime you haven't committed,
> of a murder where the body is still missing, […]] (*MF* 192)

Rarely has a poet testified, in a way so simple and so arresting, to human indignity.

L'Exode finishes with a vision of the Apocalypse. Would another life begin "dans un monde sans commencements ni fins" [in a world without beginnings or ends]? The reader can no longer follow along with the vision of the poet who contents himself with shouting, "C'EST!" [IT IS SO!].

For Fondane, the poem—a scream or a prayer—is the only language, the only source for changing the world, the only means of awakening God. The poet must "sécréter tous les jours la dose d'affirmation dont l'humanité a besoin pour vivre" [give out a dose of affirmation every day necessary for humanity to live], says Fondane, in the *Faux Traité* (18). This is the power of poetry, the power to continue to sing, to scream, to pray: the only witness to *irresignation*, to a superior freedom.

Theatre and Cinema

Fondane became interested in theatre in his youth. The development of his dramatic aesthetic can be seen in the daily newspapers published in Romania. Exasperated with the "theatre of chatter" that reigned in Bucharest, he developed his idea of a theatre without words. This explains his attraction to the early works of Maeterlinck, as mentioned earlier. Fondane understood this kind of drama, and it can be argued that this style contained the germ of what would become the theatre of the absurd in the 1950s.

In 1922 he founded an avant-garde theatre in Bucharest, named *Insula* [Island] with his elder sister Line, an actress, as well as with her husband Armand Pascal, who was at the same time an actor and screenwriter and who had worked with Copeau at the Vieux-Colombier. Among other works, they put on Maeterlinck's *La Mort de Tintagiles* [The Death of Tantagiles] and Molière's *Le Médecin Volant* [The Flying Doctor]. This theatrical experience, however, was but a short one. Fondane was forced to close his theatre because of financial difficulties. This failure contributed to his decision to leave Romania.

In Paris, from 1926 to 1930, Fondane passionately followed Artaud's performances at the Alfred Jarry Theatre. In a long letter to Artaud, Fondane encouraged him to pursue his interest in liberating the theatre from text. This desire for a "pure" theatre soon merged with Fondane's passion for silent cinema. At the beginning of the 1930s, Fondane rewrote plays in French that he had drafted in Romanian. His most interesting play was the *Festin de Balthazar* [Balthazar's Celebration], which can, in certain ways, be compared with Camus's *Caligula*. (It has to do with the insolence of a king who provokes God.)

During the years following the First World War, cinema was at the center of many intellectual debates. Fondane participated in these debates with penetrating commentaries that he published in the journals of the time. Also important was the publication of his *Ciné-Poèmes* in 1928. Before the advent of sound, cinema inspired quite a few delusions. It was thought, for example, that it would allow for the creation of a new language.

By the beginning of 1930, Fondane had acquired a working knowledge of cinema, as he had ended up working as a screenwriter for Paramount in Joinville. In 1933, he collaborated on the making of a film adapted after a novel by Ramuz. In 1936, he left for Argentina to make the film *Tararira*—"un film absurde sur une chose absurde pour satisfaire son absurde goût de liberté" [an absurd film on an absurd thing to satisfy his absurd taste for freedom] (*Écrits pour le cinéma* 105). The producer, put off by its audaciousness, refused to distribute it. No trace of this film—which was burned—has since been found.

From the letters that Fondane wrote from Buenos Aires to his wife and his sister, it appears that he was leaving to settle in Argentina, because he was well aware of the Nazi danger. If *Tararira* had been a success, he would have obtained other contracts. In 1942, his Argentinean friends tried to bring him back to Argentina, but it was no longer possible to obtain a visa.

During the war years, Fondane did not take the precaution of changing his address. He was arrested on March 7, 1944, and turned over to the Gestapo at the same time as his sister Line. The two were incarcerated at Drancy. Fondane's wife, Geneviève Tissier, succeeded in obtaining his freedom as the "spouse of an Aryan." But Fondane refused to be freed without his sister. He was sent to Auschwitz on May 30 in the next-to-last deportation convoy. The day before, Fondane had written a clandestine farewell letter to his wife, accompanied by guidelines for the publication of his work. Those who knew him at Auschwitz could attest that, even to the end, Fondane remained man and poet. He was killed in the gas chambers on October 2, 1944.

Fondane seems to have wanted to play the role of "ferryman" between Romanian and French literature. During the 1920s, as the Parisian correspondent for the avant-garde Romanian journal *Integral*, he published a special issue on the French surrealists. In 1932, in the *Journal des Poètes* in Brussels, he published several pages of anthologies of Romanian poets that he had translated into French.

In Paris he was constantly in contact with Romanian writers and artists. In particular, he was close to Constantin Brancusi, Victor Brauner, and Grégoire Michonze, and, among the poets, to Tristan Tzara, Claude Sernet, and Ilarie Voronca. As for philosophers, he allied himself with the likes of Stephane Lupasco and Emile Cioran.

In his French-language poetry, there are often memories of his Romanian poetry, with evocations of the little Jewish village "hung on air" as in the paintings of Chagall. One of his last poems, "The Unsent Letter," was written as an elegy to the memory of Marior. Fondane also dedicated one of his books of Romanian poetry to Marior.

Situated at the crossroads of Romanian, French, and Jewish cultures, Fondane enriched French poetry with an original tonality that opened up new vistas for contemporary readers. His essays on Rimbaud and on Baudelaire, as well as his *Faux Traité*, remain standard points of reference and have seen a resurgence of interest in the postmodern era. His existentialist philosophy, so well appreciated in the 1930s, then forgotten after the war, has resurged in the philosophical debates of our time.

Works Cited and Selected Bibliography[11]

Works in French

Fondane, Benjamin. *Baudelaire et l'expérience du gouffre.* Paris: Seghers, 1947. Re-edited Brussels: Complexe, 1994. (*BG*)

_____. *Benjamin Fondane et les Cahiers du Sud. Correspondance*. Eds. Jean Ballard, Monique Jutrin, Gheorg Has, and Ion Pop. Bucharest: Fondation Culturelle Roumaine, 1998.

---

[11] For a more complete bibliography, see the following: *Cahiers Benjamin Fondane* and www.fondane.com.

_____. *Brancusi*. Saint-Clément-la-Rivière: Fata Morgana, 1995.

_____. *La Conscience malheureuse*. Paris: Denoël, 1936. Re-edited Paris: Plasma, 1979.

_____. *Correspondance Fondane-Maritain*. Paris: Paris-Méditerranée, 1997.

_____. *Écrits pour le cinéma*. Paris: Plasma, 1984.

_____. *L'Écrivain devant la révolution*. Paris-Méditerranée, 1997.

_____. *L'Être et la connaissance: essai sur Lupasco*. Paris: Paris-Méditerranée, 1998.

_____. *Faux Traité d'esthétique*. Paris: Denoël, 1938. (Also re-edited Paris: Plasma, 1980; Paris: Paris-Méditerranée, 1998). (*FT*)

_____. *Le Festin de Balthazar*. Saint-Nazaire: Arcane 17, 1985.

_____. *Fundoianu/Fondane et l'Avant-garde*. Eds. Petre Răileanu and Michel Carassou. Bucarest: Fondation Culturelle Roumaine, 1999; (Also re-edited, Paris: Editions Paris-Méditerranée, 1999).

_____. *Images et Livres de France*. Trans. Odile Serre. Intro. Monique Jutrin. Paris: Paris-Méditerranée, 2002.

_____. *Le Lundi existentiel et le dimanche de l'histoire*. Monaco: Editions du Rocher, 1989.

_____. *Le Mal des fantômes*. Paris: Plasma, 1980. Re-edited Paris: Paris-Méditerranée, 1996. (*MF*)

_____. *Rencontres avec Léon Chestov*. Paris: Plasma, 1982.

_____. *Rimbaud le voyou*. Paris: Denoël, 1933. Re-edited Paris: Plasma, 1980, and Brussels: Complexe, 1990.

_____. *Au seuil de l'Inde*. Saint-Clément-la-Rivière: Fata Morgana, 1994.

_____. *Titanic*. Brussels: Cahiers du Journal des Poètes, 1937.

_____. *Trois scenarii: ciné-poèmes*. Brussels: Documents Internationaux de l'Esprit Nouveau, 1928.

_____. *Ulysse*. Brussels: Cahiers du Journal des Poètes, 1933.

_____. *Le Voyageur n'a pas fini de voyager*. Paris: Paris-Méditerranée, 1996.

Works in Romanian

Fondane, Benjamin. *Imagini şi cărti din Franţa*. Bucarest: Socec, 1922.

_____. *Iudaism şi elenism*. Ed. Léon Volovici and Remus Zastroiu. Bucarest: Hasefer, 1999.

_____. *Tăgăduinţa lui Petru*. Jassy: Chemarea, 1918.

_____. *Privelişti*. Bucarest: Cultură Nationala, 1930.

Critical Essays on Fondane

Jutrin, Monique. *Benjamin Fondane ou le périple d'Ulysse*. Paris: Nizet, 1989.

Salazar-Ferrer, Olivier. *Benjamin Fondane*. Paris: Oxus, 2004.

French as the Language of *Libre Échange* in the Works of Panaït Istrati

Catherine Rossi
Université de Bourgogne

Panaït Istrati's decision to compose the entirety of his literary output in French is remarkable simply by virtue of his Romanian heritage. But considering that he learned the French language completely on his own—without any formal schooling—his place in the realm of francophone literature is unique.

Istrati did not adopt the French language because he was exiled in France or because he was born into a French-speaking Romanian family (such as the families of Noailles and Bibesco, for example). It was not a case of necessity or of obligation; it was also not a case of continuing some cultural tradition that had begun in Romania. It cannot even be considered an attempt at assimilation. Rather, his was a voluntary act, one of choosing to belong, irrespective of any societal pressures. It was not, however, a painless process: the trouble of learning a complex language remained.

In this essay, I will discuss how and why Istrati chose French as his preferred language of composition and how that choice was transformed into a kind of conquest in its own right. I also hope to elucidate some of the ways this choice affected the construction of his identity—as a writer, certainly, but also as a human being.

An Unexpected Education

French language and culture were highly visible in the Romania of the turn of the century, both in urban centers and rural areas.[1] Istrati's town of Braïla was no exception. A cosmopolitan port city, it had become something of a crucible where East met West. Every language, it seemed, could be heard there.

Istrati was born a peasant, one of the rural poor. His mother raised him alone, and her work as a laundress forced them to leave the coun-

---

[1] See *Francophonie roumaine et Intégration européenne: Actes du colloque international de Dijon*, directed by Ramona Bordei-Boca.

tryside for the working-class neighborhoods of the city of Braïla. But he did not learn French at school there: instead, he actually quit school very early in order to work and support his mother. This was his entry into the proletariat. Istrati held numerous jobs (as waiter, messenger, docker, house painter…), learning in the process a great deal about exploitation and injustice: within him were sown the seeds of revolt.

Istrati's insatiable curiosity could not content itself with these jobs, so he was compelled to discover a different world. He read voraciously and so discovered many of the great French authors,[2] thanks to the many translations available in Romania. He deprived himself of food in order to buy books; he used the time during which he was supposed to be running errands for his boss to read; and he even used the few hours that should have been devoted to sleep for reading. He quickly gained an appreciation for France and its language, driven by the kinship he felt with the notions of freedom advocated by the French Republic. His discovery of the Enlightenment thinkers was like discovering a new world, and it strengthened his desire to learn French and enter this Western world, a world where everything seemed so unlike his dear Eastern Romania.

Istrati's personal history compelled him to aid the oppressed, whose fate he recognized as similar to his own. He was horrified by their condition and became a spokesperson for employees with their employers. He was quickly, in spite of himself, at the center of this developing scene, becoming a unionist for the dock workers of Braïla in hopes of changing their situation. His meeting with Aloman, a militant socialist, would change the course of Istrati's life.

In the winter of 1913, Adrien Zograffi, also known as Panaït Istrati, left for Paris, pushed onto the train by his friend Aloman, who took a jab at his fellow vagrants in the East:

> Tu dois connaître l'Occident! Tu dois apprendre une grande langue occidentale, une, si tu ne peux pas plus. Et puisque ton tempérament s'accorde avec la culture française et avec les libertés qui règnent en France, tu partiras ce soir même pour Paris!

---

[2] Balzac, Bernardin de Saint-Pierre, Daudet, Hugo, Fénelon, Montaigne, Montesquieu, Madame de Staël, and Zola.

[You have to visit the West! You must learn a major Western European language, one only, if you can't manage
more. And since your temperament aligns with French
culture and with the freedoms that are so common in
France, you ought to leave for Paris tonight!]

(Istrati, *Méditerranée* 592)

Adrien-Panaït was twenty-nine years old. The 1913 voyage only
lasted a few months, but it was a pivotal experience. Istrati decided
that he wanted to learn French.

It was not until 1916 during an enforced stay at a Swiss sanatorium—where he fought a recurrent case of tuberculosis—that Istrati
decided to finally learn French by reading the great works in their
original language, with the help of a dictionary:

Je ne connais pas [*sic*] la langue que pour demander du
pain et produire l'hilarité; je prends Télémaque et un dictionnaire et je commence à déchiffrer. C'est ainsi que j'ai
appris le français [...]. C'est ainsi que j'ai lu une bonne
partie des classiques français.[3]

[I only know enough of the language to ask for bread and to
incite hilarity; I pick up Telemachus and a dictionary and
from there I decode. That's how I learned French [...].
That's how I read a large portion of the French classics.]

At the end of 1918, after a long journey through the cantons of
Switzerland, Istrati was again hospitalized at a sanatorium in Sylvana-
sur-Lausanne. In January 1919, he made the acquaintance of José
Jehouda[4] who recommended to him *Jean-Christophe*, the monumental
work by Romain Rolland. Istrati could see the work that went into
producing such a text. This discovery was something of a revelation
for him.

Istrati decided to write to Rolland to express his admiration,
addressing a long letter to him on August 19, 1919, while Rolland
was traveling through Switzerland. Unfortunately, the letter was
returned to Istrati with the stamp "parti sans laisser d'adresse" [de-

---

[3] Letter from Istrati to Romain Rolland, August 20, 1919.
[4] *La Famille Perlmutter* was the result of a collaboration between Istrati and José
Jehouda. The editor had asked Istrati to develop the Jewish traits of his characters.
This new version was worked out in Istrati's story, "Isaac, le tresseur de fil de fer."

parted without leaving an address]. This was, for Istrati, a profound disappointment.

In 1920, Istrati returned to France. He was miserable and unemployed, and his health also began to deteriorate. In Nice he found work as a traveling photographer, but his morale was at its lowest point, as the work exacerbated his disappointment in humanity and the world at large. On January 1, 1921, he wrote a letter to Romain Rolland in which he poured his heart out. But he could not bring himself to mail it. Two days later, he attempted suicide by cutting his throat but fortunately, he survived. The police found the letter addressed to Rolland at his house when they arrived and released it to the newspaper *L'Humanité*. A few months later, the letter finally made its way to its intended recipient, Rolland, who encouraged Istrati to compose in French.

Rolland's response sparked a veritable "volcanic eruption" from Istrati: "Votre vocation d'artiste est évidente.—Et en quelque langue que ce soit, vous seriez—vous êtes un écrivain"[5] [Your calling as an artist is clear.—And in whatever language it might be, you would be—you are a writer]. Thus began Istrati's frenzied battle to master the French language: "Je bûche comme un aveugle, me cognant la tête à toutes les règles d'une grammaire dont j'ignore le premier mot" [I'm slaving away like a blind man, banging my head against all the rules of grammar about which I don't know the first thing] ("Préface à Adrien Zograffi" 8).

Mastering the Language

Istrati became a famous writer by the age of 40. He found himself suddenly thrown into the literary scene when his first book, *Kyra Kyralina*, was published with Rieder in the collection *Contemporary French Prose Writers*. Rolland encouraged him to continue writing and expressed confidence in his young protégé. However, writing in French remained difficult for Istrati:

> J'obéis donc, avec élan. Mais, dès le début, l'ignorance de la langue me fit payer chèrement la joie d'écrire, et d'écrire en français. Ma poitrine était un haut fourneau plein de métaux en fusion qui cherchaient à s'évader et ne trouvaient pas de moules prêts à les recevoir. Toutes les deux

---

[5] Letter from Rolland to Istrati, March 29, 1921.

minutes j'arrêtais la matière incandescente, pour voir s'il
s'agissait de deux l ou d'un e grave, de deux p ou d'un seul,
d'un féminin ou d'un masculin. Je ne sais pas comment je
ne suis pas devenu fou à cette époque-là.

[I'm obeying it, with enthusiasm. But, from the beginning,
my ignorance of the language cost me dearly in the joy of
writing, of writing in French. My chest was a blast furnace
full of metals fusing together, trying to avoid each other
but not finding a cast ready to take them. Every two
minutes I would stop some incandescent thought to see if it
had two *l*'s or an accented *e*, if it had two *p*'s or only one, if
it was feminine or masculine. I don't know how I didn't go
crazy then.] ("Préface à Adrien Zograffi" 9)

How to describe Istrati's French? Some preferring "true" French
might consider Istrati—wrongly—as an "exotic" writer. Certainly,
Istrati's language reveals his Romanian cultural background at the
same time as it reveals certain linguistic peculiarities that no translation would be able to reproduce. Istrati was lucky enough to meet
some exceptionally intelligent proofreaders (Romain Rolland, Jean-
Richard Bloch, Frédéric Lefèvre, Marcel Martinet, and Jean Guéhen-
no), who quickly understood the meaning of his words. They did not
want to play the role of "translators" of Istrati's thoughts by using
"equivalent" phrases, preferring instead to transpose those unfamiliar
elements into a familiar setting. The text was published in its unal-
tered form (except when the rules of syntax or orthography obliged
them to do otherwise). The text was seen as authentic, inviting the
French reader to work through certain details and their articulation
and gain her own understanding of Romanian culture.

Istrati's use of unfamiliar words was not the only object of interest, however: his locutions and proverbs have also captured critical
attention. A number of studies are dedicated to analyzing Istrati's language: for example, studies by Monique Jutrin Klener, Jean Hormière,
Elisabeth Geblesco, and Cecilia Condei.[6] If Istrati's language were

---

[6] Monique Jutrin Klener, *Panaït Istrati, un chardon déraciné/écrivain français, conteur roumain*; Jean Hormière, *Panaït Istrati et les mots* (master's thesis directed by
Raymond Jean, Faculté des Lettres et Sciences Humaines d'Aix-en-Provence; Elisabeth Geblesco, *Le Temps et la Voix: Contribution à l'étude des problèmes de
l'Ecriture chez Panaït Istrati* (master's thesis, Université de Paris VIII) and *Panaït
Istrati et la métaphore paternelle*; and Cecilia Condei, *Interferenţe lingvistice
româno-franceze în opera lui Panaït Istrati* (Ph.D. dissertation Craiova University).

merely an object of fascination, he would never have had such a global influence. Indeed, the very fact of its being considered truly global literature shows its enduring value. And, Istrati's French-language works move beyond the provincial realm of "Romanianness," reflecting a much larger Eastern world and evoking a kind of human suffering that knows no borders.

Moreover, the Mediterranean brought together the two major vectors in Istrati's life, both geographically and psychologically speaking. It represented the attempt to reconcile two different worlds: the East and the West united by the French language. Istrati saw the Mediterranean as a metaphor for his personal journey: the East corresponded to his period of latency, the waiting room before the approaching furnace. But the West corresponded with his period of revelation and acted as a doorway to his own volcanic eruption (a burst of work written in French). This burst transformed into a bright flame that grew in strength, thanks to the widespread influence of the French language throughout the world—but this flame could also scorch.[7] His second journey of initiation to the West was not a literary journey; it marked the border between literature and life. Still, the voyage was indispensable: it was, in fact, a transformative stage in the development of his writing, most of which was merely tottering toward the beginnings of truth. Thus, some of the early revelations of which he wrote can be seen more clearly: the writer was metamorphosing into an accomplished man, one who would face down the world's truth such as it is.

Identity Quest

A return to Istrati's original journey is useful in understanding how his later journey—his identity quest—got under way. His initiatory trip coincided with his departure for the East and concluded with a breakdown: the end of wanderings and his departure for Paris in 1913, as discussed previously. His leaving for the West marks his second initiatory trip. Curiously, this rupture entailed the superposition of one temporal paradigm over another: Istrati's death in Romania in 1935 marked the end of his literary output, but it simultaneously ended at the moment when Adrien stepped onto the train for Paris in 1913. These two breaks marked the end of Istrati's two journeys of

---

[7] I am alluding to one of Istrati's works, titled *Vers l'autre flamme/Après seize mois dans l'URSS/Confession pour vaincus* (Paris: Gallimard, Folio Essais, 1987) (1st edition: Paris, Rieder, 1929).

initiation, but their coincidence in time had an unexpected consequence: the closing of the gap between East and West, above and beyond their differences.

The conclusion of Adrien's narrative in 1913—which coincided with Istrati's death in 1935—may have been the final word in his literary output, but certainly not with respect to what remains most important when considering Istrati. The paradox in Istrati's literary work lies in the fact that what is visible in the work also reveals a hidden aspect that itself represents a kind of germination of Istrati's true identity. The writer died in order to be a realized human being molded by the experiences that conquered and constructed his identity. This person appears in his early works as well as in his later writing (articles, confessions, correspondence). Together they make up so many invisible fragments in the strictly literary field. If Istrati's output revealed him to be a truly great writer, his humanity was revealed on the margins of literature. Still, if this maieutics operated best outside the world of literature, it nonetheless began within the literary realm. Considering the paradox at the heart of Istrati's work, that is, the role of both the visible and the invisible elements, we can see that the French language acted as the medium in the development of Istrati's literary persona. French, in fact, was a guidepost along this passage from literary to outside-the-literary: it was equally important in the process of revelation.

This identity construction might not have taken place without the aid of a language with a near-universal reach. This aspect is worth noting. It valorized (in the Bachelardean sense) Istrati's personal project of identity construction. The French language had at first been for Istrati only a dream, an object of intense longing, as well as a conquest that highlighted what must have seemed impossible to a self-taught man. It had the power to transform his reality by giving him an unanticipated strength. The determination Istrati showed in learning French was evidence of his passion, a passion that matched the language itself. And memory would not be confined to the writings of his former reality: it would be completely remodeled, amplified, "valorized."[8] The French language carried within itself "une faculté de surhumanité" (*L'eau et les rêves* 25).

---

[8] The words "valorize" and "valorization" have very specific meanings for Bachelard. The idea is one of an individual's subjective gaze, one that produces images emanating from the subconscious, or of a coloring of the imagination, of a greater meaning

Adopting a foreign language for his writing allowed Istrati to gain a certain distance from his culture and his own view of the world. But his choice of French elevated his criticism's forcefulness. He believed so because he felt that in adopting French, he was also adopting a certain ideal (of freedom of expression) and certain values (the Rights of Man, democracy). Istrati had a passionate relationship with the language. He decided on a sort of pact with the French language, one that rested on *libre échange* [free exchange]: he would take forcefully and give forcefully until his death. Much like Faust, he fell into the trap of a pact that would drive him to his death, the death of a writer and the death of a man.

Istrati quickly seized on this freedom of expression that surpasses all borders or barriers. He never doubted for a moment his ability to strike the right chord: he denounced both the injustices and hoaxes that plague the world. Istrati understood where to draw the line. But for him, the French language had the opposite effect; rather than assimilating, he created his own identity within it. The strength and reach of the French language was intoxicating, so much so that Istrati no longer recognized the dangers inherent in speaking the truth—that his truth would upset the status quo.

The impact of French on his work—and, above all, on his personality—is without comparison. The French language's global influence was essentially a sound box, allowing his works to be distributed, read, discussed, and debated. It allowed him to freely express himself, and he used this tool to proclaim to the world his thoughts, to openly rebel and to denounce injustice without restraint, from his heart. But in this sense, the language was in actuality a double-edged sword. Istrati chose sincerity and truth in his dealings with people; he felt invested with a "mission." For this, though, he would be criticized:

> Je me mêlai des affaires du monde, je discutai, avec mes amis, les idées et les problèmes de mon temps. On me le reprocha tendrement d'abord, puis comme j'insistais, on

---

brought on by dreaming. Thus, all physical materials (water, earth, fire, etc.) recall images fertilized and brought forth by the subconscious. To better understand this question, the works of Gaston Bachelard are particularly useful, including *La Terre et les Rêveries de la Volonté, La Poétique de la Rêverie, La Poétique de l'Espace*, and *La Flamme d'une Chandelle*. In addition, see *La Terre et les Rêveries du Repos* (particularly pp. 79–83 and p. 112 in the edition by Éditions José Corti, Paris, 1958 (1948).

me rudoya: "Cordonnier, tiens-toi à tes chaussures!" Alors
je me fâchai. Oubliait-on qu'Adrien Zograffi avait toujours
été moins un conteur qu'un révolté? On ne l'oubliait pas,
mais on voulait que sa révolte fût disciplinée. C'est ce qui
me fâcha plus encore. Nous nous brouillâmes. A mon re-
tour de Russie, je me séparai de mes plus grands amis.

[I mixed with the world's business, I discussed, with my
friends, the ideas and problems of my time. They would
criticize me gently at first, then, since I continued, they
mistreated me: "Cobbler, watch your shoes!" So I got angry. Had they forgotten that Adrien Zograffi was more of a
revolutionary than a storyteller? They hadn't forgotten it,
but they wanted his revolution to be disciplined. That made
me even angrier. We had a falling out. When I got back to
Russia, I separated from my best friends.]
("Préface à Adrien Zograffi" 10–11)

Knowing French was like possessing the fire of language. He
could pass along his ideas beyond borders, not unlike Prometheus,
and his "friends" quickly understood the danger this might entail.
Their first priority, then, was to muzzle the man who was attempting
to upend the order of the world as some of them had established it.
Istrati's death in 1935 would allay these concerns: the clear voice had
been quieted. All that remained was to bury his works and his early
comments. A half-century-long wall of silence descended over the
works and the man. But this failed to take into account the lasting impression that Istrati had made on his readers.[9] Over the last thirty-five
years or so, thanks to the long and patient work of the (true) Friends
of Panaït Istrait,[10] there has been a resurgence of interest[11] in this un-

---

[9] Among others, it was Roger Grenier, who proposed a new edition of Istrati's works,
thanks to his memory of his works. While working for Gallimard, he suggested a
four-volume re-edition from 1968 to 1970. In 1980, he followed through on this and
personally re-edited Istrati's works. These were published in the Folio collection and
this also allowed for an update of *Vers l'autre flamme/Après seize mois dans l'URSS/
Confession pour vaincus.* The work of Daniel Lérault should also be noted; his publications on the subject are remarkable.

[10] I am alluding to the Association des Amis de Panaït Istrati, founded in 1969 by
Edouard Raydon and Jean Stanesco. From 1976 to 1982, Marcel Mermoz, the president of the association, created and worked with the *Cahiers Panaït Istrati.* The *Cahiers* continued publication until 1996, thanks to numerous association presidents
who succeeded him. The association still exists, centered in Villeurbanne (Rhône);
the president is Christian Golfetto.

commonly gifted man, one who refused to submit to dogma and who proclaimed himself a free thinker and a citizen of the world, all thanks to the passport granted by the French language.

Nonetheless, his complete rehabilitation has not yet taken place. Left to us is the task of understanding the controversy surrounding the man who only wanted to search for truth in the world and sincerity in the hearts of people. A Franco–Romanian collaboration will be necessary to allow Istrati to take back his place as a "Romanian writer of French," not only in the literary world, but also in the history of humanity.

Works Cited

Works by Panaït Istrati

Istrati, Panaït. *Correspondance intégrale Panaït Istrati/Romain Rolland (1919–1935)*. Ed. Alexandre Talex. Preface by Roger Dadoun. St Imier: Canevas éditeur & Valence, Fondation Panaït Istrati, 1989.

_____. *La famille Perlmutter*. Paris: Gallimard, Folio, 1997.

_____. *Isaac le tresseur de fil de fer*. Postface de Roger Dadoun. St Imier: Canevas Editeur, 1993.

_____. *Méditerranée (Coucher du soleil)*. Paris: Gallimard, Folio, 1984.

_____. "Préface à Adrien Zograffi ou les aveux d'un écrivain de notre temps." *Vie d'Adrien Zograffi.* Paris: Gallimard, Folio, 1984. [1st edition Rieder 1933].

_____. *Réédition des œuvres d'Istrati en trois tomes.* Paris: Phébus, Libretto, 2005–2006.

_____. *Le vagabond du monde*. Ed. Daniel Lérault. Bassac: Editions Plein Chant. F-16120.

_____. *Vers l'autre flamme/Après seize mois dans l'URSS/Confession pour vaincus*. Paris: Gallimard, Folio Essais, 1987.

Works on Panaït Istrati

Bordei-Boca, Ramona. *Francophonie roumaine et Intégration européenne: Actes du colloque international de Dijon from 27 to 29 October 2004*. Dicolor Group, 2006. Film.

Cahiers Panaït Istrati [1991–1996]. Association des Amis de Panaït Istrati. President Christian Golfetto. Villeurbanne, France.

Condei, Cecilia. "Interferenţe lingvistice româno-franceze în opera lui Panaït Istrati." Diss. Craiova U, 2001.

---

[11] The recent re-edition of the complete works through Phébus Press (in the collection Libretto 2006), is the proof of this.

Geblesco, Elisabeth. *Panaït Istrati et la métaphore paternelle*. Paris: Anthropos-Economica, 1989.

_____. "Le Temps et la Voix. Contribution à l'étude des problèmes de l'écriture chez Panaït Istrati." MA thesis. U of Paris VIII, 1975.

Hormière, Jean. "Panaït Istrati et les mots." MA thesis. Faculté des Lettres et Sciences Humaines d'Aix-en-Provence, 1969–1970.

Jutrin Klener, Monique. *Panaït Istrati un chardon déraciné/écrivain français, conteur roumain*. Paris: François Maspero, 1970.

Works by Gaston Bachelard

Bachelard, Gaston. *L'eau et les rêves. Essai sur l'imagination de la matière*. Paris: José Corti, 1998. [1st edition 1942].

_____. *La Flamme d'une Chandelle*. PUF, 1962.

_____. *La Poétique de l'Espace*. 1944. PUF, Quadrige, 1994.

_____. *La Poétique de la Rêveries*. 1960. Paris: PUF, Quadrige, 1999.

_____. *La Terre et les Rêveries du Repos*. 1948. Paris: Edition José Corti, 1958.

_____. *La Terre et les Rêveries de la Volonté*. 1948. Paris: José Corti, 1958.

Home Is Elsewhere:
Exile in the Theatre of Ionesco

Ingrid Chafee
Morehouse College

"Je ne suis pas d'ici, je suis d'ailleurs"

[I'm not from here, I'm from elsewhere]
— Eugène Ionesco, *Journal en miettes*
[Fragments of a Journal]

The term "exile" implies separation from a remembered or imagined homeland, and is associated with estrangement that can be linguistic, cultural, literary, or political—or even metaphysical and spiritual. It is especially applicable to the life and work of the playwright Eugène Ionesco (1909–1994). Born in Slatina, Romania, to a Romanian father (Eugen Ionescu) and a French mother (Thérèse Ipcar), he was raised first in the country of one parent and then the country of the other. He first became a well-known critic writing in Romanian in pre–World War II Bucharest. Later, after his return to France in 1942 as an émigré, he wrote his theatre in French. He was regarded as a French author, but remained an important figure among the Romanian literati exiled in Paris. His double linguistic and cultural identity is reflected in plays that convey a sense of permanent and irremediable alienation. Matei Călinescu, in his study of Ionesco, recognizes this persistent tension. This dilemma of identity caused Matei Călinescu to describe his own approach to Ionesco's work as "biographique-identitaire" (9). Indeed, Ionesco's work is closely related to his life, especially his experience of exile. In his plays, he exposes the ambiguities and strangeness latent in languages and settings. His protagonists are usually writers who, like their creator, find themselves caught between two homes yet belonging to neither, and who turn to writing in the hope that it can reconstitute a third lost place: a child's remembered first world.

Ionesco was first brought to France at age two, in 1911, where his father had gone to study law. Emmanuel Jacquart relates in his biographical chronology of the *Théâtre complet* [Complete Theatre] how during World War I, the father returned to Bucharest but left his family in Paris (lxxi). Then, in 1917, the mother sent her children away from the city for fear of bombardments, boarding them for two years with a farmer's family in Mayenne, in the village of La Chapelle-Anthenaise (Jacquart, "Chronologie" lxxii). This stay was to remain an important and formative experience for Ionesco, who later evoked it lovingly in an idyllic memoir collected in the volume *La Photo du Colonel* [The Colonel's Photograph]. He told Claude Bonnefoy in their interview, *Entre la vie et le rêve* [Between Life and Dream], that his departure from this remembered first world represented for him leaving the fixed point or timeless center of a personal and mythic universe, from which he moved further and further away over the years (15). This memory is an important leitmotif in the plays, signifying a home that is forever elsewhere and to which there is no return.

After World War I, Ionesco's mother brought him back to Paris, and so he left behind his friends and foster family in La Chapelle-Anthenaise. Further displacement followed. Ionesco's mother learned that her husband had divorced her and remarried, and in the process he had gained legal custody of Eugène and his sister. Ionesco would later recount how his father, at this time, summoned the children to Bucharest to live with him and his new wife and family (*Présent passé passé présent* [Past Present Present Past], 140). The change was traumatic: the youth, now thirteen, had already begun to write school compositions and even an original patriotic play in French with the Latin title *Pro Patria*; he subsequently translated this script into his new language, Romanian (Cleynen-Serghiev 18). The necessity of starting over in Romanian was a painful uprooting—or, as he expressed it to Bonnefoy in their interview, a sensation of being ripped apart: "des déchirures" (23). Exile was cultural as well as linguistic, as the young Ionesco was obliged to assimilate a new world view in the schools of his new fatherland: "J'apprenais ainsi que ce n'étaient pas les Français mais les Roumains qui étaient les meilleurs, qui étaient supérieurs à n'importe quoi" [Thus I learned that it was not the

French, but rather the Romanians, who were the best, who were superior in every way] (57).[1]

Ionesco learned Romanian and was successful in his studies, although he remained a reluctant member of the paternal household. He was rejected by his stepmother and her family and rebuked by his authoritarian father (who discouraged his literary inclinations). He left the paternal household in 1926, living elsewhere while completing secondary school (Jacquart, "Chronologie" lxxii). He wrote poetry and literary criticism and edited literary journals while pursuing university studies. In 1934, he earned the degree of Capacitate, which licensed him to teach French in the Romanian secondary schools (Jacquart, "Chronologie" lxxv). Also in 1934, he published a collection of critical essays on Romanian literature, *Nu* [No] or *Non* in the French translation of 1986. The tone of the pieces was iconoclastic and contradictory: Ionesco, widely viewed as a young upstart, would sometimes include one essay sharply critical of an important figure in Romanian letters, and then after it an essay defending the same author. This tendency to alternate in *Non* is viewed by Jeanine Teodorescu as a reflection of Ionesco's double sense of alienation: as a consequence, he "will always resist belonging to a country, to a trend or to a coterie, always experiencing isolation and exile" (280). Similarly, Deborah B. Gaensbauer notes how Ionesco's "francophilia" while in Romania influenced his resistance to ideology and nationalism, and how the same sort of reaction later caused him, when in France, to keep a "critical distance" from postwar ideologies there (18).

In 1936, shortly before the death of his mother, Ionesco married Rodica Burileanu, a student in philosophy and law whose family, Jacquart tells us, was prominent in literature and politics ("Chronologie" lxxiii–lxxiv). By now, Ionesco's situation in Romanian letters and academe seemed promising; yet, he was alarmed at the spreading influence of fascist political ideology around him, to which his own father was a convert. One day, over lunch, father and son bitterly disagreed over politics and the Jewish question. The discussion ended as the younger Ionesco arose, bade his father "good day" and walked away—never to see his parent again (*Présent passé passé présent* 25–

---

[1] Translations of French texts and most titles in this article are my own.

27; *Un Homme en question* [A Man under Questioning] 79–80). This break with his father later intrudes in the dream scenes of the plays, replayed over and over with obsessive variations.

As Ionesco saw more and more of his colleagues seduced by fascism and the notorious Romanian Iron Guard, he began to feel marooned among hostile strangers—a sentiment he would later dramatize in his play *Rhinocéros*. In the memoir *Présent passé passé présent*, Ionesco would later bitterly recall his opposition to the political climate in late 1930s Romania and his horror at seeing even old friends being persuaded to join the movement, like a herd of so many pachyderms (170). Eventually, he found a way to emigrate: in 1938, he obtained a scholarship to study for his doctorate in Paris, the proposed dissertation subject being French poetry since Baudelaire (Jacquart, "Chronologie" xix). This scholarly project was never completed, but the Ionescos were to remain in France from then on, with one interruption: after Germany invaded France in 1940, they were obliged as Romanian citizens to return to Bucharest. However, they were able to return in 1942, when Ionesco obtained a post as translator in the office of the Romanian consular office to the Vichy government (Jacquart, "Chronologie" lxxviii).

After the war, the Ionescos settled in Paris, where they could participate in French literary and intellectual life while also forming ties and making common cause with other Romanian writers in exile, such as Mircea Eliade and Emile Cioran (Marie-France Ionesco, *Portrait* 98–126). Ionesco began to write in French again and became, after 1950, a widely acclaimed pioneer of the French theatre of what was called popularly "the absurd"—a theatre that Martin Esslin defined as striving to express "its sense of the senselessness of the human condition and the inadequacy of the rational approach by the open abandonment of rational devices and discursive thought" (24). Success followed success, and the crowning moment of Ionesco's assimilation into the first ranks of French letters was his election, in 1970, to the Académie Française.

In the final decades of his life, Ionesco ceased to write plays, but continued to publish memoirs and essays; he also turned his attention to drawing and painting. He also composed the libretto for an opera based on the life of a Catholic priest, later canonized, who was in a World War II concentration camp and voluntarily exchanged his life for that of a Jewish man who had been condemned to death by enforced starvation (*Maximilien Kolbe*, music by Dominique Probst, was first performed in Rimini, Italy, 1988).[2] For a while during his later years, Ionesco continued to travel despite his declining health, sometimes serving as a writer in residence at universities and receiving a number of honorary degrees. In 1989, he was given the prestigious Molière Award for his contributions to French theatre. He was active in the French chapter of the international organization of writers, Pen, serving in 1989 as president of its jury that awarded the Prize of Freedom to Vaclav Havel, the dissident playwright who later became president of the Czech Republic (Jacquart, "Chronologie" lxxviii). Ionesco remained throughout his last years a tireless advocate for those Romanians who opposed the reign of the Communist dictator Ceauşescu, as Marie-France Ionesco recounts in detail (*Portrait* 75). Other journals and accounts such as Sanda Stolojan's *Au Balcon de l'exil roumain à Paris* [On the Balcony of Romanian Exile in Paris] also provide insights into Ionesco's close involvement during these years with his exiled friends and compatriots in Paris. Ionesco lived to see the overthrow of Ceauşescu in 1989, but never returned to Romania. He died on March 28, 1994, at the age of eighty-four, mourned by both Romanians and French. The flags of both countries draped his casket at the funeral service, which was held in Paris at the Romanian Orthodox Church of Saints-Archanges. The service was attended by the exiled King Michael of Romania and other members of the royal family as well as by numerous luminaries of the world of French and Romanian theatre and letters (*Figaro littéraire*, "Obsèques" [Funeral Service] (25).

Despite his many honors and awards, Ionesco remained throughout his French career the target of many attacks from both conservatives and the Left: the more conservative deplored his unorthodox style; the leftists disdained his lack of clearly focused ideological commitment. Roland Barthes and Bernard Dort, writing in the journal *Théâtre populaire* [Popular Theatre], both condemned Ionesco's allegiance to an avant-garde that offered no constructive social or political solutions, by contrast to the widely admired German Communist Bertolt Brecht, whose plays met with great success in France during the same period. Kenneth Tynan in England, cited by Ionesco in

---

[2] See http://www.fatherkolbe.com for more details on Kolbe. Ionesco's opera was directed in its first performance by Tadeusz Bradecki and Krysztof Zanussi.

French translation in *Notes et contre-notes* [Notes and Counter-Notes] (137–40) also compared the dramatist's work unfavorably with that of the social realist school of dramaturgy; he was reacting to a London production of *Les Chaises* [The Chairs]. Ionesco, always the contrarian, persisted in his opposition to "committed" writing. He abhorred adherence to any ideology, as he made clear when attempts were made to convert him to existentialist or socialist views; he wrote bitterly of this quarrel in *Antidotes* (327–31). He even created satirical portraits of the theories and public personae of Barthes and Dort in his *l'Impromptu de l'Alma* [The Impromptu of the Place de l'Alma, or the Shepherd's Chameleon]. Rosette Lamont refers to this episode as the "*Théâtre populaire-Improvisation* controversy" (*Ionesco's Imperatives* 257).

In *Notes et contre-notes* (190), Ionesco defined himself in opposition to his critics, declaring that he was a modern "classicist"[3] and a defender of humanism in the traditional sense.[4] His attitude was doubtless due in part to his dual literary formation. He admired in particular French novelists such as Flaubert and Proust (Jacquart, "Préface" xxxvi–xxxvii). He also read French poets, such as Larbaud, Mallarmé, Rimbaud, and Lautréamont (*Découvertes* [Discoveries] 21), and Romanian authors, including the playwright Luca Caragiale and the Francophone poet Tristan Tzara (*Entre la vie et le rêve* 26–28). He believed in the timelessness of great art, citing the influence on his own literary development of the esthetician Benedetto Croce (*Découvertes* 19). Croce, he said, emphasized the central importance to all art of original expression. When a writer or artist succeeds in achieving a master style, the result evokes "des états d'esprit, des intuitions, absolument extra-temporelles, extra-historiques" [states of mind, intuitions, absolutely timeless and extra-historical] (*Notes et contre-notes* 65).

Ionesco's stand places him at sharp variance from postmodernist critical views that reject the concept of a human "essence" or permanent authorial "self" in favor of a culturally and linguistically consti-

---

[3] Rosette Lamont reminds us that here, Ionesco's definition of "classicism" was not French neoclassicism but "a return to the sources in ancient Greek literature" (*Ionesco's Imperatives* 202).

[4] Lioure sees Ionesco as the defender of humanist philosophy and values, keeping his confidence in them despite all qualms: "une confiance à la fois inquiète et fervente" [at the same time, an anxious and a fervent confidence] (n.pag.).

tuted "subject." In his essays and memoirs, Ionesco objected vehemently to this position, asserting repeatedly that although everyday language was filled with mindless clichés, the individual writer's voice eschews them and strives for a renewal of language and expression. Hence, he disdained literary criticism that de-centers the author and his characters or that views them as mere products of a culture received through a common language that the writer, as though taking dictation, merely inscribes. More specifically, he took issue with the view that language precedes and produces the narrator or thinking subject (*Découvertes* 35–36). In this connection, he evoked Heraclitus's famous metaphor of time and constantly changing water flowing past a fixed point. He affirmed the permanence of the authorial "self" as a stationary, unique eddy, through which the mingled waters of social and linguistic currents continuously stream. The eddy is composed of this communal water, but defines itself precisely by its resistance to the common flow, being an "organisation particulière" [individual structure] different from all the others; and, at the same time, by its own example of difference from all the rest, affirming also identity with them: "Chaque moi affirme et renie le groupe" (*Journal en miettes* [Fragments of a Journal] 210–13).

This figure of current and counter-current is central to the dramatic structure of the plays. They are based on the alienation of a central character from the others and the universe of the play, beginning with his estrangement from ordinary discourse and dramatic convention and continuing later with the strengthening of his "voice" and role. Sometimes, he (it is always a man) speaks in what seems to be a poetic language filled with metaphors; it is a discourse that the others fail to understand, as for example in the opening scene of *Tueur sans gages* [The Killer] or at the end of *Victimes du devoir* [Victims of Duty] and *Voyages chez les morts* [Journeys to the Land of the Dead]. Sometimes, this protagonist even withdraws into silence and refuses to engage in dialogue at all, as in the beginning of *Jacques ou la soumission* [Jacques or Submission], in *Le nouveau locataire* [The New Tenant], or in *Ce formidable bordel!* [Oh What a Bloody Circus!].

However, this role of the chief character creates a fundamental dilemma: just as Ionesco's eddy in the current defines itself through its opposition to the flow, so these protagonists define themselves by their resistance to the very play of which they are a part, and without which they have no literary or theatrical existence. The result is the disintegration of plot and the absence of any genuine resolution—with the possible exception of *Le roi se meurt* [Exit the King]. The hero's chief motivation is to escape to some imagined better place, a paradise; yet for him, the only exit from the stage and the text is into non-being or silence. Instead of coming to a denouement, then, Ionesco intensifies this tragicomic tension until it becomes unsustainable and the action simply disintegrates or explodes or else becomes circular or stalemated.

The early plays are reminiscent of Ionesco's own experiences as a writer twice exiled from his cultural roots. They define a gulf between the alienated protagonist and the closed world of his dysfunctional family or society, while also exposing the banality of conventional plots and dialogue in which this family seems to fit. As Ionesco explained in *Notes et contre-notes*, these "anti-plays" were reactions against the *pièce bien faite* [well-made play] of the 1930s and 1940s, which he saw as blatantly false by virtue of their predictable plots and dialogues. There was nothing in which to believe; and precisely, Ionesco sought to restore to the modern theatre a lost sense of involvement. To do so, he would use a paradoxical method: he would exaggerate the very artificiality of the familiar convention through the use of a *guignol* style based on the puppet shows that had fascinated him as a child. These shows reduced the confusing and frightening adult world to simple and brutal caricature. He termed the result "making the puppet strings show" (*Notes et contre-notes* 60). By breaking through the veneer of realistic but superficial adult dialogue offered to a complacent public, he attempted to reach the spectator at a more elemental, even a more childlike, level. His characters should be laughed at, outright. Hence, they are automatons given to stilted speech and sudden moments of violence. Their mechanical, strangely solemn yet nonsensical dialogue allows the text to veer off course, revealing language's latent possibilities for containing the strange, the surprising, and the frightening. Words and sentences are broken apart and recombined to acquire new meanings, objects multiply, and characters become engaged in angry conflict for no apparent reason. The instability of language is featured front and center: in *La cantatrice chauve* [The Bald Soprano] and *La leçon* [The Lesson], arguments begin to arise regarding identity and naming. The characters' efforts at precision in these matters only unleash misunderstanding and equivocation, until at last contradiction replaces logic altogether.[5]

There is created, then, a sort of nominalist crisis: If names and words are arbitrary signifiers, how are we to know what is true, what is real? How does knowledge relate to language? Can they relate? Even the simplest and most evident of propositions can be thrown into question: How do we know that when the doorbell rings, there is someone there? Uncertainty begins to subvert the whole system of grammar and syntax. Ultimately, even the characters' orientation in space and time is affected, resulting in Ionesco's "tragédie du langage" (*Notes et contre-notes* 247–54). This concept of language as tragic is developed further in the second play, *La leçon*, whose Professor teaches us that we can be sure of nothing in this world (*Théâtre complet* 48).[6]

Marie-Claire Hubert has analyzed how the bilingual's awareness in these early plays demonstrates that the link between signifier and signified is arbitrary ("Ionesco et le bilingisme" [Ionesco and Bilingualism] 100–101). This consciousness of a separation between language and meaning echoes the situation of every exile who must unlearn the names, concepts, and customs that he or she has always known. The newcomer's shock is dramatized perhaps most vividly in the philology lecture of *La leçon*, in which the Professor teaches his Pupil, who has not "been there long" (48) that the Italian word for "country" is "Italy," whereas the French word for "country" is "France" (67). The Professor, of course, gives specific examples of names of countries rather than translating the word "country" into each language. This sort of translation is nonsensical, but it was likely inspired by Ionesco's own culture shock upon learning at age thirteen that the greatest country in the world was henceforth to be called "Romania" rather than "France."

The game of interchange between signifiers and signifieds becomes visible with the use of stage props and gestures, such as the

---

[5] In *Victimes du devoir* (242), the character Nicolas d'Eu bases his argument for a new theatre on the Franco-Romanian thinker Stéphane Lupasco's *Logique et contradiction* (Paris: PUF, 1947). Ionesco developed a similar concept in his earlier writings in Romanian, notably in his essay on Eliade, "De l'identité des contraires" [On the Identity of Opposites] (*Non* 161–91).

[6] References to the texts of the plays, unless otherwise indicated, are from this edition of the collected theatre.

famous empty chairs filled with unseen spectators in *Les chaises*. Also, with the creation of protagonists who are would-be writers, the "tragedy of language" takes on greater complexity: language alienates the chief character from the others, but it also becomes the object of his pathetic and misplaced faith in the saving power of the text. In *Les chaises*, the Old Couple living in solitude atop a lighthouse invite guests to hear the Old Man's final "message to humanity." The message is intended to justify the Old Man's failed existence and to compensate for the frustrated quest he had begun in his youth, when he had found a garden in the City of Light but was not permitted to enter it. His wife, the Old Woman, echoes his belief in the importance of this oration for future generations: "C'est en parlant qu'on trouve les idées, les mots, et puis nous, dans nos propres mots, la ville aussi, le jardin, on retrouve peut-être tout, on n'est plus orphelin" [It's through speaking that we find ideas, words, and then ourselves, through our own words, the city also, the garden, perhaps we find everything again, we're not orphans any more] (148). The Old Couple usher in their invisible guests and speak with them, constructing an entire edifice of verbal illusions that operate as signifiers; but they can only name what is other or elsewhere: their guests, the Old Man's lost paradise, and the content of the never-delivered message. (It is ultimately delivered after their deaths by a deaf-mute Orator.) The imagined paradise is always already at an unbridgeable distance from the speaker and the closed universe of the play.

The metaphor of the text as linguistic and existential prison had been fully realized in *Les chaises*. No discourse or action is possible beyond the boundaries of its script and setting, as the Old Couple demonstrate by their suicidal departure: they jump out of the windows of their lighthouse into the sea. In his next works, Ionesco pursues this metaphor of the stage universe as a life situation from which there is no exit. The chief character is still the would-be writer or playwright cast in a predetermined role in his own play. Unable to control or advance the action, he attempts to escape from it—sometimes, as in *Victimes du devoir* or *Amédée ou comment s'en débarrasser* [Amédée or How to Get Rid of It], by trying to rise upward out of the stage setting.

Such a move is reminiscent, in grotesque-comic mode, of ritual ascent as practiced by Eastern ascetics and holy men and as described by the Romanian-French historian of religions Mircea Eliade (*Sham-*

anism 264–69). Yet, as Marie-Claire Hubert has noted, the effort here is not to transcend literally the visible world, but rather to transcend linguistically and metaphysically the ordinary rational discourse of the play's closed universe. Ionesco himself says as much, in an interview (Hubert, *Eugène Ionesco* 267), evoking "un ailleurs du langage" [an elsewhere beyond language] and defining it as the goal of his protagonist Jean in the final play, *Voyages chez les morts*. Ionesco calls Jean's final soliloquy, which ends in apparent nonsense, a grasping toward a "métalangage" or a "langage oublié" [forgotten language]— an unreachable goal, a level of silence beyond all speech.

Indeed, throughout Ionesco's plays and writings on theatre, one can discern his wish to restore a lost sacred or magic dimension to the modern stage. He regretted that the modern theatre (of the 1940s and before) was a ritual or mass emptied of belief (*Notes et contre-notes* 49). Similarly, his protagonist Choubert derides the secular rationalism underlying modern popular drama: he calls it the "detachment system" (206). Choubert is suggesting that the modern *boulevard* play has become an empty shell, separated from its religious or sacred roots. Yet unlike genuine shamans, Ionesco's would-be reformers of theatre such as Choubert cannot transcend the linguistic, representational, and secular constraints of their textual universe. They cannot get out of the "house" of modern drama's rational and literary foundations. To borrow a term used by Eliade, they cannot "break the roof" (*Le Sacré et le profane* [The Sacred and the Profane] 148) of its formulaic conventions. The titular character of *Jacques ou la soumission* declares that he is forced to live with his stage family in such a "house"—clearly, the universe of the traditional betrothal play, from which there is no exit through the roof or the windows of the visible stage set, but only through the unseen region of the cellar (108). (The reference to the cellar suggests the Freudian or Jungian unconscious, manifested in the latent irrational or mythic dimension of literature and art; this concept is developed further in *Victimes du devoir* and *Voyages chez les morts*.) Evocations of a half-remembered, half-imagined paradise or country of light and immortality appear in many of the plays, always as a goal that remains distant and unattainable from the enclosed space of the stage. It is called variously the City of Light (*Les chaises*), the Radiant Quarter (*Tueur sans gages*), or Aluminia (*Voyages chez les morts*).

Thus, when the would-be playwright Choubert asks his wife "penses-tu vraiment que l'on puisse faire du nouveau au théâtre?" [do you really think it possible to do something new in the theatre?] (207), he is really asking about escaping his limitations as a writer/character in a play bounded by the received grammar of a logical plot. He complains that traditional Western drama artificially organizes and distorts experience so as to create the familiar "detective play" with its immutable logic: you seek the guilty party, you find him. Even classical Greek tragedy is no more than "distinguished detective drama" in which the nature of the outcome is never in doubt (207). Choubert's discourse is interrupted by the arrival of an actual police detective in search of a suspect. The detective is an avowed Aristotelian who obliges Choubert to participate in the very sort of plot he most despises: the conventional "whodunit." Choubert is unable to cooperate with this detective's inquiry regarding the suspect, a former tenant of Choubert's own apartment. The suspect's name is "Mallot" or "Mallod." (Here again, the accuracy of names is in question.) Soon, Choubert's deviations from the logical path of inquiry disrupt the detective's increasingly aggressive line of questioning. The protagonist literally descends into the primeval mud of his own memory, acting out on an improvised stage the anguished scenes from his own past with his father, mother, and wife—all played by the detective and Madeleine. He is called back because he has wandered too far from the script of the detective play; he then climbs up on a table top, from where his quest takes the form of an ascent toward a mountain summit. It should be the ultimate pursuit of the rational rather than the unconscious; but instead, Choubert forgets Mallot, and again wanders off course. He has a revelation of the possibility of flight and immortality, as though he were one of the shamans of whom Eliade had written. He even attempts flight. The detective and Madeleine must stop this move; they force him back down from the table top, so that he falls into a wastebasket—the inevitable repository of both the rejected script and its character-author. Choubert's discourse now becomes incomprehensible to the others, since they cram his mouth literally with hard, crusty bread—the stuff of their earth-bound realistic plot. Finally, one of these characters (there are new arrivals at this point) kills the Detective but then assumes his role so that the play becomes a closed circle incapable of further development.

Another would-be playwright, the hero of *Amédée*, is closeted in his apartment with his wife (again named Madeleine) and with a third party—a gigantic corpse that is growing by "geometrical progression" and is threatening to occupy all the space available. Amédée's writer's block and his failed marriage are both clearly related to the presence of this monstrously growing body. Amédée has not been able to write a new line of his play for fifteen years, the length of time that the body has been in the apartment. The last piece of dialogue that he managed to create is part of an exchange between an old couple reminiscent of Ionesco's *Les chaises* and expresses an impasse: "Ça n'ira pas tout seul" [That won't work all by itself] (270). Finally, as the "corpse" of the script and marriage grows to the maximum capacity of the space, the couple must expel it from the apartment by way of the window. Amédée climbs out and pulls while Madeleine pushes, in a difficult, lengthy maneuver that is a masterpiece of the grotesque comic. As the husband now bids the wife farewell, the setting changes as we follow him into the street. In this last part of the last act, his universe is transformed. He discovers that the heavy corpse has become a banner lighter than air, liberating him and changing his perspective on writing and language. He attempts to describe his new insights to a bystander; then, to his surprise, the banner lifts him up to the sky—straight out of the décor. As he disappears, he apologizes for abandoning the realistic plot. His indignant wife shouts from below as he rises, reproaching him for not finishing his play, and her final diatribe reminds the audience that Amédée has not really resolved his plight. He has escaped, but in so doing has only confirmed the impossibility of bridging the division between mutually exclusive settings, the claustrophobic script and his poetic dreams of ecstasy (306).

In the plays following *Amédée*, the would-be-writer character is no longer confined to the closed décor of the first works; instead, like Amédée, he exits into a wider world of the street and also of his imagination—a terrain beyond the traditional picture-frame stage. It is possible to view this new dream setting in Freudian terms, as does Gisèle Féal in her book on Ionesco's oneiric plays. Ionesco used his own dreams in composing the plays of his mature period, and regarded dream as one of two levels of consciousness: the "diurnal" and the "nocturnal." As did Jung and Freud, Ionesco viewed dream (or nocturnal consciousness) as inverting or reflecting the waking perspective while also revealing what it conceals (*Journal en miettes* 46–48). Accordingly, his later plays revisit the terrain of the earlier ones, though the later plays have a darker, more personal tone and are set in a boundless, formless oneiric landscape. These dream spaces may seem open and even unending; nonetheless, they are still prisons, from which there is no exit except in waking. The structure is labyrinthine, a Lacanian chain of coded signifiers that never leads to the desired ultimate signified (the elusive first world) but only to yet another signifier. The tantalizing goal always recedes and is never reached; it remains beyond the power of language to describe or depict. And, although the insights of Jung and Freud are valuable in studying these later plays, it is important to note as well that the sense of estrangement and exile in them becomes increasingly nostalgic for a missing spiritual element, as Eliade had seen ("E.I. and the Nostalgia of Paradise").

The sign of this aborted quest for paradise is the wall, a recurrent motif in the author's own dreams as recounted in *Journal en miettes* (88–89). The wall reappears in play after play; and the hero can never penetrate it, whether it is the outer wall of the city suburb in *Tueur sans gages*, the confines of the false monastery in *La soif et la faim* [Hunger and Thirst], the barrier to the invisible anti-world of *Le piéton de l'air* [A Stroll in the Air], or the exterior of the crumbling palace in *Le roi se meurt*. We will see it first in these plays, often called the "Bérenger cycle" as the protagonist of each of them bears that name.

Bérenger of *Tueur sans gages* is one of life's misfits. He inhabits a confining room in a depressing Rainy City when one day, by chance, he discovers a perpetually sunny Radiant Quarter. He believes that this place, with its perpetually green gardens and gushing fountains and beautiful houses, is the materialization of his dreams—a fusion of his inner world of longing and his external surroundings: "un accord total entre moi du dedans et moi du dehors" (*Théâtre* 2: 73).[7] Yet, this ideal urban paradise proves to be a mirage: it consists of mere façades that conceal a dark truth: "the Killer" who stalks its inhabitants. Bérenger has fallen in love with Dany, a young resident of the Radiant Quarter; she becomes the Killer's next victim. The Radiant Quarter vanishes at once, to become once more the Rainy City,

---

[7] For this play, *Tueur sans gages*, page references are from the 1958 edition as collected in *Théâtre* 2 (1958). I have cited this edition because some passages that I regard as pivotal were omitted in later editions shortened for performance.

and Bérenger sets out on an ill-fated and misguided quest through it to find the Killer and avenge Dany's death. He makes discoveries regarding the Killer's identity and tries in vain to warn the authorities, but they ignore him and even bar his way to the prefecture of police. Other characters are obstacles in his path, especially a crowd at a political rally led by the demagogue Mother Peep, who orders the deaths of those who defy her. Bérenger manages to pass beyond these crowds, only to discover that he is still not advancing toward his goal: the prefecture is actually receding as he walks toward it. It is the fulfillment of a song sung by a concierge earlier in the play: "On n'avance pas, sûrement, quand on piétine sur place. / Mais avance-t-on vraiment quand on se dé-pla-place?" [One does not advance, assuredly, when one walks in place / But does one truly advance when one changes one's place?] (105). Finally the prefecture vanishes behind the walls of dead-end alleys where the Killer awaits to trap Bérenger, so that the search for paradise culminates in the nightmare of this cul de sac.

Bérenger of *Rhinocéros* is, like his predecessor of *Tueur*, a misfit. We first see him on a Sunday morning in the square of an idyllic country village. It is an archetypal setting for Ionesco, evoking his recollections of his childhood stay in the countryside. The tranquility of this scene is shattered as a rhinoceros runs through, upsetting baskets and trays, crushing a pet cat, and precipitating quarrels. Ultimately it becomes apparent that there is an epidemic of "rhinoceritis" in the district: the townspeople, one by one, are abandoning their humanity in favor of becoming pachyderms. As noted earlier, Ionesco cited the political inspiration for this play: the metaphor of the rhinoceros had first occurred to him in Romania in the late 1930s, as he felt himself increasingly alienated from colleagues and friends who were converting to fascist ideology (*Présent passé passé présent* 170). Bérenger cannot follow the superficially coherent logic that leads the others to these conversions; instead, he finds in himself the will to resist the popular movement. He does not have ready answers for their smoothly phrased rationalizations, and bases his resistance only on intuition (618). In the end, there is no one left even to hear his objections and his defiant wish to remain human; he is besieged in his room, surrounded by photographs of his vanished friends, now become the braying beasts outside his window. It is too late to change, even if he should desire to do so; he is condemned forever to his chosen role, in isolation from all those alien others.

The burned-out playwright Bérenger of *Le piéton de l'air* is famous, but can no longer write; he has come to view literature as irrelevant in the face of the horrors of the violence and war of the twentieth century. On vacation in the English countryside with his wife Joséphine and his adult daughter, Marthe, he has retreated to a cottage where he hopes to regain inspiration. However, his refuge is destroyed by an improbable bombing raid carried out by old World War II German airplanes. He is forced outdoors into the sunshine of a beautiful June day. He experiences a moment of euphoria, believing that he has discovered the lost link between the known world and an imagined anti-world beyond life. He has intimations of immortality and discovers or remembers, in Platonic fashion, that he can fly. He takes a walk in the sky, leaving his astonished wife and daughter and onlookers below. During his absence, their drama occupies the stage as they experience Holocaust-like scenes: Bérenger's wife is condemned to death by enormous judges on wheeled elevated platforms, and a huge John Bull marionette kills small children on the grounds that it is better for them to die sooner rather than later (618). At twilight, Bérenger descends back to earth and babbles about the infinite horrors he has witnessed: a Dante's inferno, a region of the damned trapped in unending fire and ice. He has received no message, no authorial insight, no transcendent truth beyond the known world. He will continue his interrupted walk with his family, perhaps now a little sadder. The sense of despair is relieved only by Marthe, whose hopeful vision of paradise concludes the play: "peut-être les abîmes se rempliront … peut-être que … les jardins … les jardins" [maybe the abysses will fill up … perhaps … the gardens … the gardens …] (736).

Bérenger the First of *Le roi se meurt* is a monarch of fabulous old age who is told, in the opening lines of the play, that he will die "à la fin du spectacle" [at the end of the performance] (751). He resists and refuses to believe the news, and calls out in vain for help, blubbering like a frightened child as he begins to stumble, fall, and grow feeble. He had hoped for immortality, and now his theatrical universe is shrinking and crumbling around him; the walls are cracking and the kingdom itself is falling into a pit. He calls out the window for help, in vain. The elder of his two queens, Marguerite, sternly reminds him that he must die like a king; he must utter illustrious last words as did his predecessors. He refuses to do so and dismisses such statements as mere words: "de la littérature" (769). The younger queen, Marie, reminds him of their love and happiness. But the king is soon past caring for such memories; he is by now confined to a wheel chair. Marguerite takes charge of the terrified old man, soothing his fears and leading him through a ceremony inspired by ancient funeral rituals from the *Upanishads* and the *Tibetan Book of the Dead*.[8] As she intones the time-honored words, the King is at last persuaded to accept his end with calm: to renounce his existence together with the play and his insistent illusion of an enduring physical self. It is a true ending, one of the few in Ionesco's theatre, bearing out his remark that death is the only possible ending to a play: "Autrement il n'y a pas de fin" [Otherwise, there isn't any ending] (*Entre la vie et le rêve* 86).

Le roi se meurt was a success, but subsequent works were widely criticized. They were increasingly anti-ideological, enigmatic, and autobiographical. *La soif et la faim*, at its Paris premiere in 1964, met with outright hostility, hoots, and catcalls; as Ionesco himself characterized it, the evening was "turbulente." He described with apparent relish the traffic jam and general brouhaha that developed outside the theatre after the final curtain (*Antidotes* 280–81). The play excited angry reactions with its painful brainwashing scene, a play within a play in which a Christian and an atheist, under torture, are forced to swap their beliefs. This scene attacks and satirizes all systems of thought with officially approved positions and vocabulary: it spares neither leftist nor right-wing partisans.

For the purposes of our discussion, though, we are concerned with politics less than with the protagonist's search for perfect love and immortality, and his willingness to abandon his wife and child in pursuit of these illusory goals. He says, as he begins his pilgrimage, "Il me faut l'air de la montagne, quelque chose comme la Suisse, un pays hygiénique où personne ne meurt" [I must have mountain air, something like Switzerland, a hygienic country where nobody dies] (815). Hence, he flees the cramped, oppressive apartment he shares with his family, but instead of finding his utopia, he stumbles upon a wayside

---

[8] Barranger offers an informative analysis of elements borrowed from these rituals and incorporated into Ionesco's play. See also Eliade, "Eugène Ionesco and the Nostalgia of Paradise" (22–23).

inn run by bogus monks. These "brothers" offer him food and lodging in exchange for the terrible price of his freedom. He may leave, but only if he can satisfactorily complete impossible tasks. The first of these is a narrative of his journey. He fails at this first assignment, as he is unable to recite more than a catalogue of disconnected words, and these are not in the approved lexicon of the brothers. They exact a punishment: he must witness the didactic spectacle already described, the conversions under torture. He must then also watch twenty-nine other such spectacles, and when he refuses he is condemned to the task of perpetually serving soup to his jailers. Like Tantalus, he has not surrendered hope; he can see and hear his wife and child in the home he has abandoned, realizing, too late, that his home with them was his true goal. The wife and daughter beckon to him forever, just beyond the impassable monastery walls; but he is captive both to the brothers and to his own stubborn will, as in the end he has refused to learn the "lessons" they teach: acceptance of a dialectical system of finite goals and renunciation of his desire for an "elsewhere."

Ce formidable bordel! has a protagonist who is taciturn, often even silent. The play is based on Ionesco's novel *Le solitaire* [The Hermit] (1973). In both novel and play, the central character inherits a fortune and buys an apartment far from the center of town. Here, he can lead a life as a hermit, arranging his possessions around him and shutting out the noisy world. In both novel and play, a violent civil war soon breaks out. The hero barricades himself in the apartment for the rest of his life. The novel's narrator engages in long chains of circular reasoning in his search for metaphysical enlightenment. The play's protagonist silently imbibes cognac unless interrupted by a rare visitor. Both texts end with the protagonist's final moments, when he has an epiphany—a glorious but absurd vision. In the play, it is a flowering tree, causing the hero to burst into laughter at the miraculous cosmic joke that has been played on him. It demonstrates to him that all his serious meditations have been futile. Ionesco said he was inspired in choosing this ending by an anecdote in a Zen text about a monk who had a similar vision and a similar reaction to it (*Entre la vie et le rêve* 172).

L'Homme aux valises [Man with Bags] and *Voyages chez les morts*, the last plays, are autobiographical dream journeys through a remembered past in both Romania and France, in search of a mother toward whom the protagonist feels guilt and a father with whom there is a complex love–hate relationship. They can be seen as formless dramatized memoirs; yet, they are best understood as a progression that uncovers successive layers of memory so that one sees how past and present interact.

The protagonists of both plays (often discussed and performed together) are famous elderly playwrights who are attempting to return to the countries of their youth or to the land of their dead. They search, of course, for the lost remembered Eden of their childhood. A constant barrier, particularly in *Voyages chez les morts*, is the forbidding father—who at each stage interposes himself between the protagonist and the vanished home of the mother. The situation, especially given the oneiric quality of the narrative, recalls Freudian or Lacanian psychological theories of the Oedipus complex. Yet Lacan in particular seems relevant, since his thought, as set forth in *Écrits*, adds a linguistic perspective to the psychological: the father in Lacanian theory is the authority whose realm is language, and he is associated with the child's initial separation from the mother at the time language begins to develop. In these last plays of Ionesco, it is the father who bars the way to the mother, and who is at the same time the arbiter or guardian of language, texts, and naming (including addresses and other information about the mother's location). The father in *Voyages chez les morts* is even an author in his own right, for here in the afterlife he churns out popular potboilers approved by the administration of the place. He declares these works to be far superior to the writings of the son; and the latter's work crumbles to dust whenever he attempts to show it to his disapproving father.

This Lacanian slant on the Oedipal conflict is here both nostalgic and idealistic. The roundabout route to the mother is the child's longing both for her and for the imagined realm she represents—the primordial home that predates both experience and the text. This elusive dream will never be realized, as is made clear when Jean finally confronts the mother. She is not the kind, nurturing female of the male child's dreams and longing, but rather an avenging ancestress—or, as Lamont puts it, an ancient goddess and a Gnostic figure of transformation and revenge (*Journey to the Land of the Dead* 116). The dream journey homeward has, in the end, branched into two paths, one leading to the father's house (or country) and one to the mother's. Neither is home. The quarrels between the two families, in the penultimate scene of *Voyages chez les morts*, make it clear that this estrangement is irreconcilable and eternal. The avenging maternal ancestor tears the father's family members to pieces. Yet they are restored, being only demonic ghosts; and so the battle will go on forever.

In these last two plays, with their voyages to the past and to the land of youth, exile is not only a question of language, nationality, family, and identity; it is also the separation between past and present, and hence the impossibility of bridging the gap between history and myth. In *Voyages*, the protagonist, Jean, cannot go to his mother's house except in a horse-drawn carriage, a conveyance from the past. She lives on a street that has disappeared. The protagonist (who had been bilingual) can no longer remember or speak the language of his youth in the father's country. The forgetting of archaic Romanian becomes a barrier in the search for the mother's grave. Jean cannot read the service for the dead or decipher the lists of those who are buried in the cemeteries of old churches. In *L'Homme aux valises*, the nameless "Premier Homme" [First Man]—i.e., the first male character on stage—has even lost the documents attesting to his identity. Indeed, he cannot recall his own name or replace a lost passport. This linguistic estrangement is sinister: loss of memory and texts is also loss of power, resulting in imprisonment or even death. It erases history and the mythic past and the map needed to complete the quest journey. The First Man, whose manuscript (his third dimension, as he puts it) has been lost or destroyed, must in consequence wander forever. Even a reunion with his wife does not restore the lost structure.

It is fitting that the last play, *Voyages chez les morts*, should end in the present with a defiant soliloquy on a bare stage—the one mentioned by Ionesco in the previously cited interview with Hubert. This soliloquy disintegrates into stream of consciousness prose in the manner of the surrealists' automatic writing. It is, as Rosette Lamont has pointed out, an "exercise in deconstruction" (*Journey* 116). It is a deliberate dis-articulation of text, narrative, and drama so as to make a statement about the limitations of ordinary syntax, ending with the assertion "Je ne sais pas" [I don't know] (1361). Ionesco saw it as a reaching beyond language, but it is also an obliteration of the script, recalling Eliade's *anâmnesis*—the ritual erasure of memory and history, a return to the beginnings as practiced by primitive religions (*Aspects du mythe* [Aspects of Myth] 112). It is the protagonist's farewell, and it is also the playwright's. One of the last statements refers to a melting-down and recasting in a "furnace"—which can refer to the creative process itself, which erases all and begins again: "Une voix sensée est-elle pleine de sens ou de sang? Ils avaient des noms. Pas les mêmes. Les noms changent dans les fournaises" [Is a sensible voice full of sense or blood? They had names. Not the same ones. Names change in the furnaces] (1358).

We can say, in general, that Ionesco's self-referential representation of the protagonist in these later plays dramatizes the writer's unending dilemma: the impossible search through the creative process for an end to spiritual exile and the affirmation of a permanent literary or theatrical identity. The impasse is inevitable, for one cannot transcend either existence or one's own script, either through writing or erasures: as Alexandra Hamdan observes, Ionesco explores the "impossibility of writing" (22). Hence, despite claiming to be a "classicist," Ionesco depicts a contemporary concern: the dilemma of those who would signify, through the text alone, the permanence of the self as a linguistic, national, familial, or social entity. We have attempted to show how this overall perspective evolved, beginning with the satirical anti-plays and continuing with the development of the idealistic writer-protagonist's efforts to restore his City of Light and return to his origins. We have seen that the identity to be preserved was actually lost in space and time—altered even by the writing or the dramatic process—just as raw materials are melted down in the "fournaise" of the finished manuscript.

Paradoxically, though, Ionesco's plays—precisely because they are metaphors of exile, separation, and distance between language and reality—can have a transformative effect in performance. Perhaps the best example of this phenomenon occurs at the end of *Les chaises*, in the silence following the exit-suicide of the visible characters. At that moment, the audience hears yet cannot see the crowd of invisible and previously silent spectators, who whisper, giggle, and shuffle their chairs as they rise to exit. This ending conveys the seemingly impossible: an experience of absence, the spectator being led to believe in the reality of the unseen guests. Similarly, in the final moments of *Le roi se meurt*, the last words of the ritual and the extinction of the lights at the death of King Bérenger merge with the experience of each spectator imagining his or her own dying. The spectacle of the "other" expiring on stage and relinquishing his very being, his "self," becomes for a moment an undeniably real future event for each spectator. At such moments, the protagonist's experience of being isolated is, strangely, shared by each member of even a large audience—in a communion that is based on the disappearance of ritual language and shared faith, rather than on their celebration. Such a moment can exist, if at all, only in an era like our own, in the secular theatre.

This experience of solitude in a crowd resonates for a century of spectators who have known displacement from vanished homelands. And, in revisiting this theatre, I have viewed these plays as expressions of a postmodern consciousness—despite their continuing link with the author's own avowed reverence for the classical heritage. For though Ionesco's work is rich in myth and history, it also manifests a lucid, pained disenchantment with the possibility that writing might end exile, together with a Sisyphean determination to pursue the effort. The plays spoke to the author's own era of disruption and estrangement; they continue to speak to ours.

Works Cited

Barranger, M.S. "Death as Initiation in Exit the King." *Educational Theatre Journal* 27 (1975): 504–507.

Călinescu, Matei. *Ionesco: Recherches identitaires*. Trans. Simona Modreanu. Paris: Oxus Editions, 2005.

Cleynen-Serghiev, Ecaterina. *La Jeunesse littéraire d'Eugène Ionesco.* Paris: PUF, 1993.

Eliade, Mircea. *Aspects du mythe*. Paris: Gallimard, 1963.

_____. "Eugène Ionesco and the Nostalgia of Paradise." *The Two Faces of Ionesco*. Ed. Rosette C. Lamont and Melvin J. Friedman. New York: Whitston Publishing Co., 1978. 21–30.

_____. *Le Sacré et le profane*. Paris: Gallimard, 1965.

_____. *Shamanism: Archaic Techniques of Ecstasy*. Trans. Willard R. Trask. London: Routledge and Kegan Paul, 1964.

Esslin, Martin. *The Theatre of the Absurd*. 3rd ed. London: Penguin Books, 1980.

Féal, Gisèle. *Ionesco: un théâtre onirique.* Paris: Éditions Imago, 2001.

Gaensbauer, Deborah B. *Eugène Ionesco Revisited.* Twayne's World Authors Series 863. New York: Twayne Publishers, 1996.

Hamdan, Alexandra. *Ionescu avant Ionesco*. Paris: Peter Lang, 1993. Publications Universitaires Européens Série XXIV, Langues et littératures ibéroromanes. 40.

Hubert, Marie-Claude. *Eugène Ionesco.* Paris: Éditions du Seuil. Collection les Contemporains, 1990.

____. "Ionesco et le bilinguisme." *Euresis: cahiers romains d'études litté-raires* 1.2 (1993): 98–102.

Ionesco, Eugène. *Antidotes*. Paris: Gallimard, 1977.

_____. *Découvertes*. Geneva: Albert Skira. Les Sentiers de la Création, 1969.

_____. *Entre la vie et le rêve: Entretiens avec Claude Bonnefoy*. Paris: Gallimard, 1996.

_____. *Un Homme en question*. Paris: Gallimard, 1979.

_____. *Journal en miettes*. Paris: Gallimard, 1973.

____. *Maximilien Kolb*. Trans. Rosette C. Lamont. *Performing Arts Journal* 17.6 no. 2 (1982): 32–36. (Opera libretto with music of Dominique Probst).

_____. *Non*. Trans. Marie-France Ionesco. Paris: Gallimard 1986.

_____. *Notes et contre-notes*. Paris: Gallimard, Collection Idées, 1966.

_____. *La Photo du Colonel*. Paris: Gallimard, 1962.

_____. *Présent passé passé présent*. Paris: Mercure de France, 1968.

_____. *Théâtre complet*. Ed. Émile Jacquart. Paris: Gallimard, Bibliothèque de la Pléiade, 1991.

_____. *Tueur sans gages*. Vol. 2 of *Théâtre*. Paris: Gallimard, 1958. 59–172.

Ionesco, Marie-France. *Portrait d'un écrivain dans le siècle: Eugène Ionesco 1909–1994*. Paris: Gallimard, Collection Arcades, 2004.

Jacquart, Emmanuel. "Chronologie." *Théâtre complet*. By Eugène Ionesco. lxviii–cvi.

_____. "Ionesco aux prises avec la culture." *Ionesco: Situations et perspectives: Colloque de Cérisy*. Eds. Marie-France Ionesco and Paul Vernois. Paris: Belfond, 1980. 55–84.

_____. Préface. *Théâtre complet*. By Eugène Ionesco. xi–lxiii.

Lacan, Jacques. *Écrits*. Paris: Éditions du Seuil, 1966.

Lamont, Rosette C. *Ionesco's Imperatives: The Politics of Culture*. Ann Arbor: U of Michigan P, 1993.

_____. "*Journey to the Kingdom of the Dead*: Ionesco's Gnostic Dream Play." *The Dream and the Play: Ionesco's Theatrical Quest*. Ed. Moshe Lazar. Malibu: Undena Publications, 1982. 93–119.

Lamont, Rosette C., and Melvin J. Friedman, Eds. *The Two Faces of Ionesco*. Troy, New York: Whitston Publishing Co., 1978.

Lioure, Michel. "L'humanisme d'Eugène Ionesco." *Lingua Romana* 3.1 (2004) n.pag. <http://linguaromana.byu> [Accessed 30 August 2010].

Mouraud, Yves. "Ionesco: Un Théâtre de l'exil et du rituel." *Ionesco: Situations et perspectives: Colloque de Cérisy*. Eds. Marie-France Ionesco and Paul Vernois. Paris: Belfond, 1980. 75–100.

"Obsèques d'Eugène Ionesco: L'hommage des anonymes." *Le Figaro* April 2–3 1994, literary supplement: 25.

Stolojan, Sanda. *Au balcon de l'exil roumain à Paris: avec Cioran, Eugène Ionesco, Mircea Eliade, Vintilă Horia*. Paris: l'Harmattan, 1999.

Teodorescu, Jeanine. "'*Nu, Nu* and *Nu*': Ionesco's Non! To Romanian Literature and Politics." *Journal of European Studies* 34.3 (2004) 267–287. <sagepub.com/cgi/reprint/34/3/267>.

Vodă-Căpuşan, Maria. "Ionesco—Le Paradoxe de l'exil." *Euresis: Cahiers roumains d'études littéraires* 1.2 (1993) 94–97.

Traditionalism and Protochronism in the European Context[*]

Ashby Crowder
University of Maryland

A significant aspect of the literature on twentieth-century Romania involves the communist period's various points of continuity and rupture with pre-communist developments.[1] The relationship of the protochronist movement of the 1970s and 1980s to the interwar "Great Debate," however, has not been sufficiently examined within this useful framework. The literature has tended to portray protochronism as a resuscitation of the interwar debate over Romania's future and its place in Europe. The only extended analysis of protochronism available in English remains Katherine Verdery's chapter "Romanian Protochronism" in her book *National Ideology under Socialism: Identity and Cultural Politics in Ceauşescu's Romania*. Since the protochronist phenomenon remains a distinguishing and widely known feature of the Ceauşescu period, more research and theorizing on the topic are warranted. This essay will examine the contentions and intellectual lineages of representatives of both interwar "traditionalism" and the late communist period's protochronism in order to assess the extent to which protochronism constitutes a continuation of the interwar debate. It attempts to trace the French and German influences on

---

*A version of this essay appears in *Balkanistica* v. 24 (2011) under the title "Lineages of Romanian Cultural Protectionism: From the 'Great Debate' to the Protochronists."

[1] Keith Hitchins, for example, considers the proclamation of the Romanian Popular Republic in December 1947 an event that "marked the subordination of the country to the Soviet political and economic model at home and to Soviet aims in international relations. At a deeper level it served notice that the modern era of Romanian history, which had begun with the loosening of ties to the East and the opening to the West, had come to an end" (Hitchins 547). Vladimir Tişmăneanu, examining the question of continuity from a different perspective, argues that the Ceauşescu regime adopted much of the imagery, rhetoric, and nationalist style of the pre-communist right. In this view, the fascist–communist nexus, and not the concept of rupture, must guide our understanding of Romanian communism's development and evolution (see Tişmăneanu, 12, 22, 220).

these two schools of writers as a basis for establishing degrees of continuity or rupture.

The following pages will argue against the reflexive tendency to link the interwar movements to the Ceauşescu era's protochronism, noting a number of serious divergences and proposing an alternative explanation for the development of each. To argue, as Verdery does, that protochronism constituted "an intensified resuscitation of interwar indigenist arguments about the national essence" in a different context is to insufficiently appreciate the very different claims and preoccupations of the two movements' spokesmen on the topic of Romanian culture's relationship to others and its place in the world (168). An alternative explanation proposes that each movement should be primarily seen as a product of its own time. The protochronists represented an innovation more than they did a continuation of interwar indigenism. The interwar Romanian right, meanwhile, should be understood in the context of European-wide developments that even render problematic the ingrained labels "traditionalist" and "Europeanist" that Keith Hitchins advances in his comprehensive history of modern Romania, *Rumania 1866–1947* (292). In short, traditionalism is a movement whose body of characteristics is specific to the interwar period, whereas Romanian protochronism is specific to Romania's late communist period. It is striking how little protochronism really shares with traditionalism—the former having been produced to complement Romania's peculiar place in the geopolitical environment of the Cold War. Protochronists, moreover, specifically reject the main tendencies of the traditionalists.

This chapter consists of a critical appraisal of the views of Hitchins and Verdery, followed by a note on communist historiography and, finally and most importantly, an examination of selected works of some principal writers from both periods. While a number of traditionalists and protochronists published fiction, poetry, and literary criticism as well as political and philosophical works, it is the political and philosophical works—the ones most likely to discuss intellectual history and cultural and national ideology—that deserve attention here. From the traditionalist camp, the views of Lucian Blaga, Nichifor Crainic, and Constantin Rădulescu-Motru will be considered. From the protochronist school, I will discuss the writings of Edgar Papu, Ilie Purcaru, and Dan Zamfirescu.

The labels "traditionalist," "Europeanist," "protochronist," and "anti-protochronist" are problematic for an additional reason other than the one mentioned above. As Hitchins has noted in the case of the "Great Debaters" and Verdery with respect to the protochronists and their opponents, members of the same camp were not always in agreement (Hitchins, 298, 305; Verdery 170–72). Some were more extreme in their views than others. Livezeanu observes that the terms scholars have used to discuss the groups that emerged in interwar intellectual life—"traditionalist," "authochtonist," and "indigenist"—do not adequately account for the "cultural complexity and new divisions that arose after the Great War" (Livezeanu, "Generational Politics" 210). Nevertheless, the broad categories with respect to the protochronists are sound enough to be conceptually useful. While noting the problems and inconsistencies these terms carry, this essay nevertheless continues to use them to designate the various groupings of writers to be discussed. As any alternative set of labels would pose its own new problems and likely lead to more confusion, I make no attempt to propose one here. As Livezeanu demonstrates, one can "contextualize and complicate" our understanding of these "by now classic categories of analysis" without setting them aside altogether (Livezeanu, "After the Great Union" 110). Regarding the interwar thinkers, current labels are more problematic.

The issues at stake in the interwar Great Debate were not novel or unique to the period. Verdery remarks that we cannot "divide the nineteenth century cleanly from the twentieth," since arguments from the interwar period were so often continuations of debates from earlier years (41–42). As Hitchins notes, it had already become clear to contemporary thinkers in the second half of the nineteenth century that Romania would develop in one of two ways:

> Two general directions presented themselves. One, drawing upon the Western European experience, would lead to industrialization and urbanization and bring radical change [while] [...] the other was based upon Romania's agricultural past and emphasized the preservation of traditional social structures and cultural values. (55)

To understand the interwar right, we must first understand the Junimea movement—a society of young, conservative, Western-educated Moldavian intellectuals—that developed in Iaşi in the mid-nineteenth century. In contrast to the Francophile tradition that had dominated the Romanian elite for decades, the Junimists drew on German Romanticism and German philosophy's "principles of organic social development." Junimists considered society an organism that must evolve gradually rather than change through sudden rupture. They aimed their criticism at the Romanian revolutionaries of the "Springtime of the Peoples," the *paşoptişti* [1848ers] for ignoring the deep structure of Romanian culture and society in favor of grafting a superficial Francophile Westernness onto a social environment fundamentally different from France's (60–63). Yet the Junimists, Hitchins is careful to note, were not extreme autochthonists. They accepted the imminent Westernization of Romania in some form, but believed that this transformation should come as a gradual and synchronistic evolution (64).

The interwar Great Debate is essentially a continuation of the Junimist vs. Francophile argument in a sharper key. In *Rumania 1866– 1947*, Hitchins discusses the various currents of thought in the interwar polemic surrounding Romania's cultural and political orientation and describes the personalities involved. He divides the debate's participants into two broad categories: the Europeanists and the Traditionalists. While Europeanists viewed Romania as an underdeveloped part of Europe that had no other choice but to model its future course on the Western European experience, traditionalists considered the imposition of Western forms onto the agrarian and Christian Orthodox country an artificial course of development ill-suited to Romania's realities (292–93). As Hitchins notes, the Europeanists identified with the Francophile tradition, while the traditionalists, like the Junimists before them, built upon German preoccupations with culture, civilization, and national character. Eventually, a strain of Germanic anti-rationalism and mysticism, Hitchins explains, "exercised a profound influence on Romanian thought." Traditionalists, therefore, in addition to supporting an inward-looking course of development, had militated against the "steady moral and spiritual decay of Romanian society since the 19th century" (298–99).

The term "Europeanist," for Hitchins, suggests a forward-looking, progressive conception of European development that we can use Mark Mazower's work to critique. Extremism, Mazower shows, fits well into the European mainstream. We should, therefore, consider Europeanness as a deeply conflicted state of being in which liberalism competed with a number of darker approaches to dealing with the dilemmas of modern life (Mazower ix–xv). It is also well to note the contribution of Maria Bucur to understanding this problem in its Romanian form. Bucur, in *Eugenics and Modernization in Interwar Romania*, has addressed the problem of terminology in regard to the interwar cultural and political debates. She demonstrates that the eugenics movement in interwar Romania "shows the limited explanatory power" of a model setting "secular western" values against "antisecular nativist" ones. "Modernism," Bucur observes, "was not always progressive, nor was traditionalism always reactionary." Bucur finds that Romanian eugenicists' "synthesis of tradition and modernization" helped to "negotiate the apparently irreconcilable interwar debates [...] between traditionalist conservatives and their opponents—the Europeanizing modernists." Bucur does not, however, find a "direct and unequivocal link between the Romanian extreme right and the eugenics movement" (4, 11–12). Livezeanu, too, observes the modernist influence on Romanian traditionalism. Traditionalists, she notes, had ideologically eclectic backgrounds, and some of their publications were "stamped by European modernism" ("After the Great Union" 111).

Communist-era Romanian historiography is exceptionally weak on the interwar period. Rarely did a work appear, even during the thaw of the early Ceauşescu years, that offered more than a few sentences on the cultural, political, and social dynamics of these decades; it seems that there was simply no extensive and comprehensive analysis of the interwar period published. As Vlad Georgescu points out in his *tamizdat* analysis of Romania's communist-era historiography, throughout every phase of the Romanian Communist Party's rule the desire to "minimize the role of undesirable personalities in [...] history" remained strong (8, 34).[2] The 1969 tome *Istoria României* [The History of Romania], in a brief chapter on the interwar period, devotes only a few sentences to the interwar polemics in a subsection on the press. *Istoria României* states that "newspapers like *Curentul* [The Current] and reviews like *Gîndirea* [*The Thought*] insistently propagated reactionary, chauvinistic, mystical concepts, and the fascist press tried to prepare public opinion in view of the expansionist, bellicose plans of German imperialism" (Constantinescu 538). The text

---

[2] This and all other translations are mine, unless otherwise noted.

states that the interwar period enjoyed a "rich and valuable cultural heritage," but it omits the details of the main personalities and controversies of the epoch (542).

The university manual *Istoria României între anii 1918–1981* [The History of Romania during the Years 1918–1981], published in the early 1980s, offers similar observations while reflecting the changed terms of discourse that characterized the late Ceauşescu years. The work contains no detailed discussion of the Great Debate, but it does mention a "confrontation between materialism and idealism, between the new and the old [that] embraced all spheres of spiritual activity." This confrontation takes place between those who hold "materialist and democratic" positions and those who have succumbed to "fascist influences" or "retrograde currents":

> [The] spokesmen [for the latter movement] were a series of pseudophilosophes and publicists linked to the legionary and Cuzaist movements, like Nae Ionescu, Emil Cioran, Nichifor Crainic, [...] Vasile Bancila, Nicolae Roşu, etc.
> (Petric 207)

The interwar right's major personalities are mentioned, but not elaborated upon. Like the 1969 compendium referred to above, this 1981 volume contends that the interwar period, despite the fascist threat, was, at least in part, an era of progress because it saw the flourishing of a "unitary national Romanian state" [*stat naţional unitar român*] (207, 211). Yet official publications admit no ideological continuity between interwar indigenist thinkers and the protochronist movement that was flourishing when the *Istoria României* manual was published. Moreover, the problem intellectuals faced in not being free to discuss in any depth such a crucial period in recent history created an opening for a movement like protochronism to grow and flourish.[3] In this sense, too, protochronism is a product of its own context.

A fresh examination of the interwar publications of some of the major figures of the indigenist movement helps to clarify the relationship of the interwar right to the nineteenth-century conservatives and, finally, to the protochronism of the late twentieth century. *Puncte cardinal în haos* [Cardinal Points in Chaos], the writer, philosopher,

---

[3] I thank John R. Lampe for sharing this observation.

and poet Nichifor Crainic's influential treatise on what he considered fundamental challenges to culture and civilization, has a deeply troubled and apocalyptic tone. Crainic's objective in the work is to find a means of escaping from existential crisis and chaos into "saving light" [*lumină salvatoare*]. Affirming the priority of spiritualism over materialism and idealism as the proper "mode of considering the world," Crainic declares that like Benito Mussolini, he chooses a "manly" struggle with "the monster" that is threatening civilization: "I do not believe [...] that [the] poor [species of] man must be under the sway of his times [*sub vremi*]; I believe with Benito Mussolini that the power of man breaks the neck of the monster" (Crainic, *Puncte cardinale în haos* 19).[4] Who, or what, is this "monster"? Along with materialism and idealism, Crainic notes the threats of skepticism, cynicism, and nihilism:

> Is there, according to this doctrine, love of one's nation [*neam*]? No. Is there love of one's fatherland? No. Is there love of the people and of its institutions? No. There exists only treason against all of these. [...] The materialist man is by definition anarchistic and revolutionary: Nothing interests him other than his personal success. (20)

Crainic militates against a perceived assault on traditional values and institutions. A defender of Christianity, he credits the youth for defending the "sacred institution of the people" from those materialists who sought its destruction (46).

Crainic explains that the "materialist conceptions" that dominated the end of the nineteenth century and reached their "paroxysm" in the 1930s provoked the "alternating sentiments of uncertainty, of revolt, and of universal panic" that are responsible for the "chaos in which the world now lives" (20). Democracy, socialism, and communism are "political formulas rooted in the materialist doctrine" that Crainic so thoroughly condemns (22–24). He states that while Mussolini and Hitler might not have found the formula for resolving life's problems, they are to be admired for having recognized the chaos of their time and proposing a solution. Crainic admires above all these movements' strict hierarchy. This organizational structure, he believes, reflects the "natural order" of human society (25).

---

[4] This work was originally published in 1936.

Crainic discusses at length the contributions of several contemporary German thinkers. He refers to Oswald Spengler's contribution to the quasi-biological understanding of a national culture as a living "organism in constant growth, with roots in the sap of the people" (70–72, 153). He notes Herman Keyserling's views on the "autochthonous cultural spirit" of each people. He praises the German philosopher's view that the Romanians have a "European mission" to "reawaken a new Byzantinism" (138).

The notion that Crainic is somehow an inward-looking nationalist and nothing more is misguided, for he is firmly engaged in the European context. For Crainic, the crisis of modern times requires a Europe-wide movement to tackle the threats to civilization. Crainic's discussion of the nature of "Christian nationalism" is especially revealing. Fundamental to his Christian nationalism is the concept of "demofilia." Different from national pride, "demofilic nationalism" constitutes the "loving of one's people on the model of Jesus Christ." Demofilia, he continues, is a European phenomenon affecting Dostoevsky, Rousseau, and Tolstoy, one that is "creating a general atmosphere of vague naturalist mysticism around the people" (33–35).

Crainic considers Romanticism, too, a Europe-wide phenomenon that, unlike the attempts of willy-nilly Europeanizers on the French model, does not interfere with natural development but rather catalyzes it. "Romanticism," according to Crainic, "draws from local sources, teaching them to become autochthonous. Historic Romanticism guides towards one's forbears; poetic romanticism towards folklore" (123). The "Intellectualists," on the other hand, are reformulating the "Francomania" of times past. They are "'intellectuals' in so far as they are Francomaniacs [*franţuzomani*]; they are Europeanizers [*europeanizanţi*] in inverse relationship to [their] autochthonism. […] What they call Europeanism is nothing more than Franceism […]" (123). Taking aim at Eugen Lovinescu, the principal "Europeanizer" of the interwar generation, Crainic argues that the "Lovinescan doctrine is anti-traditionalist, *tabula rasa*," and "integrally revolutionary" (152). "We do not know well the soul of our people," Crainic complains. "We have looked at it from a distance through the colored window of foreign ideologies" (139). Crainic, however, was a Europeanist in his own way inasmuch as he identified the struggle with modernity as a continental, and not a merely national, problem. This aspect illustrates a problem with Hitchins's assumption about what is and is not European.

In *Etnicul românesc* [The Romanian Ethnic], Constantin Rădulescu-Motru, a philosopher, psychologist, and politician with indigenist and peasantist views, analyzes the psychology of the Romanians as an ethnic group. He divides consciousness into three categories: "consciousness of a community of origin, consciousness of a community of language, and consciousness of a community of destiny" (13).[5] Like Crainic, he adopts a biological understanding of culture, noting that "the soul of a healthy people is an organism in constant growth" (77–78).[6] Indeed, the modern biological lexicon of the interwar traditionalists distinguished them from their nineteenth-century conservative forbears. Rădulescu-Motru specifically credits German Romanticism for facilitating the development of Romanian peasant culture and national literature and poetry (79–80). In the political realm, he discusses the type of leadership that a "community of destiny" requires:

> The community of destiny, in order to have among members of the ethnic [group] a strict discipline, needs a leader. […] In the leader is symbolized the destiny of the nation itself, because on his thought and his action the future depends. In these conditions the new German National Socialist state was formed, under the leadership of Adolf Hitler, a shield for assuring the German nation in the face of dangers with which it was threatened. Perils being the same for other nations, it is natural that the organization of the German state be adopted also by other nations. (126)

Rădulescu-Motru goes on to endorse the German notion of a "vital space" for each nation, adding that "it cannot enter any other territory inhabited by any other foreign nation, but only the territory inhabited by a nation rooted by destiny" (127). Although *Etnicul românesc* offers evidence of the strong German influence on Rădulescu-Motru's concept of the nation, he was hardly unfamiliar with French intellectual culture. In fact, he had significant involvement in both French and German academic circles. Rădulescu-Motru studied in both Germany and France, and served as a member of the

---

[5] This work was first published in 1942.

[6] For a different view on Rădulescu-Motru, see Verdery (50).

advisory committee of the French *Journal de psychologie normale et pathologique* [Journal of Normal and Pathological Psychology] and was a member of the editorial committee of the German periodical *Forum Philosophicum*. Dumitru Otovescu describes him as "not only a point of connection between Romanian and European philosophy, but a representative [to it] of [Romanian philosophy's] avant garde" (Otovescu 17). Despite his ties to France, Rădulescu-Motru remained firmly grounded in a German-inspired cultural and national philosophy.

Philosopher and poet Lucian Blaga, as Hitchins notes, expressed somewhat more moderate views than did his fellow "traditionalists," and it is, therefore, only with some unease that he is incorporated into the same philosophical camp with Crainic and Rădulescu-Motru. As Livezeanu notes, Blaga "represented a new generation and a new mixture of authochtonism and modernism that the older generation of literati and academics barely understood and instinctively disliked" (Livezeanu, "Generational Politics" 210). As Blaga was interested first and foremost in the features of Romanian character and the essence of rural existence, his writings, even the later ones, are not overtly political like those of his colleagues discussed above.[7] He was concerned with the relationship between the spatial landscape and the "national soul," with national institutions such as the church, with the defining features of rural life, and with spiritualism and transcendence (Blaga, *Trilogia culturii* 2: 25–27). Blaga cites the contributions of German thinkers such as Spengler and Herder, and considers the "national idea" a development that crystallized abroad and that only later was adopted by the inhabitants of Southeastern Europe. "The strategy of liberation," he writes, "with inevitable concessions that had to be made to the situation and the conditions of the epoch, obliged us [...] to accept certain influences of European spirit and civilization" (192).

Although he is not a Europeanist in Hitchins's rubric, Blaga by no means sought to isolate Romania from larger European currents. Though captivated by village life, he observed that the village could not rapidly develop to accommodate the "complex network of European interdependence." Rural Romania would require time to evolve into its continental European context. This continental context itself,

---

[7] For an excellent discussion of Blaga's thought in relation to that of other interwar writers, see Hitchins (305–13).

moreover, needed time to develop in a way that would be favorable to culture and to the human spirit. Blaga considered that "we [Romanians] cannot [...] maintain ourselves and develop ourselves as a state without integrating ourselves into Europe" (189). However, he rejected modernity's homogenization, mechanization, and rationalism, contending that both the Romanian and the broadly European spirit needed to be reconsidered to bring the world into line with what he considered healthy and appropriate philosophical and spiritual values (Hitchins 306–307).

In a revealing essay that speaks to the spiritual and intellectual lineage of the traditionalist school, Blaga compares French and German influences on Romanian thinkers. Both French and German cultures represent, for Blaga, aspects of the great "European spirit." While French cultural influence was "more massive and more sustained," German influence did far more to stimulate Romanians' native creativity. Whereas French culture posits a "universal model" of "universal validity" that reasonable individuals would naturally choose to adopt, German philosophy represents "a call [...] to one's own ethnic soul." Blaga explains:

> French culture dictates to any foreigner that comes close to it: "Be like I am!" The Frenchman will never understand the foreigner who responds: "No!" [...] German culture, being oriented in a totally different manner, will never raise the pretension: "Be like I am!" German culture is conscious of its own grandeur, but it feels itself unto its own [...] it takes into account local and individualist character. [...] When appearing in front of a foreigner, it, despite its own pride, advises: "Be yourself." [...] What is interesting is that the influences of a catalytic nature came to us, in the form of a call unto ourselves [*un apel la noi înșine*], almost always from the Germans. (196–99)

Blaga mentions the indispensability of German influence on the works of linguist Gheorghe Lazăr and the national poet Mihai Eminescu. Blaga is convinced that the "ethnic coefficient"—the German conception of blood versus the French one of *citoyenneté*—explains the difference between French and German cultural traditions (192–200). These views on German philosophy, central to the thought of the traditionalist camp, were rejected outright by the protochronists, as we will see shortly.

A strength of Hitchins's *Rumania 1866–1947* is its lengthy discussion of the German influence on the nineteenth-century conservatives and the interwar right. While other scholars have insisted on the primacy of French influence on Romanian intellectuals, the significance of German thought, especially to rightist Romanian thinkers, should not be overlooked.[8] Nevertheless, Hitchins's choice of the label "traditionalist" to broadly designate the thinkers of the interwar right is as problematic as his notion that only their opponents were Europeanists. As evidence for the broadly European orientation of the traditionalists, we note that Crainic and Rădulescu-Motru discussed developments in Germany and Italy widely, appearing to consider their own views part of a transnational initiative against the features of modernity that they abhorred. They shared concerns with rightists and cultural protectionists across the European continent. To consider their views anti-European, purely autochthonist, or traditionalist is, therefore, something of a conceptual error. Still, even Crainic himself uses the labels traditionalist and autochthonist, suggesting that even if a new vocabulary is needed to understand these contradictory currents that were neither conservative, nor moderate, nor revolutionary, we may be bound to existing labels.

Anthropologist Katherine Verdery, in her influential study *National Ideology under Socialism: Cultural Politics in Ceauşescu's Romania*, discusses the interwar debate treated above. The purpose of her description of the Europeanists and the traditionalists is to furnish a background for her argument about the expressions of "national ideology" of the Ceauşescu period, the protochronist phenomenon of the 1970s and 1980s included. The protochronist movement, Verdery explains, rejected the importation of foreign concepts and "encouraged critics and literary historians to look for developments in Romanian culture that had anticipated events in the better-publicized cultures of Western Europe" (167). Protochronism asserts not merely a separateness from Western Europe, but seeks to "up the ante" vis-à-vis Western European contributions, portraying Romanian artistic, cultural, intellectual, and literary developments as anticipatory and prophetic.

---

[8] See, for example, Anne Quinney, "Cultural Colonies: France and the Romanian Imagination," in *Contemporary French and Francophone Studies*. Boia, however, like Hitchins, is an exception, for his *History and Myth in Romanian Consciousness* contains a section comparing the "French myth" to the "German countermyth." See Lucian Boia, *History and Myth in Romanian Consciousness* (160–65).

Protochronism, therefore, would seem to be much more than a continuation of the interwar traditionalist position. But we must understand the traditionalists if we are to make sense of the protochronists because the latter group inherited the former's organic nationalist views.

While Verdery's work is not a history of protochronism per se, her study furnishes plenty of historical insight. She has examined the writings of the main protochronist and anti-protochronist figures to develop an argument about resource competition among intellectuals under socialism, and the role of national images in this competition. Verdery is primarily interested in how the protochronist phenomenon fits into her conception of the "economy of shortage" that governed cultural production in socialist Romania (168). We learn much about the intellectual history of protochronism from her book, but intellectual history is not her focus.

National Ideology under Socialism, although it is about much more than protochronism, offers the only substantial piece of scholarship devoted to the subject that has been published in English. Its sophistication and comprehensiveness are perhaps reasons that more contributions have not appeared. Verdery connects the intellectual discourse of the 1970s and 1980s to the Great Debate of the interwar period, discussing at length the protochronists' dismissals of Lovinescu and other Westernizers. In turn, she covers the anti-protochronists' retorts. One weak point concerns the intellectual lineage of the traditionalists and, by extension, of the protochronists. An account of the intellectual foundations of Europeanist thought is evident in the Europeanist program. The Westernists' Francophilia is well established. The intellectual lineage of the protochronists and traditionalists, however, is more difficult to trace, as noted above in the discussion of Blaga. Verdery recognizes the traditionalists' "recourse to organic imagery and to metaphors of kinship," but she almost completely ignores the German roots of this perspective (211). In her chapter "Antecedents: National Ideology and Cultural Politics in Presocialist Romania," Verdery discusses traditionalist thinkers extensively, but without mention of the foreign, the *German*, inspiration for and influence on their work. The Romanian traditionalists' ideas are hardly original, but this is how Verdery presents them. Moreover, Verdery's basic historical argument that "protochronism was an intensified resuscitation of interwar indigenist arguments about the national essence," albeit in a different context, deserves to be questioned.

The term "protochronism" [*protocronism* in Romanian] was popularized in Romania in the 1970s, but it can now be employed to refer to similar cultural movements in other national contexts. The father of Romanian protochronism was the essayist Edgar Papu. Papu studied philology and philosophy at the Universities of Bucharest and Vienna. At Bucharest, he did so under Tudor Vianu, himself a student of Rădulescu-Motru.[9] Papu's 1977 book *Din clasicii noștri: contribuții la ideea unui protocronism românesc* [From Our Classics: Contributions to the Idea of a Romanian Protochronism], which developed out of a 1974 essay on the subject published in the review *Secolul 20* [Twentieth Century], reveals the far-fetched, but compared to what came later less extreme, beginnings of the *soi-disant* protochronist movement.[10] Papu suggests Romanian anticipations "in all domains" of later developments "on the universal plan" in art, music, and literature (Papu, *Din clasicii noștri* 7). To be sure, it is possible to identify protochronist-like arguments *avant la lettre*, and Papu concedes that his theory is not wholly original (Cristea 88). His work did, however, spark a movement that would become a significant feature of Romanian intellectual life for more than a decade.

A principal preoccupation of the protochronists is not merely to locate anticipatory Romanian precedents for European and global trends, but also to prove Romania's position in the world as a major player in culture, art, literature, and politics. In other words, protochronism is not a purely academic tendency; it is profoundly intertwined with the political preoccupations and insecurities that characterized the Ceaușescu years. Protochronists, in short, were wedded to Ceaușism, and their writing was designed to defend and promote the communist regime. Protochronism represents, as even the more moderate Papu writes, an effort to alter "consciousness about our position in the world," to transform Romanian identity from one of the periphery to one of the center (Papu, *Din clasicii noștri* 10–11).

---

[9] See Vasile Lungu, *Viața lui Tudor Vianu* (79); Dumitru Otovescu, *Cultură, personalitate, vocație: în concepția lui C. Rădulescu-Motru* (20); Alex Ștefănescu, "Edgar Papu," *România literară* (10–11); and Anda Teodorescu and Andre Bantaș, *Romanian Essayists of Today* (5).

[10] See Mircea Martin, "Cultura română între comunism și naționalism," *Revista 22* 660: 44 (2002).

Papu complains that "we have the consciousness of being behind, nurturing the illusion that we have entered into the world circuit later, in other words only with the nineteenth century. In fact, this idea is inexact" (Papu, "Am o mare încredere" 85).

Papu's arguments have been taken more seriously than those of the later protochronists who borrowed—some say corrupted and transformed—his ideas. Sympathetic Romanian scholars writing since the revolution portray him as a serious intellectual, noble in intentions, whose reasonable approach to identifying universal themes in Romanian literature was distorted into a national Stalinist propaganda movement by the likes of Ilie Purcaru and Dan Zamfirescu.[11] Papu possessed the academic credentials and intellectual heft that the other protochronists lacked. But it would be a mistake to see his argument as developing outside a certain political environment that was setting the boundaries for cultural production and interpretation. Papu presented his argument in the years immediately following Ceauşescu's promulgation of the 1971 "July Theses," which aimed to turn cultural production into a propaganda service. The Theses signaled a renewed effort at socialist realism in art and literature—a neo-Stalinist hyper-ideologization of cultural production. The capstone of the re-radicalization of the Ceauşescu period, the Theses marked the definitive end of the comparative liberalization that characterized Ceauşescu's first years in power.[12] Language in the July Theses called for combating foreign influences while celebrating the Romanian people's own achievements,[13] and Papu's arguments met these criteria marvelously by repatriating ideas once considered of foreign origin. Using this strategy, Papu simultaneously rejected foreign influence and celebrated native achievements. Even if Papu's writings were less extreme than what would come later, it would be a mistake to build too high a barrier to separate him from the other protochronists.

---

[11] For a sympathetic analysis of Papu's protochronism in post-communist Romanian scholarship, see Ovidiu Ghidirmic, *Studii de literatură română modernă şi contemporană* (223–269) and Alex Ştefănescu, "Edgar Papu" (10–11).

[12] See Dennis Deletant, *Romania Under Communist Rule* (119–120) and Vlad Georgescu, *Politică şi istorie* (44–75).

[13] See Titu Popescu et al., "Tezele din iulie" (32–46). The text of the July Theses, officially called "Propuneri de măsuri pentru îmbunătăţirea activităţii politico-ideologice, de educare marxist-leninistă a membrilor de partid, a tuturor oamenilor muncii," is reproduced in this article.

Literary historian and critic Dan Zamfirescu rendered his proto-chronist interpretations in more stridently nationalist language. He earned a doctorate in philology and spent his career as an editor and writer for numerous publications, from literary reviews such as *Luce-afărul* [The Morning Star] and *Contemporanul* [The Contemporary] to party-state propaganda organs like *Scînteia* [The Spark] and *Scîn-teia tineretului* [The Spark for Youth]. Zamfirescu considers the es-sence of Romanian culture to be its independent spirit, and he offers a protochronist interpretation of the history of Romanian independence. His ideas on Romanian independence complement official foreign policy priorities nicely. Zamfirescu holds, for example, that the "struggle for independence is permanent in our history," and that Ro-manians must "remember that the Geto-Dacians, our forbears, glori-ously confronted the greatest empire of antiquity" (Zamfirescu, *Inde-pendenţă şi cultură* 5–8). In the 1977 volume *Independenţă şi cultură* [Independence and Culture], Zamfirescu contends that "the results of these never-ending battles for independence is Romanian culture, which is among the richest and most original of the cultures of our continent" as well as "one of the most pregnant revolutionary histories of a European people" (132). He writes that "the leaders who arose from among this people have been, just through their representative character, powerful personalities not only of the national history, but also of universal developments" (5). Zamfirescu's objective is explicitly to argue for a special and esteemed place for Romania in global history and culture. "The present volume," he writes in the introduction,

> pleads for a new conception about the place and the role of the history and culture of the Romanian people in the en-semble of universal history and, especially looks separate from the experience of the past for the reasons for our be-lief in the great work of the socialist present and in the fu-ture towards which we aspire. (5–6)

Romanian culture, he argues elsewhere,

> must use the chance it has today to become the dough [*alu-atul*] of a new humanity, a humanity of human solidarity. [...] [I]t is not a small thing to be the spiritual dough of a new humanity. [...] The Italians were in the Renaissance and they showed us how a people that was never the most

> numerous nor the most powerful in Europe created never-
> theless the basis of modern Europe.
> (Zamfirescu, "Cultura română" 136)

Protochronism, therefore, is both inward-looking and outward-looking at the same time. Protochronists looked to the West for guideposts of the developments for which they needed to find internal, Romanian, antecedents. Again, the notion of Romania as a European leader complemented the foreign policy of the Ceauşescu regime.

The interwar traditionalists and the protochronists offer quite different accounts of the historical and contemporary influences on their work and on Romanian culture as a whole. Whereas Blaga, Crainic, and Rădulescu-Motru refer often to German thinkers, the protochronists offer few clues about their own intellectual heritage. As asserting Romanian primacy was part and parcel of the protochronist movement, claiming a foreign influence would have been problematic. Papu's, Purcaru's, and Zamfirescu's approaches show no discernible French influence either. Although admitting a foreign, especially German, influence might have led to conflict with censors in the mid-1970s and 1980s—the years of redoubled ideological pressure on cultural producers in the wake of the 1971 July Theses—the very ideology of protochronism made it unlikely that its proponents would claim one. Still, some protochronist publications contain hints whose meanings are debatable. Papu, for example, considers the role of German Romantic influence on Romanian literature, asserting a protochronist antecedent to the Romantic movement:

> We are accustomed to search in German Romanticism (and
> especially in Herder) for the source of national literary
> movements in Europe. The type of national patriotism that
> is almost modern, the enthusiasm of the "national rebirths"
> we find, yet, in the time of Şerban Cantacuzino, in his work
> *Stolnicul* [...] the first rhapsody of Dacianism [...].
> (*Din clasicii noştri* 11–12)

Zamfirescu makes a similar observation, claiming that the Romanians' "modern national movement" began a century before what is called "the century of nations." "The idea of political and national independence," he continues,

> is not an idea borrowed by Romanians from the literature of
> the Romantic century, but is an idea that rests at the foun-
> dation of their political existence from the first day, from
> the road of liberation of nations from under the pretensions
> and yokes of empires. And the formulation [of the idea of
> independence] in its quintessential form [...] we find in the
> ingenious contemporary of Machiavelli, who was Neagoe
> Basarab. (*Independenţă şi cultură* 119)

Romanians, therefore, "did not need to learn modern patriotism
from the Western Romantics" (120). Taken literally, this passage
represents a genuine if ironic attempt to claim a protochronist antici-
pation of German Romanticism. Whereas Hitchins's interwar traditionalists celebrated German influence, the protochronists denied its
significance altogether. We may inquire whether Papu, Purcaru, and
Zamfirescu truly felt this way, or if they simply recognized that they
operated in a cultural-political atmosphere in which citing German
Romantics approvingly was at the very least problematic. However,
the clear meaning of the text is to downplay the import of German
Romanticism, the same Romanticism to which the interwar writers
paid homage.

The protochronists occasionally mention the interwar period, but
they reinvent it in order to connect their own concerns with ones pro-
jected back onto the 1920s and 1930s. The work of Ilie Purcaru serves
as an example of this tendency. This poet and political writer has an
academic background in literature and spent his career in publishing.
He founded the review *Ramuri* [Branches] and was chief editor of
Tribuna României [Tribune of Romania]. Like Zamfirescu, he worked
on the party propaganda dailies *Scînteia* and *Scînteia tineretului*, both
of which he served as editor. Purcaru presents the interwar period as
a time when "our culture participated effectively, frequently in a
distinguished manner, in the great planetary debate which, placing in
relation culture, currents, styles, defined what may be named, across
frontiers and across national particularities [*specificul national*], the
profile of human spirituality in the 20th century" (Purcaru 5). This
fantastic version of the interwar debates serves as the background for
the current one, according to Purcaru:

> Let us take up [this debate] again with the present volume.
> [...] Are we able to say the word not only in relation to our
> own problems, but also in relation to the problems of the

> world? Are we really liberated of local, zonal problems that hold to a peripheral autochthonism, and disposed to enlist our own contribution in the process of constituting a new spirituality, one that integrates cultures and that may be named a new humanism? (6)

Romanian culture, Purcaru argues, was not "subaltern" until the nineteenth century, when

> there arose the problem of a handicap—one that Romania must overcome—in the face of Western cultures. Older Romanian intellectuals, as Mircea Eliade shows ... did not know the complex of inferiority in the face of the West. In the time of Miron Constin, of Cantemir, or of Milescu, Romanian culture dialogued as an equal with Western Cultures. [...] [Romanians] did not have the sentiment of humility [...] in the face of their cultural neighbors. [...] This is the place that returns now, in corollary, to Romanian socialist culture. Our function as a bridge between cultures is now more important than ever. (6)

Purcaru's protochronism, in other words, is presented itself as reconnecting with a Romanian tradition of assertiveness and global engagement. Details of the interwar debate, though, are conveniently omitted, as discussing them would pose major ideological problems.

One partial exception includes the discussion of Lovinescan synchronism in the Romanian literature of the 1970s and 1980s. Indeed, Lovinescu's position in the interwar period is an indispensable background for understanding the concept of protochronism. Papu, the father of protochronism, did not attack Lovinescu by name, but his view that protochronism represented an alternative to synchronism invokes Lovinescu without always saying so (Maier 4). Still, Lovinescu was not as wholly objectionable to authorities as those interwar figures who were openly pro-fascist, such as Nae Ionescu, or those whose works appeared to support a strain of rightist-nationalist or anti-communist thought, such as Crainic and Rădulescu-Motru. Unlike the work of these indigenists, Lovinescu's writings, albeit in abridged and edited versions, were published during the Ceauşescu period.[14] The ideological climate of the Ceauşescu period appears to

---

[14] See Eugen Lovinescu, *Istoria civilizaţei române moderne*. For a discussion of editorial manipulations of Lovinescu designed to make his work more palatable to the regime's censors, see Boia, p. 76.

have been friendlier to interwar Francophiles than it was to the Germanophiles.

The protochronists attempted to defuse the stark choice between traditionalism and Europeanism that was at the heart of the interwar debate. Papu, for example, proposes a synthesis of the two (Papu, "Am o mare încredere" 87). Praising some of Lovinescu's contributions, Mihail Ungheanu, too, rejects the "fatal alternative" of choosing between synchronism and protochronism (Ungheanu 63). The link to Lovinescu by way of rejection remained one of protochronism's trickiest ideological problems. Papu's implicit dispute with Lovinescu allowed critics to charge that protochronists were simply adopting the position of the interwar right (Maier 4; Cristea 90–91). Given that the positions of these two cultural protectionist movements differed so much, it would be a mistake to take away from this polemic too much of analytical value.

Zamfirescu, in *Independenţă şi cultură*, has a fascinating way of disconnecting protochronism from the interwar period. Unlike Purcaru and the official history texts, which find some positive developments in the interwar period, Zamfirescu considers the early twentieth century to be a time of

> development not without dramatic moments and sliding into errors, tendencies which led, especially in the so called "interwar" period, towards an irredeemable diminishing of substance, a reflex of the twilight of the capitalist order and of the type of civilization linked to this order.
>
> (*Independenţă şi cultură* 164–65)

In a move unusual for the period, Zamfirescu then mentions a number of influential German philosophers, including Nietzsche and Spengler, who, he notes, took steps towards creating a "scientific criticism" and a "philosophy of culture" (174). Zamfirescu then discusses the work of Lucian Blaga, which, he argues, is far superior to that of the Germans he cites. Blaga was

> one of the great Romanians of our century who, starting from the contents of another cultural tradition than that which gave birth to Nietzsche, Spengler, or Paul Valéry, dared to face the inexorable decline of European creativity. Blaga's gesture was to transform the philosophy of culture from a philosophy of the inexorable decadence of Euro-

> pean culture into a philosophy of belief in creation, of hu-
> man creativity, with direct application to Romanian culture.
> (175)

In this sense, Blaga was, for Zamfirescu, an exception to the de-
cline of the interwar period. Blaga, as noted, clearly saw himself as
writing in interaction with, and under the influence of, some of the
same German thinkers that Zamfirescu mentions. But in order to discuss Blaga, Zamfirescu must purify him by disassociating him from
the atmosphere of his time, and especially from the substantial German influence under which he was formed and operated (Hitchins
305–14).

The protochronists were more likely to find a useable past in the
period from the Middle Ages through the seventeenth century. It is
this period of time, safe from modern ideological baggage, from
which a number of protochronists draw examples to support their
arguments. For example, Zamfirescu writes that "today [...] we ourselves live in a national epoch [that] [...] has brought us into communion with our forefathers. We have this sentiment that it seems as
if all our history is near us" (Zamfirescu, *Independenţă şi cultură* 9–
10). Contemporary Romanians were joined with those of centuries
past to form a "community of defense" of the nation (12). Which figures from the past does Zamfirescu highlight? Basarab, Vlad Ţepeş,
and other less well-known sixteenth-century personalities such as
Petru Rareş and Despot-Voda. This kitsch invocation of ancient personalities was an ubiquitous feature of the Ceauşescu period, and one
that is substantially reflected in the protochronists' writings (12–17).[15]

The publications in which many protochronist texts appear tell us
something about the protochronists' relationship to the Cold War atmosphere. Zamfirescu, for example, originally published a number of
the articles—later collected into volumes—in military journals such
as *Apărarea patriei* [The Defense of the Fatherland]. They carry titles
such as "The Strategy and Tactics of Independence in the History of
the Romanians."[16] Their objective is to historicize the Ceauşescu regime's doctrine of the *lupta întregului popor*, or "the struggle of the
entire people," in the face of foreign invaders. "The entire history of

---

[15] See also Vlad Georgescu's chapter "Kitschul Istoric" (75–80).
[16] See Zamfirescu, "Cultura română" (96). For a discussion of the "militarization" of
historiography during the Ceauşescu years, see Boia (81).

our people," Zamfirescu explains, "constitutes itself as a constant struggle for the defense of its ethnic, political, and spiritual liberties and identities in uninterrupted confrontation with a series of factors which put them in danger" (Zamfirescu, *Independenţă şi cultură* 118). The "fundamental text that explains the entire concept of Romanian policy about independence and defense," Zamfirescu claims, is the sixteenth-century treatise of the voivode Neagoe Basarab, *Învăţăturile lui Neagoe Basarab către fiul său Teodosie* [Lessons of Neagoe Basarab to His Son Teodosie] (119). In this argument, Zamfirescu combines a protochronist argument for an anticipatory Machiavellian text with an assertion of the age-old Romanian attribute of vigorous self-defense. Elsewhere, he elaborates on Romanians' "inferiority complex" vis-à-vis other cultures and nations:

> I name this complex the "Phanariot complex," for it is the product of this epoch between 1711 and 1821, which saw the systematic destruction of belief in the Romanian people in itself, in the virtues of its language, in its force of creation. It was an epoch of political humility, of cultural isolation, of domination by a foreign imperium through foreign interposers, or foreignized souls [*înstrăinaţi sufleteşte*].
>
> ("Cultura română" 130–31)

It requires little imagination to recognize the sixteenth-century Phanariots as stand-ins for twentieth-century Bolsheviks and "anti-national" Romanian communists. Both author and reader thus became participants in a hidden text in which all are aware of what is suggested, but remains unwritten. This technique of invoking a distant and ideologically unproblematic individual or issue as a stand-in to make a veiled point about some aspect of current international affairs was common in Romanian academic writing from the communist period.[17]

In a published interview with fellow protochronist Ilie Purcaru, Zamfirescu notes that it is the charge of the "third Europe" to bring about the "spiritual regeneration of our old continent." He explains,

---

[17] Scholarly works in the field of international relations, for example, refer to obscure treaties from the fourteenth century to object to coercion and interference in others' internal affairs. It is clear that they are engaged in veiled criticism of Soviet foreign policy. See, for example, Edwin Glaser, *Dreptul statelor de a participa la viaţa internaţională* and *Statele mici şi mijlocii în relaţiile internaţionale*.

> I consider that a true Europe of peace and understanding
> can benefit massively from the existence of an active con-
> sciousness of southeastern Europeans about the past, about
> their historic and cultural solidarity and about their actual
> changes and future. This "third Europe" can contribute
> massively to the birth of that "Europe of the European
> soul" so hoped for and yet still not achieved [...] that
> would lead us to consider naturally that any inter-European
> conflagration [would be] a monstrosity.
>
> ("Cultura română" 134–35)

Zamfirescu's comments on the Phanariot mentality and on raising the European and global profile of Southeastern Europe appear carefully crafted to support the official position of Romania's communist government. This position involved maintaining a degree of autonomy within the Eastern bloc and cultivating independent regional associations with other East European states as well as pan-continental ties with other European communist parties.[18] These ideas formed the core of the Romanian "third way" between high Stalinism and Hungarian "independence." And throughout the 1980s, "evidence" of Romanian independence was ubiquitous in party-state propaganda. Especially after Yugoslav leader Tito's death, Ceaușescu aspired to emerge as Eastern Europe's—and even the world's—primary spokesman for a global third-way movement (Deletant, *Ceaușescu and the Securitate* 324).

In contrast to the interwar right, which focused on the threat of modern life to the spirit, the protochronists' objectives complemented the foreign policy goal of raising Romania's international profile. Zamfirescu attempts to link Romania's cultural profile with its geopolitical clout:

> In the past ten years, the dynamism of economic and social
> life, and the powerful affirmation of Romania in the inter-
> national arena have created an acute interest in the past of
> our country, for the history, culture, and language of Ro-
> mania. The foreign consciousness, surprised at the coher-
> ence and maturity of a policy manifest so vigorously, looks
> for the historic roots for an explication of what is more and
> more often called the "Romanian phenomenon."
>
> (*Independență și cultură* 15)

---

[18] See Ashby Crowder, "Romanian Interpretations of the Prague Spring: Cadres, Diplomats, and the 1968 Crisis, Episode I," *Archives of Totalitarianism*, 2007.

In other words, an aspect of protochronism's politico-cultural project is to support the notion of Romania as a major player in world affairs.

The conclusions presented here do not dispute Verdery's contention that the "discourse on nationality" became, in the interwar years, "a basic ideological premise of all argumentation in Romania." This was indeed the case then, and it was also the case during the Ceauşescu years, as the protochronist phenomenon testifies. However, the two movements' conceptions of the Romanian nation's relationship to other parts of the world differ significantly (Verdery 63, 70–71). The very different thrusts of the writings of the interwar and the late communist periods suggest that drawing a direct line from the former to the latter would be at the very least an oversimplification. The interwar texts of the leading traditionalists make no pretenses about Romanian culture's contribution to world culture. Blaga, for example, considered Romania a great cultural contributor not unto others but unto itself. Crainic's and Rădulescu-Motru's writings show evidence of a fear and rage that is not at all a feature of protochronist writings, whose tone has more in common with the boilerplate official propaganda of their own era. Indeed, a number of the protochronists, including Purcaru, Ungheanu, and Zamfirescu, had served on the editorial boards of the Romanian party-state's propaganda organs. The more thoughtful and measured academic texts of Blaga can hardly be seen as the clear antecedents of protochronism, a movement deeply connected with Romania's particular place in Cold War geopolitics. Also notable is the complete absence of religious references in the protochronists' work. Orthodox Christianity had been, for so many interwar thinkers, at the very foundation of Romanian culture and identity.

It is possible to argue that protochronists necessarily had to cleanse interwar thought of its German association and its religious themes in order to rehabilitate it. But without the German and Christian Orthodox influences, the framework connecting the two movements is left threadbare. The ideological thrust of Romania's international strategy in the Cold War accounts for more aspects of protochronism than does the argument for intellectual continuity with pre-communist thinkers. Moreover, the interwar traditionalists could more correctly be called Europeanists inasmuch as they formed part of a Europe-wide intellectual phenomenon in the interwar period. The protochronists certainly did not—so innovative were they that a new word had to be introduced to explain what they were doing. It must be noted, however, that something akin to protochronism did develop in other Eastern bloc countries such as Albania and Bulgaria around the same time, although these phenomena were neither as developed nor as extreme as Romanian protochronism.[19] The fact that these countries did not have in their own public discussion about modernization in the interwar period a polemic as strong as the Romanian Great Debate only strengthens the argument for decoupling protochronism from interwar indigenism.

Another explanation for the way in which protochronists treat the interwar period must be faced. This alternative suggests that protochronists were consciously continuing the interwar debate and explained the resemblance away out of ideological necessity. This notion, while attractive, is not convincing. Protochronism repeatedly explains itself as being based on a rejection of what the interwar right stood for. It is more likely that the communist–nationalist nexus that was a feature of Ceauşescu-era Romania opened up a new kind of category of thought that we cannot properly understand by viewing it as a resuscitation of interwar polemic. Vlad Georgescu's comments on the pervasiveness of Ceauşist megalomania in all areas of discussion are informative:

> The people, the country, their history, they all lose their real dimensions, they explode in the universe, they are giganticized, all becomes epochal, historical, immense, without comparison, a model envied by others. [...] Under such a standard, any affirmation becomes possible.
>
> (77–78)

Just as Ceauşescu himself was neither a Bolshevik nor a fascist, the protochronist movement of the late Ceauşescu period had its own foundation particular to its era's cultural and political environment.

This study has argued against the prevailing interpretation that Ceauşescu-era protochronism and interwar indigenism are two manifestations of the same cultural phenomenon. While understanding these two movements as resurfacings of the same species of cultural

---

[19] See Ivanka N. Atanasova, "Lyudmila Zhivkova and the Paradox of Ideology and Identity in Communist Bulgaria," *East European Politics and Societies*, and Vesselin Dimitrov, *Bulgaria: The Uneven Transition* (1–2).

protectionism in different political environments may be tempting, a thorough look at indigenist and protochronist writings, combined with a consideration of the cultural and political environments in which they operated, exposes weaknesses in this standard view. First, the existing scholarship's labels such as "Europeanist" and "traditionalist" risk obfuscating more than they reveal, as interwar traditionalists were engaged in a broadly European debate about culture and modernity. Second, these "traditionalists" do not appear to have inspired the protochronists to anywhere near the degree the scholarship has asserted. As this essay has demonstrated, protochronists specifically rejected the ideas of the interwar right and made substantially different arguments about Romania's place in the world. Finally, the protochronists abandoned the interwar controversy over whether to draw on French or German inspiration. Scholars are inclined to look back in time to find the intellectual roots of later phenomena. We are less adept at recognizing a new phenomenon—one that is rooted in its own political and cultural epoch—when we see it. This essay has argued that protochronism is one such phenomenon.

Works Cited

Atanasov, Ivanka N. "Lyudmila Zhivkova and the Paradox of Ideology and Identity in Communist Bulgaria." *East European Politics and Societies* 18.2 (2004): 297–314.

Blaga, Lucian. *Trilogia culturii. 3 vols*. Bucharest: Humanitas, 1994.

Boia, Lucian. *History and Myth in Romanian Consciousness*. Budapest: Central European UP, 2001.

Bucur, Maria. *Eugenics and Modernization in Interwar Romania*. Pittsburgh, PA: U of Pittsburgh P, 2002.

Constantinescu, Miron, ed. *Istoria României: Compendiu*. Bucharest: Editura Didactică şi Pedagogică, 1969.

Crainic, Nichifor. *Puncte cardinale în haos*. Iaşi: Editura Timpul, 1996.

Cristea, Darie. "Sociologia vieţii intelectuale în România postbelică: dezbateri asupra chestiunii protocronismului." *Geopolitica* 2.4 (2004): 87–101.

Crowder, Ashby. "Romanian Interpretations of the Prague Spring: Cadres, Diplomats, and the 1968 Crisis, Episode I." *Archives of Totalitarianism* 15.56–57 (2007): 99–116.

Deletant, Dennis. *Ceauşescu and the Securitate: Coercion and Dissent in Romania, 1965*–1989. Armonk, NY: M.E. Sharpe, 1995.

_____. *Romania under Communist Rule*. Portland, OR: Center for Romanian Studies, 1999.

Dimitrov, Vesselin. *Bulgaria: The Uneven Transition*. New York: Routledge, 2001.

Georgescu, Vlad. *Politică şi istorie: cazul comuniştilor români 1944–1977*. Munich: Jon Dumitru Verlag, 1983.

Ghidirmic, Ovidiu. *Studii de literatură română modernă şi contemporană*. Craiova: Scrisul Românesc, 2002.

Glaser, Edwin. *Dreptul statelor de a participa la viaţa internaţională*. Bucharest: Editura Politică, 1982.

_____. *Statele mici şi mijlocii în relaţiile internaţionale*. Bucharest: Editura Politică, 1971.

Hitchins, Keith. *Rumania: 1866–1947*. Oxford: Clarendon P, 1994.

Livezeanu, Irina. "After the Great Union: Generational Tensions, Intellectuals, Modernism, and Ethnicity in Interwar Romania." *Proceedings of the International Symposium of the Center for the Study of the Imaginary, April 6–7, 2001: Nation and National Ideology: Past, Present, and Prospects*. Bucharest: Center for the History of the Imaginary, 2001.

_____. "Generational Politics and the Philosophy of Culture: Lucian Blaga between Tradition and Modernism." *Austrian History Yearbook* 33 (2002): 207–237.

Lovinescu, Eugen. *Istoria civilizaţiei române moderne*. Bucharest: Editura Ştiinţifică, 1972.

Lungu, Vasile. *Viaţa lui Tudor Vianu*. Bucharest: Editura Minerva, 1997.

Maier, Anneli. "Romanian 'Protochronism' and the New Cultural Order." *Radio Free Europe Background Report*. Nr. 226. 16 November 1977.

Mazower, Mark. *Dark Continent: Europe's Twentieth Century*. New York: Knopf, 1999.

Martin, Mircea. "Cultura română între comunism şi naţionalism." Pt. 2. *Revista 22* 660:44 (2002): 13: 660. http://www.revista22.ro/cultura-romana-intre-comunism-si-nationalism-ii-241.html.

Otovescu, Dumitru. *Cultură, personalitate, vocaţie: În concepţia lui C. Rădulescu-Motru*. Craiova: Scrisul Românesc, 1990.

Papu, Edgar. "Am o mare încredere în înzestrările excepţionale ale poporului roman." *Literatură şi naţiune*. Ed. Ilie Purcaru. Bucharest: Editura Eminescu, 1986: 82–94.

_____. *Din clasicii noştri: contribuţii la ideea unui protocronism românesc*. Bucharest: Editura Eminescu, 1977.

Petric, Aron. *Istoria României între anii 1918–1981: Manual universitar*. Bucharest: Editura Didactică şi Pedagogică, 1981.

Popescu, Titu, et al. "Tezele din iulie." *Revista Literară Vatra* 8 (2001): 31–66.

Purcaru, Ilie, ed. *Literatură şi naţiune*. Bucharest: Editura Eminescu, 1986.

Quinney, Anne. "Cultural Colonies: France and the Romanian Imagination." *Contemporary French and Francophone Studies* 11.3 (2007): 445–452.

Rădulescu-Motru, Constantin. *Etnicul românesc: comunitate de origine, limbă şi destin*. Bucharest: Editura Albatros, 1996.

Ştefănescu, Alex. "Edgar Papu." *România literară* 8 (2002): 10–11.

Teodorescu, Anda, and Andre Bantaş. *Romanian Essayists of Today*. Bucharest: Editura Univers, 1979.

Tişmăneanu, Vladimir. *Stalinism for All Seasons: A Political History of Romanian Communism*. Berkeley: U of California P, 2003.

Ungheanu, Mihai. "E captivant să urmărim literatura română în faza ei de proiect." *Literatura şi naţiune*. Ed. Ilie Purcaru. Bucharest: Editura Eminescu, 1986: 59–73.

Verdery, Katherine. *National Ideology under Socialism: Identity and Cultural Politics in Ceauşescu's Romania*. Berkeley: U of California P, 1995.

Zamfirescu, Dan. "Cultura română trebuie să folosească şansa de azi spre a deveni aluatul unei noi umanităţi." *Literatura şi naţiune*. Ed. Ilie Purcaru. Bucharest: Editura Eminescu, 1986: 130–139.

_____. *Independenţă şi cultură*. Bucharest: Editura Militară, 1977.

Isidore Isou's Spirited Letters

Jean-Jacques Thomas
University at Buffalo (SUNY)

It is paradoxical to consider that today Isidore Isou, probably one of the least-known Romanian-born French writers and philosophers could have become the most famous and most highly regarded Romanian intellectual of the twentieth century. It was probably his insatiable desire for public fame and recognition that prevented him from achieving such a destiny that would have placed him at least on a par with Tristan Tzara or Eugène Ionesco.

Isou was an extremely well-read intellectual—an indefatigable writer and thinker; in fact, there are very few aspects of human knowledge, be they letters, arts, or sciences that, at one point or another did not attract his intellectual attention and his knowledgeable study. Totally convinced of his own worth and exceptional nature, he compares in several essays his nature and intellectual status to that of Leonardo da Vinci, estimating even that his own capacity to construct a unified system of organization of human knowledge placed him above da Vinci who could only systematize and understand fragmentary aspects of the same.[1] For many of his contemporaries, it is this hubris (megalomania) coupled with a sharp and relentless criticism ("chiseling" would be his word in its literal sense) of the mediocrity of the other intellectuals, writers, and thinkers of the immediate post–WW II period in France that explains Isou's paradoxical status as a marginal intellectual generally at odds with the different intellectual and literary movements that span the period of 1945–1970 in France. Two terms are directly related to his early literary accomplishments and innovations: *lettrisme* [Letterism] and *métagraphie* [Metagraphy].

---

[1] "People have described Leonardo da Vinci's work as an ideal of intellectual totality. However, he only left us paintings, in which his contribution is merely a great figurative capacity […]. It was only after the death of this famous Renaissance artist that people discovered a trove of non-authenticated notes that were considered […] as pertaining to medicine, physics, technology […]. I believe I have […] produced more original revelations in more fields than Leonardo da Vinci" (Isou, *Créatique* 1110).

Isou was born Ioan-Isidor Goldstein on January 31, 1925, into a Jewish family in Botoșani, the main capital of the Botoșani county of the current Bucovina region, the northeastern part of Romania, near the border with Ukraine. As a city, Botoșani was an important Jewish center as, according to statistics from 1930, half the population of thirty-two thousand was of the Jewish faith. Ioan-Isidor was the only son of an upper-middle-class family who owned several grocery stores in town, and he had one older and one younger sister. The complicated history of the Bucovina region during WW II and the fact that this was the Romanian geographic area in which the Jewish deportation was the most important during the dictatorship of Ion Antonescu (1940–1944) explain why little is known of the actual circumstances of the Goldstein family during the war years. In addition, it is only clear that Ioan-Isidor was able to study assiduously and to acquire an excellent education at school and with the help of independent tutors. Botoșani, the largest center of trade in Moldavia, always had a rich international cultural life with a multitude of theatres, libraries, and art centers. It is in this context that Ioan-Isidor was able to read Mallarmé, Baudelaire, Balzac, Flaubert, and, under the guidance of an academic friend of the family, he had his first experiences of French theatre, French novels, and French poetry. As he narrated it in the "Introduction en forme de système autonome" of *Fondements pour la transformation intégrale du théâtre* [Prolegomenon to the Complete Transformation of Theatre], Ioan-Isidor wrote and produced several plays while in high school. According to his recollections, he was working feverishly on a major new play when, in 1944, the police of the Antonescu regime became suspicious of his membership in the Zionist movement Haschomer Hatzair, which was considered a cover for the underground Young Communist group. As it was believed that Ioan-Isidor would be questioned and eventually arrested, his family asked him to give all his papers to a neighbor in case a few of his notes contained suspicious political sentiments. Ioan-Isidor's mother, however, asked the neighbor to discreetly destroy the papers. Because of this destruction of his work, Ioan-Isidor broke violently with his family, and according to his memoirs, became the leader of the Zionist group right after King Michael's coup on August 23, 1944, which put an end to Antonescu's dictatorship and hastened the entry of the Red Army into Romania. Because by then the victory of the Allied Forces was a certainty, Ioan-Isidor, by personal ambition, in order to be able to come to France, became a member of the Young Communists. Through his relationship with the members of the still illegal Romanian Communist Party, at the end of 1944 he met with Ştrul Herş Moscovici (Serge Moscovici) who would also later immigrate to France and become a famed French social psychologist and director of the European Laboratory of Social Psychology. Together, they founded an artistic and literary review *Da*, which was almost immediately censored by the police of King Michael's new soviet regime. Ioan-Isidor immigrated to France during the summer of 1945 at age twenty through an international Zionist organization. By then, he had collected a large number of papers and documents. And, after publishing in 1946 "Appendice à la dictature lettriste" in which his new (1942) term "lettrism" appears, through his Zionist network he was able to meet with Jean Paulhan who by then had returned to Gallimard as the head of the *Nouvelle Revue Française*—a position of intellectual preeminence that he had left in 1940 at the beginning of WW II. It was nevertheless not with a book on theatre that Ioan-Isidor started his French career in 1947, but with a book on poetry: *Introduction à une nouvelle poésie et à une nouvelle musique*, a collection of notes dated from February 1941 to March 1944. From then on, designating himself as a "lettrist," he created a literary movement around this poetic system of sound poems based on a rhythmic and tonal system of combined phonemes represented by a transcription of Letterist graphics.

For this first Parisian publication, Ioan-Isidor had already adopted his newly naturalized French literary pseudonym: Isidore Isou. During his later years, he would reinstall Ioan as "Jean" and sign as *Jean Isidore Isou*. Yet, at this early stage of his French career, he only kept Isidore as a reference, in the French literary field, to the then still not well-known writer Isidore Ducasse, who, under the nom de plume, Comte de Lautréamont, was the author of the sulfurous *Les Chants de Maldoror* [The Songs of Maldoror] and who, prior to WW II, had been idolized by the Surrealist group.

Beyond the elementary idea that there was a need, in the immediate post–WW II world, to tone down his Jewish affiliation by abandoning the name Goldstein, there is no direct explanation for the choice of the pseudonym "Isou." There is a constellation of connotations that all point to the same attachment to the idea of centrality or preeminence. "Iso-" designates the first element, and through its

Greek etymology it refers to a broad concept of equilibrium, equality, and similarity, all classical qualities related to a vision or order (of the world, of a hierarchy, etc.). The name may also have been chosen because, through its Hebraic associations, it refers to a mystic paradigm of biblical rulers or prophets. The explanation is not too far-fetched for a reader familiar with Isou's constant proclamation of self-worth and affirmation of the exceptional quality of his creative powers: "Isidore Isou, with his mastery of the method of discovery, was becoming the master of innovators, and my system should have gained authority over all other forms of authority, as a never before seen agency of control and domination, justifying the reorganization *of all rules of causes and effects*" (Isou, *Créatique* 20). In Chapter II of *La Créatique ou la novatique* [Creationic or Novationic] devoted to a study of hyper-theology, Isou, often speaking of himself in the third person, elevates himself and his demiurgic work to a mystical level: "Isou believes that his writings will bring forth the reality of a felicitous world; they will transform the world into a state of ultimate happiness. They will reveal the meaning of the reigning Jew. They will help the realization of the Judaic messianic word. If Isou believes himself to be the Messiah, it is because in his Name by his work he will bring about in the human order the values that necessitate the third and last apparition. The most fundamental change in human perspective will lead to that universal divinity" (Isou, *Créatique* 296). This prophetic and pathetic rhetoric through which Isou elevates his literary pseudonym to a mystic and biblical level was already present in the fiction of his first *hyper-graphic* novel, *Les Journaux des Dieux*, published in 1950. The book is, in fact, a rewriting of the Bible by Isou and, while the original structure of the Old Testament is respected, the story is an epic chronicle, often burlesque, or trivial, or critical, of events that had affected Isou's life or Paris literary life in recent years. The word "journal" (newspaper) plays on the ambiguity, being at the same time a "diary" (a daily biography) as well as a daily paper, on the tabloid side, including nudity and sexuality. Nevertheless, the mystical dimension of the main characters is respected. In the chapter "La Postérité de Teroch" [The Posterity of Thare], one can find an actual picture of Isou in the hyper-graphic text and he becomes himself part of a holy divine Trinity (Figure 9.1).

If one remembers that Romania takes its name from the strong historical attachment to the Roman Empire and to the Latin language, it is philologically elementary to see the paradigm that unites the name "Jesus" to "Isou." In addition, Isou being a Letterist and thus using phonemes as the materials for his sound poetry, the connection between the two names must have been easy to decipher. Since the original Latin alphabet does not have the letter "J," it always appears under the form "I." The sound [y] that exists in French and other contemporary languages did not exist in Latin, as that sound is a remnant of the Celtic linguistic substratum; thus, the letter "u" would have been pronounced [u] so as to give the compound phonemic unit [izu] (Isou). While this is just a hypothesis, the presence in many parts of Isou's writing of an explicit mantic dimension attached to the name is, in my view, a clear indication of the mystagogic dimension that Isou wanted to give to his writing project. His writings are Holy Scriptures in the order of human knowledge; it is no leisurely activity. Writing has a purpose and a serious social and spiritual mission. In an interview with Roland Sabatier,[2] Isou confides that "Isou" was the (nick)name that his mother had given him and thus he adopted it as his name. It is possible that his mother used Isou as a term of endearment based on Isidore; however, this does not explain how it became the "Name" that would become the crucial object of the aggregation with the Messiah (Isou, *L'Agrégation*).

When Isou arrived in France in August 1945, in the immediate post-war period, intellectual life in Paris was in turmoil. The intellectual powers that had survived the German occupation of France found themselves to be out of favor, and many were accused of "collaboration." Those who had maintained a public presence under the Vichy regime, including popular newspapers, publishers, singers, and actors were put on trial; many were condemned to a self-imposed exile or they simply decided to abandon any form of public life. Paris's intellectual landscape appeared ready for a clean slate, and certainly the intellectual and media movements issued from the Résistance (Gaullist or Communist) decidedly seized the day and with new newspapers such as *Combat*, new journals such as *Les Temps modernes* and *Les Lettres Françaises*, the time was favorable for a total renewal of the intellectual hierarchy that would dominate the Parisian intellectual world. Even pre-war intellectual movements such as Surrealism,

---

[2] Published in *La Termitière*, no. 8, November 15, 1999.

whose principal members had been able to select exile (mostly in the US) were slow to reestablish themselves after four or five years of absence from Paris. The intellectuals, *issus de la Résistance*, progressively dominated on two fronts. The previously underground poetry of the Résistance (such as that of René Char) and the Existentialist philosophical group (around Sartre and de Beauvoir) rapidly dominated Paris's landscape. They established their new area of influence around the Saint-Germain-des-prés neighborhood, as during the war, the Occupation years, the two main cafés, Le Flore and Les Deux Magots, were the main public places where Sartre and de Beauvoir spent the day writing and meeting with their followers.

Figure 9.1. Isou, "Les Journaux des Dieux."

While these two groups were the central movers of the intellectual renaissance of post-war Paris, because of the brutal and systematic elimination of any past establishment, a large part of the intellectual Parisian universe was open to newcomers as long as they were untainted by participation in the intellectual scene of occupied Paris. With his credentials, his Zionist network, and his direct connection to a reinvigorated Gallimard publishing house now again under the leadership of Paulhan at the helm of the NRF, Isou was immediately accepted as a new figure of the intellectual Paris scene. And, with his natural taste for showmanship and intellectualism as performance, he was able to maintain his position as a key figure in Paris's new intellectual scene from 1946 to 1952. It was during this period that he established himself as the founder of Letterism, recruited disciples, and found the resources to develop theoretical interventions in the domains of poetry, fiction, theatre, and cinema. If one considers that his indisputable influence declined after 1953, it was because of his monomaniac desire to be recognized as the sole and uncontested leader of the true intellectual vanguard and his theoretical argumentative method that was almost exclusively polemical in nature. Once he had early assured his solid status as the founder of Letterism, it became a crusading mission for him to convince everyone that he was the only "novator," the only one capable of proposing and formulating new and unexplored directions for the development of contemporary intellectual life. This insatiable desire to be recognized as the sole agent of intellectual permanent invention led him to issue challenges to two main groups, first the Résistance poets and then the Existentialists.

Encouraged by the immediate success of his *Introduction à une nouvelle poésie et une nouvelle musique* and the popularity of his Letterist Manifesto (a strategy of occupation of the prime local intellectual territory directly borrowed from a similar campaign conducted by Breton and his Surrealist group in the early 1920s), Isou insisted that in this era of new intellectual beginnings the main project for poetry and arts and letters in general was to conceive a new understanding of literary form; thus, he was abrupt in rejecting what he perceived as a misguided modish interest for the poetry elaborated by writers of the nationalist underground during the German occupation. For him, this interest in theme and its denotative connotations (to resist the enemy, freedom, democracy, human dignity, justice, etc.) was too often presented as the heavy content of a poetry that was archaic in its poetic versification, poorly written stylistically, embedded in the most traditional fixed poetic forms, and, worst, totally devoid of any attempt to even consider the need to investigate new formalist solutions that would echo the semantic content calling for a change in the political status of a subjugated France. While these texts as content were clamoring for change, formally they were prototypical of the less desirable formal continuation of stale metrics and antiquated poetic models. This attack on the flag literature of the (by now heroic) Résistance years almost automatically created trouble for Isou with the Existentialist group with which many of the Résistance intellectuals were associated. According to his writings, Isou understood immediately how his status as an immigrant placed him in a position of inferiority in this debate with a group that had a special "untouchable" status in the post-war society of France. On the one hand, as a Jewish war refugee he appeared ungrateful to his benefactor country of asylum. Now, too, as his country of origin, Romania, was becoming perceived as a communist satellite country of the Soviet Union, he was perceived in certain circles of the former French Résistance as a subversive element with a political allegiance to the communist wing of the French Résistance. Yet, in fact, as a refugee who had actually lived under a communist regime, badly bruised by the brutality of its Soviet protector, he already had ambiguous feelings vis-à-vis the Soviet Russian communist regime while the position of the French Communist Party and its leader, Maurice Thorez, were still following a strict Stalinist line.

Nevertheless, true to what he perceived as his mission of intellectual truth as the only way to contribute to the creation and furthering of human knowledge, Isou found himself more and more involved in attacks against Sartre's Existentialism. During Isou's formative years in Romania, under the dictatorship of Antonescu, the philosophical teaching of Nietzsche and Heidegger (for Isou, unequivocally a "Nazi" philosopher) were encouraged; thus, Isou was able to define Sartre as an ersatz Heidegger and his Existentialism as a pale hybrid recombination of well-established philosophical theories: "The person whose main intellectual interest is in general existential metaphysics can only consider the French group that was formed after this war (Wahl, Sartre, Merleau-Ponty, etc.) as a mere secondary extension of the great German philosophical movement, as an effort of general vulgarization and an attempt to simply explore in detail limited aspects of the system whose masters and first class creators were, in Germany, Husserl, Heidegger, Jaspers" (Isou, *Pompiers du Nouveau* 17). Isou also came to attack Sartre's views on poetry and literature as misguided and elementary. The strongest criticism focuses on Sartre's "neo-naturalist" prescription that any novel be first and foremost a commitment to an "engagé" plot involving the place of man in his current social environment. (For the existential critic, the author is celebrated only if he is immersed in contemporaneity). Isou concluded his utter rejection of Sartre by indicating how irrelevant his views were in relation to Isou's own intellectual passions: "Sartre only pursues and talks about matters for which I do not give a damn" (Isou, *Pompiers du Nouveau* 18).

The attacks against Existentialism whose influence on the arts, politics, and philosophy was becoming an overwhelming force in France and in the post-war world was certainly damaging to Isou's own public and preeminent status. Almost immediately, his critical proclamations generated questions from these groups and their followers on the true "newness" of his invention of Letterism. It was suggested that movements such as Futurism with the typographic work of Iliazde and mostly early Dada, through the "phonetic" poems of Hausmann, Schwitters's "Ur Sonata," and the "poems to sing and dance" of Albert-Birot, had in fact "invented" what Isou had (falsely) presented as his innovative Letterism. To defend the integrity of his discovery, Isou had to show how Letterism was different from Dada's phonetism; he had to directly attack older, still-respected figures of the Dada/Surrealist period, in particular André Breton, who still maintained a certain influence on the Paris intellectual scene even if his movement was no longer in a vanguard position. Several of Isou's texts of the late 1940s and early 1950s were thus "distractions" not really devoted to the presentation of new developments but documents defending his invention and, often to the detriment of his reputation, describing the degradation of his relationship with previous supporters who were now attacking him. His *Réflexions sur M. André Breton* is certainly an example of this type of appalling polemic literature: "I know that all this is very petty, very low, but I had warned the reader that I would not elevate the debate higher than the level of the interlocutor, and that is very low" (Isou, *Réflexions* 21).

Isou's fall from Parisian grace and (according to his own metaphor in *Les Journaux des Dieux*) expulsion from the Latin Quarter's intellectual paradise came in 1952 when Paulhan refused to publish several of Isou's pieces in the NRF where he had been previously welcome. Following this rupture came an acerbic polemic. Paulhan went directly for the jugular indicating that he had "never learned anything new from Isou." Because Isou felt that any intellectual legitimacy he had was the result of his own exceptional capacity to invent new models of human knowledge and understanding in a world replete with copyists, followers, and epigones, he lashed back and presented Paulhan as the ultimate "grammarian," who could only repeat existing rules and principles and who could not recognize newness even if it were to hit him in the face: "Paulhan has never learned anything and he wants to offer the key of everything [...]. The Rimbauds always terrorize the Paulhans" (Isou, *Fondements* 23).

The final marginalization of Isou can be considered the result of his Romanian origins and the specific political perspective that his historical background had given him. As indicated, at the fall of the Antonescu regime, Isou confessed that his desire for expatriation and travel to Paris had led him to become politically involved with the Young Communists movement as a way to be part of the new political order and to put himself in a position to court political favors, including, eventually, authorization to leave Romania. His departure for France did not happen under these political circumstances; nevertheless, his probable political zeal, as the rest of his life demonstrates, facilitated his reading of the necessary political literature required to excel in the highly ideological regime newly established with the entrance of the USSR troops to Romania. Isou claims that, as a result, he familiarized himself with the political, economic, and social writings of Smith, Ricardo, Rodbertus, Menger, Engels, Marx, etc. This fast education as a social scientist led him to become an active member of the National Democratic Front (FND), a political party formed in October 1944 that involved the regrouping of the Communist Party and a few secondary "democratic" parties favorable to the communists and the Soviet administrators; the appointment of Petru Groza as prime minister in February 1945 signaled the triumph of the FND and the de facto communist takeover of Romania. By then, according to Isou's own work, he had become singularly disenchanted with the Marxist mentality and the limitations of "dialectical reasoning": "My friend [...] who had been incarcerated was only liberated when the Red Army arrived. Indoctrinated by his fellow prisoners he had become a *real* communist. When he was liberated we worked together for a few days at the FND. I did not want to stay in Romania and I was highly disgusted by the formulaic manner in which the 'dialecticians' were operating. My friend had become cynical and busy with menial daily activities like a grocer [Isou's family trade n.a.]. Nothing looks more like a grocery clerk than a member of the Communist party" (Isou, *Fondements* 11).

Based on his own experience as a youth in Romania and his reading of Carl Menger's theory of marginal utility, Isou proposed a system of early liberation of the youth in *Le Soulèvement de la jeunesse*, a study written, apparently in a rudimentary form, when he was fifteen and sixteen in Romania. According to him, young people are outside the market system, but nevertheless reduced in slavery through the work conducted within the family economy and rejected outside of the creative sphere, as they are forced to produce efforts through a hierarchical frame (school, family) with no direct impact on society as a whole but simply in relation to their own chance to "advance," "evolve, "and "become." It is remarkable that in the 1950s—before the baby boom of the next decade and the societal changes that would accompany it—Isou had come to understand the economic status of youth as an important political and social consideration. Isou had theorized the emancipation of a social category that, contrary to prior social analyses, was not (yet) fully recognized as an economic segment of production and consumption in Marx's and Menger's models. Isou sent an open letter to Jacques Duclos (then secretary general of the French Communist Party) and Florimond Bonté (a known pro-Soviet communist representative at the French National Assembly, mostly known for his opposition to the European construction debated at the time). The general topic of the letter was Isou's criticism of the lack of creativity, on many issues, including the question of the status of youth, of the French intellectuals who belonged to the French Communist Party. At the time when Isou was progressively being rejected from the dominant intellectual Parisian "bourgeois" intelligentsia, he could have chosen to progressively move towards the Communist Party, which, until the late 1960s, had real power within intellectual institutions such as the print media and the university. Isou certainly had intellectual knowledge and political experience that could have helped him achieve a position of power within the cultural apparatus of the Communist Party. There again, his passion for creation and his disdain for intellectuals who simply relied on the rhetoric and grammar of the accepted discourse prevented him from joining the communist group to maintain a certain power and preserve his intellectual status. Isou, in fact, did proclaim his contempt for Aragon: "I cannot be accused of liking Aragon very much" (Isou, *Réflexions* 13), certainly the most well-known and respected communist intellectual of the period; for Isou, Aragon was a "reactionary esthete" who published surrealist poetry and hid it under realistic declarations" (Isou, *Pompiers du Nouveau* 34). In the late 1950s, Isou's social, economic, and political views attracted new disciples to his Letterist group seminars and meetings.

It is always indicated in relation to Isou's biography and the history of Letterism that Guy Debord, who was one of the founders of the International Situationist Movement and wrote *La Société du spectacle* [The Society of the Spectacle] started his political and intellectual career within Isou's Letterist group of the early 1950s. ("The Internationale Situationniste was a small transnational group of artist-revolutionaries that came out of the neo-Dadaist Lettriste movement" (Hastings-King 26). If I have indicated that in the early 1950s Isou was indeed developing a social, political, and economic doctrine ("the future will recognize Isou as an economist even greater than Marx" [Lemaître, n.pag.]), it was, however, not the radical social aspect (which would become central for the Situationist Movement under the direct leadership of Debord during the 1962–1967 period) that brings Debord to Isou's Letterist movement. Instead, it was a common interest in experimental cinema. In April 1951, Isou presented his film *Traité de bave et d'éternité* [Venom and Eternity] and his film theory at the Cannes Film Festival (where Debord was then living), and on this occasion Isou and Debord met. In October 1951, Debord officially became a member of the Letterist group and at the 1952 Cannes Film Festival, all the Letterists including Debord and Isou signed the anti-commercial pamphlet *Fini le cinéma français* [No More French Cinema]. Later that year, Debord and several other members of the group secretly decided that Letterism should have a more international ambition than simply limiting itself to Paris and French intellectualism; thus, a sub-group, the International Letterism, was created within the main group without Isou's knowledge. Following the production and dissemination of Debord's first film, *Hurlements en faveur de Sade* [Howls for Sade], in June 1952, Debord met with the Belgian group Revolutionary Surrealism in Brussels and with the members of the sub-group International Letterism disturbed the press conference at which Chaplin was presenting his new film, *Limelight*. The founding Letterists, Isou, Pomerand, and Lemaitre, who were not aware that this action had been planned, publicly dissociated themselves from the public disturbance of the sub-group. And, as a result, in a paradoxical reversal, the members of the sub-group "excluded" them from Letterism and proclaimed their own legitimacy as the main Letterist movement under the title of "International Letterism." A mission document appeared in December 1952 ("Position de l'Internationale lettriste") in the very first issue of the newly created journal *L'Internationale Lettriste*; a founding conference for the movement took place in December in Aubervilliers near Paris; and, in January 1953, a Manifesto signed by twelve members appeared in the second issue of *L'Internationale Lettriste*. Thus, a more international and more politically revolutionary leftist Letterism started to exist in 1953 under the leadership of Guy Debord, but none of the founders of Letterism were part of it. In 1957, through the regrouping of three different European radical groups, *L'Internationale Lettriste* officially became *l'Internationale Situationniste*, a move that would favor the ascendency within the movement of the experimental social theorists to the detriment of the radical experimental artists. As a result, most of them left or were excluded from the new organization in the early 1960s. The social and economic activism of *L'Internationale Situationniste* is widely credited as the intellectual force that made the radical social upheaval of the student movement of May 1968 in France and Europe possible.

As can be deduced from this brief and somewhat reductive presentation, for a few years just after his arrival in Paris from Romania, Isou had become a star in the literary Parisian world of the then Saint-Germain-des-Prés. He was known and accepted as the founder of a new literary movement, Letterism. Within five years, though, his social and intellectual status had fallen considerably, and in 1953, he could only watch in humiliation, as the movement he had created was taken away from him to become something he could only condemn (*Contre l'Internationale Situationniste* 2001). It is ironic to consider that his fate is strangely similar to that of Tzara, another Romanian-born French intellectual who came to Paris in 1921: originally celebrated as the creator of Dada, Tzara found himself three years later upstaged by Breton, who had joined him as a Dada convert. The poetic similarity in destiny is even more striking if one considers that the first victim of Isou's desire for Parisian fame was Tzara himself.

Right after his arrival in Paris, on January 21, 1946, as Pomerand narrates the story, Isou went to the Vieux-Colombier Theatre, where Tzara's play *La Fuite*, directed by Lupovici and preceded with a presentation by Michel Leiris was being premiered in the presence of Tzara himself. In the purest provocative Dada fashion, the Letterists who were there interrupted Leiris by shouting "We know about Dada, M. Leiris—tell us about something new! For example—letterism! Dada is dead! Letterism has taken its place! Let's hear the Letterists!" Paradoxically, Tzara's lyrical play is about two themes that could not leave Isou indifferent: exile, as it is a departure, a severing of old ties, and the passing of generations, a new one always replacing the previous. Since Leiris did not know anything about Letterism, he finished his presentation and, after the play, Isou jumped on stage to present his ideas and read a few Letterist poems. The next day, *Combat* ran a story about the Letterist public disruption of the previous night and so, in early 1946, Letterism took center stage in Paris (Leiris, *Brisées* 96–100).[3]

Even after being eclipsed in the public eye after 1953, Isou continued to pursue his *novatique* [innovative] and *créatique* [creative] work, investigating newness in many branches of knowledge all at once. During the fifty-four years until his death (2007), Isou endlessly tried to fulfill his goal of covering all the branches of human knowledge in order to discover the unique principle governing the general rules of the universe. According to him, the governing principle is that the universe does not like stagnation and thus the only responsibility of special beings is to invent and create. In 2003, the publishing house of Al Dante (Paris), known for its support of the most extreme contemporary vanguard publications, released Isou's *La Créatique, ou la novatique: 1941–1976*, a 1,390-page book that can be considered the sum of his reflections on the question of the creation. The endeavor is exceptional, as publishers usually consider the publication of a book longer than five hundred pages to be a dangerous project. The situation was even more astonishing at the time because, on this very question, a serious quarrel between the publishing

---

[3] In his personal diary, Leiris, on March 10, wrote: "Plusieurs camouflets ces temps derniers: chahut 'lettriste' au Vieux-Colombier pendant que je lisais ma présentation de la pièce de Tzara (j'ai pu sauver la face, mais je sais bien qu'il s'en est fallu de fort peu pour que je ne tienne pas le coup) [...]" (Leiris, *Journal* 427).

house Le Seuil and one of its most well-known writers, Jacques Roubaud, had become public. Roubaud had proposed a six-hundred-page manuscript as the fifth installment of his autofiction "le grand incendie de Londres," [The Great Fire of London], and it had been refused with the recommendation that the final published text (the "version mixte") be around three hundred pages. The contrast between the two situations, especially considering the difference in social capital of the two writers in Parisian circles at the time, demonstrates Al Dante's confidence in Isou's book and its ability to find a proper readership despite its complexity and the idiosyncratic vocabulary and high conceptualization of its author. The magnitude of the publishing project revealed a high degree of respect for the integrity of his work and treats *La Créatique, ou la novatique* as an important intellectual contribution to human knowledge at the beginning of the twenty-first century, when certain intellectuals of the preceding century, Schwitters, Hausmann, Etiemble, to cite only a few, with whom Isou had acrimonious polemical battles early in his career, were almost completely forgotten.

To conclude, it seems thus fitting, to go beyond the totalizing scope of Isou's project and without necessarily accepting his positional principle that human knowledge should always be envisioned with a view to the globality of its branches (kladology) to consider some of the contributions that Isou's work has made. That is, in some domains, Isou's work has proven helpful and visionary. Further, it is still highly contemporary.

Three domains of art, literature, and society have been directly and durably impacted by Isou's ideas: sound poetry ("Letterism" proper), experimental cinema, and the discourse of reality. This distinction between three domains exists only to facilitate the presentation of the arguments; in fact, today, in a theoretical approach there is a need to address these questions in a unified way. Isou himself would have considered that the unified way is the only way to approach any question of human knowledge, since no aspect of human knowledge is an "organism" in itself but simply a "branch" of a global system.

While I have no position vis-à-vis Isou's central kladological doctrine, my claim that even if these three domains constitute separate intellectual entities they should be looked at *in fine* as fields related by an underlying common problematics about twenty-first-century collective expressiveness. Isou's views in the early 1950s anticipated this contemporary discussion because he was notably the first intellectual to insist on their connection and to insist that all three have something to do with what could be called "expression as plasticity." In his approach to each of these three domains, Isou attempted to modify the established linguistic frame of common communication and to invent new ways by which human communication could go beyond words, beyond established conventional signs, and construct a highly creative interpersonal understanding based on the de-semantization of human language and its functional transformation into an uncanny configuration of material shapes immediately capable of conveying the necessary significance in a non-verbal way.

Letterism

During their first year in Zürich, the members of the newly created Dada group had to find acts for their daily show at the Cabaret Voltaire.[4] Early on, they resorted to the production of sound poems as the Futurists had started to do before WW I ("motlibrist" by Marinetti, etc.). Dada systematized the principle and invented at least four recognized ways to perform a sound poem (non-semantic): bruitist poem, phonic poem, simultan poem, and exotic poem. For this performed non-sensical poetry, the minimal unit was the phoneme. Several of these poems have been transcribed and several are well known, such as "Karawane" (1920) and "Poem Without a Title" (1919) by Raoul Hausmann; "L'amiral cherche une maison à louer" [The Admiral Is Looking for a House to Rent] (1916) by Huelsenbeck and Tzara; and "Ursonate" (1926) by Schwitters. Any transcription of these sound poems would deliver an apparently haphazard collection of *letters*, apparently organized at random, as the sound poem (by principle an a-semantic construct) cannot be based on accepted words (Figure 9.2).

Isou's 1942 Letterism certainly built on that existing legacy in order to establish his own theory and movement. Isou's Letterist poems may appear, at first glance, very similar, as final printed products, to the sound poems of the Dadaists who had engaged in similar language exploration twenty years earlier; letters seem to be distributed

---

[4] For details regarding the poetic inventiveness of Dada in Zurich, Paris, New York, and Berlin, etc., see the chapter "Dada Means Nothing" in my book co-authored with Steven Winspur, *Poeticized Language*.

Lanke trr gll

P P P P P

oka oka oka oka

Lanke trr gll

pi pi pi pi pi

züka züka züka züka

Lanke trr gll

rmp

rnf

Lanke trr gll

Figure 9.2. Schwitters, "Poème sans titre," 1923.

9. — *LARMES DE JEUNE FILLE*
— *POÈME CLOS* —

M dngoun,m diahl ⊖hna iou
hsn ioun inhlianhl ſipna iou
vgain set i ouf! sai iaf
fln plt i clouf! mglai vaf
ℕ'o là ihi cnn vii
snoubidi i pnn mii
A'gohà ihihi gnn gi
klnbidi ∆'bliglihli
H'mami chou a sprl
scami Bgou cla ctrl
gué el inhi ni K'grin
Khlogbidi Σ'vi binci crin-
cncn ff vsch gln ié
gué rgn ss ouch clen dé
chaig gna pca hi
⊖'snca grd kr di

Figure 9.3. Isou, "Larmes de jeune fille–poème clos" ("L'Agrégation" 323).

at random to produce a phonic ensemble that is not part of the graphic compound recognized by any given dictionary as an established word immediately interpretable by a linguistic community (Figure 9.3).

Looking uncritically at this graphic ensemble, as a "bag" of letters, it is thus easy to understand the severe criticism that Isou encountered in the early 1950s and the accusation of plagiarism that was voiced vis-à-vis his main poetic early work by former Dadaists and contemporary critics familiar with the Dada phonetic production of the 1920s. This graphic ensemble is nevertheless not the only "text" that was printed. Secondary symbols appear in the text, and a code is given that regulates other aspects of the phonic performance: tone, accentuation, speed, pitch, vital sounds, etc. (Figure 9.4).

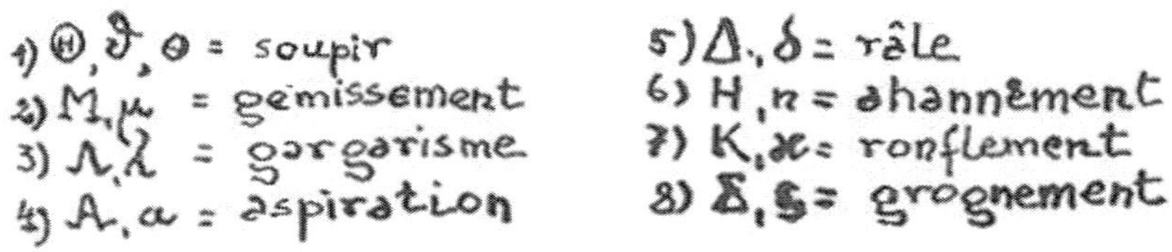

1) $\oplus, \vartheta, \theta$ = soupir   5) Δ, δ = râle
2) M, μ = gémissement   6) H, κ = ahannement
3) Λ, λ = gargarisme   7) K, $\varkappa$ = ronflement
4) A, α = aspiration   8) δ, ς = grognement

Figure 9.4. Isou, "Larmes de jeune fille–poème clos" ("L'Agrégation" 323).

Also, I have chosen a model of poem very similar in its free flow to the typography and *dispositio* of the Dada model provided by Schwitters's model; however, other Letterist poems by Isou and the other Letterists show a constricted systematization based on repetitive paradigmatic patterns and highly constructed phonetic combinatorics (Figure 9.5).

Obviously, even in "Ur Sonate" by Schwitters, incontestably the most complex and sophisticated sound poem of the Dada period, one cannot find this degree of systematization (lasting many pages for each poem) and this type of multilevel composition that develops an expressive construct for the whole performance.

It is precisely these two characteristics, systematization or the organization of the sound system and complexity of the expressive composition, that allow Isou to make his case for originality. His argument is that when Dada was creating its sound poems based on the sound of the poem, the activity was its own end: for Dada the goal was to ensure the collapse of communication as it had led to the destruction of WW I. To reduce signs to their meaningless and empty sounds was akin to bringing humanity back to the level of the primal

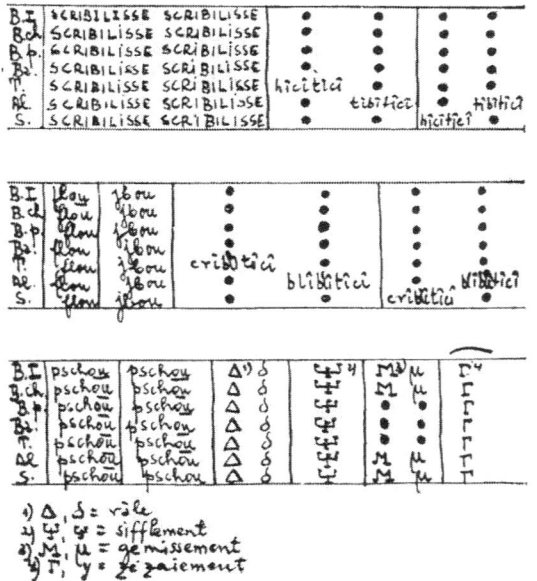

Figure 9.5. Isou, "1ère symphonie" ("L'Agrégation" 371).

cry. The act of destroying language was used as the allegory for the collapse of the "civilized" world. The production of sound poems outside of any context of interpersonal communication was fundamentally a nihilistic gesture. On the contrary, for Isou, Letterism is a positive and optimistic endeavor in the sense that it is an innovative process by which mankind can develop new means of communicating not necessarily based on the structure of the linguistic sign. Certainly, letters are used as units of sound production, but they are no more than the musical notes on a music score. The second argument used by Isou to establish his originality is the intellectually rigorous conception of the Letterist principle of systematization. While "chance encounter" was the principle mostly invoked by the Dadaists to validate their composition, Isou bases his Letterist composition on number and rhythm. Letterist poems become akin to composing music, and this is the reason for the title of Isou's first book: *Introduction à une nouvelle poésie et à une nouvelle musique.* For Isou, Letterism requires a fundamental competence to read expressively out loud: "Between the man who does not know how to vocalize correctly and the Letterist poem there is an impassable obstacle akin to a concrete wall!" (Isou,

L'Agrégation 293). Performing a Letterist poem is not "amateur night" as many of these Dada evenings at the Cabaret Voltaire seem to have been.

Because Letterist poetry accepts the principle of free verse, the poetic music of Letterist poetry is atonal in nature. The melodic aspect of traditional and well-established poetry ("amplic" in Isou's vocabulary) is replaced by an emphasis on the rhythm that is articulated on the distribution of internal sound blocks similar to what the rhyme was in the old system. (This reuse under a different compositional principle of a component of "amplic" poetry outside its original context is recognized by Isou as a "chiseling" principle of the new Letterist composition; in terms of contemporary theory that would be a case of "deconstruction.") In order to elaborate the system of sound repetition in a way that will nevertheless favor diversity, variety, and different modes of expressivity, Isou proposes a set of constraining "rules" that will achieve the best possible composition: "Rules about internal rhymes," "Rules about rhythmic groups," "Rules regarding consonants and vowels," etc.

Because the final production of a Letterist poem is always a collection of letters organized in a certain order on a page, the text can be "read" in a simple graphic manner; thus, certain Letterist poems have achieved notoriety, not because they have been vocally performed, but because of the quality of their graphic design (Figure 9.6).

In recent years, public urban graffiti has often been considered a dominating form of social and collective Letterist expression and more and more the graphic aspect of Letterism is used as a stylistic system of abstract representation. Also, through the New Letterist International movement, Hurufism (the graphic art related to the Arabic alphabet) has been associated with contemporary Letterism.

Experimental Cinema

It is often considered that the Nouvelle Vague directors such as Godard, Truffaut, and Rohmer invented modern French cinema in the late 1950s and early 1960s. It is thus astonishing, now that these "experimental" and confidential films by Isou and Debord are becoming more accessible, that in the early 1950s the revolution and experimentation had already started in French film. In *À bout de souffle* [Breathless] by Godard (1960), Belmondo walking the streets of Paris, alone

Figure 9.6. Isou, "Self-portrait," 1952.

or with Jean Seberg, is a moment of film anthology as it shows the commitment of the French New Wave to shoot outside of the studio setting and its indisputable eagerness to capture the outside world (sounds and sights) in a light style that represents wandering in the city and participation in city life as a daily cinematographic event. It is thus stunning to discover that during the entire first part of Isou's first long film, *Traité de bave et d'éternité* (1951), the camera follows Isou as he wanders through the familiar streets of the Parisian Latin Quarter and in particular the Bonaparte Street part of the Saint-Germain-des-prés area that was precisely, during these early years of the 1950s, the nervous system of post-war Parisian intellectualism (Figure 9.7).

In the first part of the movie, Isou expresses several of his innovative and creative ideas about cinema, photography, movement, images, and the development of a visual culture that he hopes to harness through his "méca-estheticism" to give his contemporaries "headaches" for thinking rather than simply falling victim to casual eye fatigue. And, certainly, Isou's first film is the antinomy of an

*Figure 9.7. Isou wandering at Saint-Germain-des-prés
in "Traité de bave et d'éternité," 1951.*

escapist movie. The film constantly challenges the spectator and
through theory and practice imposes a frustrating evaluation of what
film and cinema could be as instruments of discovery, as means that
would allow access to expressive newness since Isou insists that cinema is there to challenge our *passéisme*, our complacency.

Two concepts deserve particular attention as they are presented
here for the first time, though they will become ordinary components
of the vulgate of experimental films. First, Isou demands the realization of "discrepant" films, i.e., films in which there is a disconnect
between the sound and the image. This way we will not simply follow
the image but we will have to pay (separate—and he hopes more intense) attention to the discourse present on the sound track. In fact, the
first sequence of the movie is a direct practice of that principle: while
we follow Isou wandering the Paris streets, the soundtrack transports
us to an unruly public meeting of the Letterist group during which
Isou exposes a few of his ideas to a resisting audience that disrupts his
speech, challenges his propositions, insults him, and treats his remarks
on the vanguard of film and cinema with ridicule. The contrast is
powerful because within the constructionist discrepancy between
sound and image the film is actually performing what the speaker is
advocating. The "discrepant" technique appears in many variations in
"vanguard" films of the period including at the beginning of *À bout de
souffle* when Belmondo is seen driving his "belle américaine" on the
N7 road and abruptly stops watching the road to turn sideways ninety
degrees toward the (not present in the film) camera and addresses a
few comments directly to the spectators about the necessity of

Figure 9.8. "Détournement" of a military ceremony in French Indochina and "chiseling" in the film stock in "Traité de bave et d'éternité," 1951.

choosing between sea, countryside, and mountains, as the best place to take a vacation. In this case, the dialogue has absolutely nothing to do with the action depicted by the images of the film. The second concept proposed by Isou is the necessity of including pre-existing materials in the film (clips of other films, images, etc.) and to simply offer them visually as gratuitous images totally decontextualized from their original source and integrated in an awkward fashion in the new film. This technique will be known as "détournement" (Figure 9.8). As in the case of discrepancy, this second recommendation is used extensively in the second part of the film, which contains sequences apparently borrowed mostly from newsreels: workers in factories, school, sports events, and several sequences about the French occupation of Indochina. In addition to these two techniques, throughout the film, Isou imposes Letterist recitation (accompanied by a white or black screen and the spectator can see the letters related to the poem appear in a fashion today reminiscent of texts readable on a large screen during public sessions of karaoke). Also, often, the images that come from a détournement effect have been physically modified as the film or the still images have been scratched or etched so that letters, numbers, and other symbols can appear as moving signs on the screen as the film is presented. These alterations are part of the necessary elevation to newness recommended by Isou as a chiseling of the old to create the new. At the same time, these are experiments in visual graphism through which the conventional design of the socially accepted letters becomes something else, a sign in evolution.

Many of these cinematographic effects were to be copied by the other Letterists involved with cinema. In particular, after he joins the Letterist movement, Debord will experiment with them in his first film *Hurlements en faveur de Sade* (1952), which exaggerates the black screen of the first twelve minutes of Isou's *Traité de bave et d'éternité* (it will be extended to most of the duration of the film with the exception of a burst of white light). Debord also uses the principle of the détournement technique (as his next films include clips borrowed from films made by other directors), but, while Isou gives an aesthetic dimension to the process (he uses the existing amplic film copia, and deconstructs—chisels—it to produce something new), Debord gives the process a "revolutionary" economic and social dimension by "recycling" what exists without acknowledging previous ownership and rights; things are there to be used, copied, and integrated at will in new constructions without consideration for a possible capitalistic conflict of interest.

Plasticity and Vision of the Upcoming Visual Turn

Very early in his Parisian career Isou proclaimed that "In order to create, one has to be situated at the very vanguard of the vanguard of research and of the modern works" (Isou, *Créatique* 23). As an illustration of his own exceptionally advanced intellectual position in the domain of poetry, he proposed this schema of the evolution of French poetry (and thus of the world's poetry, as he totally shared the view that Paris was the intellectual capital of the world) (Figure 9.9) for what was then for him the last century (Baudelaire's *Fleurs du mal* was first published in 1857).

In this schema, one can recognize Isou's view that literary movements during the history of humanity start with an innovator (here Baudelaire is credited with that status) and then go through a phase of development (the amplic period) during which the ideas put forth by the innovator are exploited differently and amplified by followers, until the movement has exhausted its capacity to expand and it is necessary for a new innovator to intervene and to create the means of the development of a new amplic phase. In this case, Isou designates himself as the innovator acting in his capacity as the one placed by nature, fate, and destiny at "the vanguard of the vanguard." With

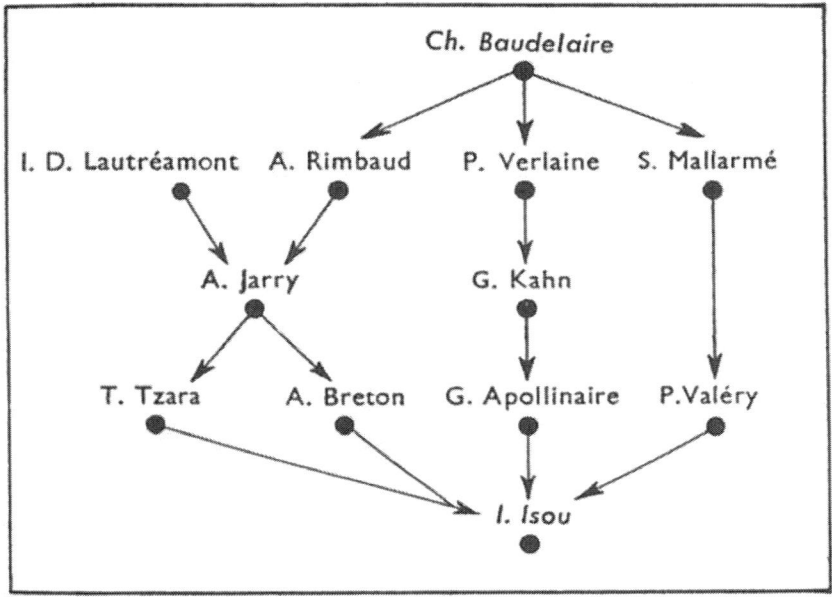

Schèma I : L'évolution spirituelle de la poésie.

Figure 9.9. French poetic evolution since Baudelaire
according to Isou ("L'Agrégation" 32).

the benefit of fifty more years to look at the subsequent evolution of French poetry and the evolution of the theory that has developed, it is appropriate to admit that Isou in his theoretical writings and in a few of his actual poetic works offered certain propositions that are in line with the current reflections of the extreme contemporary creative movement. It is also necessary to acknowledge that this convergence of views exists mostly with no direct influence of Isou on the field and in total ignorance of Isou's theories given his marginal status vis-à-vis the French intelligentsia and the lack of recognition afforded him by the majority of influential intellectual institutions such as the publishing houses, the media, and the universities.

Isou was working in a very different world and if, today, there is the possibility of recognizing a visionary dimension to his ideas and work, it is entirely due to his analytical skills and his own individual capacity of understanding. Thus, while it is difficult to consider him the prophetic innovator of things to come in the formulation of poetry, it is not far-fetched to include his vision as part of the collection of pertinent ideas that have led to the current thinking of the vanguard (under its present label of "extreme contemporary") about the status of poetry and its necessary reformulation in this age of the "visual turn."

Today with images as the ever-present representational surroundings of everyday life, social and aesthetic theoreticians consider that our contemporaneity can be defined as a mostly visual symbolic space. While articulated language is still present as a major source of information and knowledge, it is being increasingly replaced by plastic representations attached to realist or abstract images that become the primary blocks of memory and that complement each other, in a somewhat warehouse fashion, to organize our perception of the world and its hierarchy of values. We no longer rely on the assimilation of discourses, verbal definitions that include their own rhetorical and argumentative structures of understanding and ethical, social, and aesthetic commandments. Plasticity has become the organizational order of our understanding. With the pun intended, it should be recognized that Isou had long perceived the *letter* of that type of future, if not its spirit. The limited universe in which he lived with the daily restrictions imposed by the scarcity of goods at the end of WW II did not allow him to remotely imagine the image technology that is our daily environment. Also, while he was very much a man of the book, we live now, according to contemporary philosophers such as Derrida, in an era that can be defined as the "end of the book."

The 1942 Letterist Manifesto offers as its primary concept the destruction of the *word* as the main unit of the poetic piece. The poem should no longer be understood as a collection of words, but it becomes a "lettrie," a collection of letters assembled in a certain order in order to represent the sound patterns to be performed out loud. Isou was writing before the structuralist movement (he provided a few uncomplimentary comments on Barthes's *Le Degré zero de l'écriture* (1953), but the general movement passed him by); therefore, he had a very non-technical use of the term "sign." Thus, he could not propose that his Letterism was displacing the question of the expression of poetry from the plane of the "signified" to the "signifier," be it graphic (letters) or phonic (the sound system of the performance). Today, it is easy to recognize that this systematized and theorized removal of poetry from the universe of signification to the more contemporary world of significance was a decisive step into the future and in what is still our intellectual and aesthetic universe. Once Isou had advocated a universe of expression not based on semantics, he understood that it was his responsibility to explore how poetic significance should be produced. His book, *Introduction à une nouvelle poésie et à une nouvelle musique*, probably under the influence of previous work by Mallarmé and the Symbolists, looked at solutions in the world of music. The day-to-day practice of composing Letterist poems, however, because it forced him to reflect on issues directly related to graphic expressivity, led Isou to the conviction of the importance of poetic graphic plasticity. In other words, poetry is no longer a question of linguistic or neo-rhetorical established forms (verses, rhymes, fixed forms, word choices, syntactic arrangements, etc.); instead, it becomes a question of physical and material shape. Once, as Isou does, letters are removed from the coercive structure of the word and from the functionality of language, they become graphical artifacts and simple iconographic motifs that can be shaped in many different ways and organized in a multi-dimensional space. They become commodities of a visual system under the rules governed by aesthetic plasticity. While Letterism was conceived as a new poetic movement in which poetry should be heard, its ultimate expansion, and its current contemporaneity, is its ability to take place in an overwhelming visual universe that is everywhere to be seen. Isou should be fully credited for understanding that potential visual dimension of poetry and for offering preliminary reflections on that dimension that time has proven insightful and still relevant to today's poetics: "Today poetry, tired of the old format, invents new models (forms). Letterism, by creating a new plastic matter that cannot enter into the old poetic mold, will have, through trial and error, to develop a new mold. […] Like the plastician who can rely on so many materials, like the music composer who relies on so many instruments and voices, poetry will collect a new material compound available for its new composition. After the words, letters will lead to new forms" (Isou, *L'Agrégation* 27).

Isou's early understanding of the graphic and visual dimension of future poetic expression will lead, later in his life, to his proposal of a new graphic system that will encompass all forms of aesthetic expressiveness. The Metagraphy (métagraphie) first imagined as a phonetico-pictographic way to go beyond the original graphic system solely conceived around the physical shape of the letter as a transcription of a sound, will become, for Isou, a "global system of *écriture*" destined to trace and memorize the contours of human experience and knowledge. This last claim remains to be proven, but, as the recent publication of Isou's intellectual works by the publisher Al Dante demonstrates, fifty years after Isou's first Parisian appearance, his work still earns him a place at the very core of the most extreme contemporary Parisian reflections on poetry and symbolic representation.

Works Cited

Barthes, Roland. *Le Degré zéro de l'écriture*. Paris: Le Seuil, 1953.

Debord, Guy. *La Société du spectacle*. Paris: Champ Libre, 1967.

Hastings-King, Stephen. L'Internationale Situationniste, Socialisme ou Barbarie, and the Crisis of the Marxist Imaginary. *SubStance* 28.3, 1999. 26–54.

Isou, Isidore [Ioan-Isidor Goldstein]. *L'Agrégation d'un nom et d'un messie*. Paris: Gallimard, 1947.

_____. *La Créatique, ou la novatique: 1941–1976*. Paris: Al Dante, 2003.

_____. *Fondements pour la transformation intégrale du théâtre*. Paris: Bordas, 1953.

_____. *Introduction à une nouvelle poésie et à une nouvelle musique*. Paris: Gallimard, 1947.

_____. *Les Journaux des Dieux*. Paris: Aux escaliers de Lausanne, 1950.

_____. *Les Pompiers du Nouveau Roman. Lettrisme* 17, 1971.

_____. *Précisions sur ma poésie et moi*. Paris: Aux Escaliers de Lausanne, 1950.

_____. *Réflexions sur M. André Breton*. Paris: Editions Lettristes, 1948.

_____. *Le Soulèvement de la jeunesse*. Paris: Aux Escaliers de Lausanne, 1949.

Leiris, Michel. *Brisées*. Paris: Gallimard, 1966.

_____. *Journal 1922–1989*. Paris: Gallimard, 1992.

Lemaître, Maurice. Préface-défi de l'éditeur-métagraphe. *Les Journaux des Dieux*. By Isidore Isou. Paris: Aux Escaliers de Lausanne, 1950. n.pag.

Thomas, Jean-Jacques, and Steven Winspur. *Poeticized Language: The Foundations of Contemporary French Poetry*. University Park: Penn State P, 2000.

Emile Cioran and the Politics of Exile

Anne Quinney
University of Mississippi

Emile Cioran, the Romanian philosopher who lived in France from the late 1930s until his death in 1995, devoted his life to what American novelist and critic William Gass was quoted as calling "a philosophical romance on modern themes of alienation, absurdity, boredom, futility, decay, the tyranny of history, the vulgarities of change, awareness as agony, reason as disease" in the *New York Times* obituary of Cioran ("E.M. Cioran, Novelist and Philosopher of Despair").[1] The subjects of the void, suffering, and nothingness were the impetus behind Cioran's autobiographically inspired, highly eccentric literary production. His interviewers, biographers, and close friends spoke of him as "obsessed with the worst," "misanthropic," "insolent," and a "brilliant rebel" for awakening his readers to the "nothingness of human existence" ("E.M. Cioran"). Elsewhere, he is described as a "champion of pessimism" and an "anti-prophet of universal disenchantment" (Vernescu 73). Edward Said called him "a mocking ghost of all traditions" and considered him a fanatic without convictions (29).

With statements such as, "l'unique moyen de sauvegarder sa solitude est de blesser tout le monde, en commençant par ceux qu'on aime" [the only way to ensure one's solitude is to wound the world, beginning with those one loves] (*IEN* 121), it is no surprise that he was left, in the end, with few friends and peers among the literati in Paris.

A self-identified exile and iconoclast whose work varies in form from meandering philosophical essay to terse aphorism, Cioran refused to belong to any literary or philosophical movement in France although he lived in the heart of the literary sixth *arrondissement* in Paris for over fifty years and counted Eugène Ionesco and Samuel

---

[1] I am grateful to Yves Gaonac'h at the Bibliothèque littéraire Jacques Doucet for allowing me access to the Cioran documents.

Beckett among his friends. He preferred solitude to affiliation and cultivated a reputation for mystery and notoriety as a literary genius, a Romanian transplant, and a misanthropic "penseur d'occasion" [second-hand thinker] (Bollon 32). His uncertain status as either a philosopher or as a French literary stylist has also put into question his position in twentieth-century French literary history. Readers and critics have found his work inaccessible, often dismissing it on the basis of its futile pessimism or for its *illisibilité* (a reference to the proliferation of paradox and contradiction in his aphorisms). How to categorize him has as much to do with what he writes as how he writes, in other words, the form he chooses to express his bitter thoughts. Cioran employed short essays and aphorisms to affirm, sometimes in the same sentence, the most disturbing illusions and the most extreme lucidity, the mystical power of revelation and an attachment to materialism, and the most primitive recourse to instinctual drives along with the search for universal wisdom. On the one hand, Patrice Bollon, author of *Cioran, l'hérétique*, sees Cioran as definitely not a philosopher but as a "penseur des caprices" [whimsical thinker] (32), one who does not respect the implicit rules of philosophy as a systematic structure of thought. For Susan Sontag, on the other hand, Cioran reflects more than anyone since Kierkegaard or Wittgenstein the state of modern philosophy, that is, a discipline that no longer rests on establishing authority or universals and whose single rhetorical mode is auto-destruction: "Philosophy becomes the activity of a tortured mind, of a mind that devours itself, and which continues intact, moreover blossoms, despite or perhaps because of this repeated self-cannibalism" (Sontag 11).[2]

Controversy surrounding Emile Cioran has not, however, been limited to debates about the validity of his status as a philosopher. Revelations about his experiences in Romania in the early part of this century have shattered the image of the reclusive, timid philosopher whose self-imposed solitude and obscurity elicited unquestioned re-

_____

[2] Sontag's essay appeared as the Introduction to *The Temptation to Exist*. Here she writes, "One response to the collapse of philosophical system-building in the nineteenth century was the rise of ideologies—aggressively anti-philosophical systems of thought, taking the form of various "positive" or "descriptive" sciences of man. […] Another response to the debacle was a new kind of philosophizing: personal (even autobiographical), aphoristic, lyrical, anti-systematic. Its foremost exemplars: Kierkegaard, Nietzsche, and Wittgenstein. Cioran is the most distinguished figure in this tradition writing today" (11).

spect among the reading public. Much attention has been accorded to his experiences in Romania in the early part of this century.[3] More precisely, his participation in the Iron Guard movement, a proto-fascist, anti-democratic movement inspired by mysticism and German National Socialism that reached its zenith during his adolescence and years as a college student in Bucharest, has caused a buzz of specula-tion and outrage. Cioran may not have been a member of Corneliu Codreanu's Iron Guard, a movement described as "one of the oldest, most obscurantist and mystical, the most murderous in the physical sense of the word, that history has ever known in this category of po-litical movements."[4] What is certain, though, is that "il a vécu in-tensément le phenomène légionnnaire" [he experienced intensely the legionnaire phenomenon] (Mutti 105) as expressed by the author of one study of fascism's influence over young Romanian intellectuals in the 1930s. The extent to which he became an enthusiast of the move-ment serves as an important metric for Cioran's capacity for negative passions, as his lifetime of writing demonstrates.

I hypothesize that the body of his work written in French is a re-sponse to his alienation from his homeland and the family and friends he left in Romania. To a lesser degree, his work in French served as an attempt to exorcise certain demons haunting him from the past. Cioran's misanthropy, his *ressentiment* towards Romania's history and what he saw as its national temperament correspond to his radical switch to writing in French, his immigration to France, and most em-phatically to his pessimistic philosophy. Why would this desperate cynicism follow in the aftermath of his politically extremist sympa-thies in his youth? What quality in the experience of suffering was capable of supplanting Cioran's previous passion for a fanatic drive to

---

[3] For a thorough discussion and in-depth account of Cioran's life during this period, see Marta Petreu, *An Infamous Past: E.M. Cioran and the Rise of Fascism in Roma-nia* (Chicago, Ivan Dee, 2005). See also Alexandra Laignel-Lavastine, *Cioran, Eli-ade, Ionesco: L'oubli du fascisme* (Paris, PUF, 2002).

[4] Isac Chiva, "À propos de Mircea Eliade: Un témoignage," *Le Genre Humain*, 26, November, 1992, 92. See also Patrice Bollon *Cioran l'hérétique*. Bollon follows on the heels of other recent studies of wartime writing that claim to reveal particular writers' past political affiliations and wartime activities. Bollon raises questions about the credibility of Cioran's intellectual legacy by doubting the ethical dimension of his ideas. It is no surprise that Cioran's past has gone on trial. Speculation surrounding the extent of his activity with the Iron Guard continues to animate discussions on the utility and significance of Cioran's thought for readers of this century.

transform Romania, its past and future possibilities, as a nation? Cioran's struggle to define himself within French literary culture involved a cycle of renouncing his Romanian origins to embracing only aspects of this heritage to feigning French nationality whenever possible. This cyclic pattern of defining and redefining the self within and without French institutions and traditions represented a more general effort to reconcile his feelings of nostalgia and rage toward his native Romania—an effort that can be traced in the repetition of certain themes throughout his work. Suffering expressed in the most impersonal of literary forms dominates his work both in Romanian and in French. Eventually, suffering became precisely the idiom that served to define Cioran against his contemporaries in a struggle for literary and philosophical authority in mid-century France.

Youthful Errors

Emile Cioran was born on April 8, 1911, in the Transylvanian village of Rǎşinari, at the time still under the reign of the Austro-Hungarian monarchy, to a Romanian orthodox priest and his wife. In every account of his childhood, Cioran described it as a happy period, an Edenic moment that was followed necessarily by the proverbial loss of innocence. In an interview with Helga Perz in 1978, Cioran stated, "Si j'avais eu une enfance triste, j'aurais été beaucoup plus optimiste dans mes idées. Mais j'ai toujours senti, même inconsciemment, ce contraste, cette contradiction entre mon enfance et tout ce qui est venu ensuite. Cela m'a détruit intérieurement en quelque sorte" [If I had had a sad childhood, I would have been much more optimistic in my ideas. But I always felt, even unconsciously, this contrast, this contradiction between my childhood and everything that came afterwards. That destroyed me internally in some way] (*E* 33). After deciding to leave Romania definitively and to adopt French as his literary language, Cioran wrote persistently of his estrangement from his past, Romania, and the Romanian language in terms of an irrevocable loss and destruction.

In his reconstruction of the lifelong history of his affliction, Cioran blamed his preoccupation with suicide and suffering on his insomnia, which he called "the greatest drama of my life." What insomnia prevented him from doing ironically assisted him otherwise: it called for a creative outlet and led to his prolific literary and philosophical production. As he admitted, "Tout ce que j'ai écrit, tout ce

que j'ai pensé, tout ce que j'ai élaboré, toutes mes divagations trou-
vent leur origine dans ce drame: aux alentours de mes 20 ans, j'ai perdu le sommeil" [All that I have written, all that I have thought, all that
I have elaborated, all my ramblings originate with this drama: around
the age of twenty, I lost sleep] (*ML* 19). Insomnia dominated his
memories of childhood, provoked intense bouts of profound despair,
and ultimately determined the themes that preoccupied his writing
from its inception. "Ces nuits de Sibiu sont donc à l'origine de ma
vision du monde" [These nights of Sibiu are thus the origin of my vision of the world] (*E* 287). Despair over his inability to sleep was not
the problem; rather, the loss of innocence pitted Cioran against life in
general in such a way as to destroy everything that followed childhood. As Patrice Bollon put it:

> L'insomnie ne pourra que renforcer cette perception dé-
> sabusée, blasée, du monde. Ce qui accroîtra d'autant chez
> lui la nostalgie de l'univers de Rășinari, laquelle, plus
> qu'au rêve d'une primitivité édénique à la Rousseau,
> ressortit au deuil d'une innocence à jamais perdue, impos-
> sible à réconquerir, *tragiquement inconcevable*: au senti-
> ment d'une "chute" infinie, à laquelle toute participation au
> monde non seulement ne saurait remédier, mais qu'elle ne
> peut même qu'aggraver encore.
>
> [Insomnia only served to reinforce this disenchanted and
> jaded view of the world. What increases so much with him
> is the nostalgia for the Rășinari universe, which, more than
> a dream of a Rousseau-like Edenic primitivity, comes out
> of a mourning for an innocence that was never lost, impos-
> sible to regain, *tragically inconceivable*, a feeling of an in-
> finite "fall," which all the participation in the world not
> only would not remedy, but which would only aggravate
> even more.] (53)

It is possible that the exile from Rășinari or from childhood itself
shaped the tormented and anguished writer that Cioran became in
France. These explanations have also served, however, to divert attention from his experiences with totalitarian politics in his youth, experiences that might instead be the reason for so much retroactive
suffering and distress. Recent criticism of Cioran has tended to focus

on his apparent sympathies with the Iron Guard of Romania.[5] I say "apparent" because Cioran renounced his youthful allegiances to fascism such as they were in his youth in interviews as well as in his *Cahiers*. He denied the significance of his early writing, stating that religious and political fanaticism often attracted those with a propensity for "the bestial substratum of enthusiasm."[6] Cioran began publishing pamphlets and articles as a young college student in Bucharest. Like other members of what is known as the Young Generation in Romania, he had opportunities to publish his literary and philosophical essays in well-known newspapers and literary journals in Romania. His articles appeared for example, in the journals *Calendarul* [Calendar], *Floarea de foc* [Flower of Fire], *Vremea* [Time], *Azi* [Today] and *Gândirea* [Thought]. He started to gain a reputation as a promising young writer, publishing his first book, *Pe culmile disperării* [On the Heights of Despair], in 1934, which won the Royal Academy Prize for young authors. In a two-year period, 1936–1937, Cioran published three other books in Romanian, *Cartea Magirilor* [Book of Lures], *Schimbarea la față a României* [Romania's Transformation], and *Lacrimi și Sfinți* [Tears and Saints].

His third book, *Schimbarea la față a României* [Romania's Transformation], although it does not mention the Iron Guard, or its leader, Corneliu Codreanu, by name, is the most unequivocal embrace of fanatical nationalism he ever wrote. Not only did he confront the main tenets of the Iron Guard doctrine, according to Marta Petreu, the book was "an act of extreme candor, upsetting both the far-right movement of the Legion and Romanian nationalist movements in general" (77). In this book, Cioran calls for a total reconstruction of Romania's vision of its future as well as a re-evaluation of its past, an end to democracy, the installation of a totalitarian regime, and finally, a transcendental legitimacy of the state. It contains all the tenets of nationalist rhetoric from a mystical vision of the nation, an enthusiastic

---

[5] A recent French translation by Alain Paruit of *Schimbarea la față a României* as *La Transfiguration de la Roumanie* (Paris: L'Herne, 2009) has sparked further commentary. The critical works mentioned in note 4 were written by those who were fluent in Romanian and had access to the text in its original.

[6] In "Genealogy of Fanaticism," in *Précis de Décomposition*, Cioran writes, "There is no form of intolerance, of proselytism or ideological intransigence which fails to reveal the bestial substratum of enthusiasm. Once man loses his *faculty of indifference*, he becomes a potential murderer, once he transforms his idea into a god, the consequences are incalculable" (3).

espousal of war and violence at any cost, individual submission to the idea of the monolithic state, and a prescription for the country's heroic destiny. It was so well-received in Romania that, in the words of one critic and fellow Romanian, "one might safely say that almost all the subsequent writings of any importance on the 'Romanian spirit' or the Romanian philosophy of life are responses to Cioran" (Călinescu 204). These publications, particularly *Schimbarea la faţă a României* [Romania's Transformation], but also passages in the *Cahiers* where Cioran corrected himself to avoid reproach and accusations, reveal unambiguous anti-Semitic diatribes and highly xenophobic rhetoric.[7] Cioran later denounced these statements, writing as he did to his brother:

> Pour moi l'époque ou j'écrivais *La Transfiguration* ... me paraît incroyablement lointaine. Parfois, je me demande si c'est bien moi qui ai écrit ces divagations qu'on cite. En tout cas, j'aurais mieux fait de me promener dans le parc de Sibiu.... L'enthousiasme est une forme de délire. Nous avons connu cette maladie dont personne ne veut admettre que nous soyons guéris.
>
> [The time when I was writing *Transformation* ... seems to me incredibly distant. Sometimes I wonder if it were even me who wrote those meanderings that people quote. In any case, I would have been better off taking a walk in the park in Sibiu.... Enthusiasm is a form of madness. We were familiar with this illness of which no one wants to admit being cured.] (Liiceanu 39)[8]

Yet in the 1940 "Lettre-Préface" that Cioran wrote for the essay by Paul Giraud, "Codreanu et la Garde de fer," Cioran defended the Guard saying that it was "a school of moral and spiritual education, a school of sacrifice, of suffering, and of poverty, an initiation to love one's neighbor and a heroic acceptance of death" (Giraud 5). Later, Cioran justified his errors by claiming that Romania was suffering from a kind of collective indolence and self-loathing that could only be remedied with a total reversal of its present government and social structure. The Guard provided the solutions to longstanding social and

---

[7] For a recent study and translation of Cioran's early writing and his fascism, see Alexandra Laignel-Lavastine, *Cioran, Eliade, Ionesco: L'oubli du fascisme*.
[8] Letter to Aurel Cioran, November 2, 1973.

political problems. In what is now his most infamous book Cioran
wrote, "Je ne peux aimer qu'une Roumanie en délire" [I can only love
a delirious Romania] and called for *une Roumanie ayant la population de la Chine et le destin de la France*" [*a Romania with the population of China and the destiny of France*] (187).

It is true that, as a member of a group of rising new young writers,
philosophers, and social critics, the avant-garde of the day, Cioran
might well have embraced the ideals the group in general was espous-
ing, these ideals being largely disseminated through the charismatic
teachings of a common philosopher professor, Nae Ionescu. Nonetheless, Cioran's generation included artists and intellectuals such as
Ionesco, who, unlike Cioran, as he saw fascism gaining momentum,
grew quickly disenchanted, and escaped Romania for refuge in
France. Undoubtedly, Ionesco, whose mother was Jewish, had everything to fear from this strongly anti-Western, anti-Semitic, nationalist
ideology. Cioran, then closely associated with the dissemination of
certain political ideas, fascist and nationalistic in nature, gaining momentum within the intelligentsia of Romania, never disabused himself
of the ideas themselves, but rather made a point of denying any affiliation with the political organization responsible for spreading them. In
L'ami lointain: Paris–Bucharest, Cioran blamed his fascist sympa-
thies on his youth: "J'étais jeune et ne pouvais admettre d'autres véri-
tés que les miennes [...]. Honte de l'Espèce, symbole d'une humanité
exsangue, sans passions ni convictions, inapte à l'absolu, privée
d'avenir [...] ainsi je regardais le régime parlementaire" [I was young
and couldn't accept other truths than my own [...]. Shame of the human race, symbol of humanity bled, without passions or convictions,
absolutely incapable, deprived of a future] (9).

When questioned about his earlier statements, Cioran attempted to
nuance his once absolute denial of any involvement by arguing that
the avant-garde felt ambivalence towards the Guard's presence in
Romania. He even cited fear of ennui as a reason for his controversial
youth: "L'histoire ne serait-elle pas, en dernière instance, le résultat
de notre peur de l'ennui, de cette peur qui nous fera toujours chérir le
piquant et la nouveauté du désastre, préférer n'importe quel malheur à
la stagnation?" [Would history not be, in the last analysis, the result of
our fear of ennui, of this fear that will make us always cherish the
spice and the novelty of disaster, preferring any misfortune to stagnation?] (*HU* 181). Often, for reasons of "ennui and fatalism," this

group of intellectual youth were enticed by the extreme quality of such inherently destructive groups: "Et les intellectuals avec leurs diplômes dans les villages où ils s'ennuyaient à mourir, rejoignaient volontiers ses rangs. La Garde de Fer passait pour une espèce de remède à tous les maux, y compris l'ennui" [And the intellectuals with their degrees living in villages where they were bored to death, eagerly joined their ranks. The Iron Guard masqueraded as a kind of cure for all ills, including boredom] (*E* 17).

Given that the government in Romania after 1941 brutally suppressed the leaders of the Iron Guard, it is not surprising that Cioran, as well as his peers, including Mircea Eliade, all left Romania for France. Yet, even after he had broken ties with Romania, Cioran remained committed to the spirit of the ideas that buttressed the Iron Guard's rhetoric. That is to say that while he may have emptied his expression of references to a former teleology of the nation, a mystical vision of Romania's future under fascism, his expression was still obsessed with fanaticism and all extremist positions, with paradox, and with a kind of faith in the total negation of discourses of moderation or positivism. A "fanatic without convictions," Cioran erased the goals of fascism from his speech and was left with the power of negation, the "substratum" of sentiment. One of his aphorisms even hinted at this possibility: "Avec un peu de chaleur dans le nihilisme, il me serait possible—en niant *tout*—de secouer mes doutes et d'en triompher. Mais je n'ai que le goût de la négation, je n'en ai pas *la grâce*" [With a little warmth in nihilism, it seemed possible to me— that in, negating *everything*—I was shaking off my doubts and triumphing over them. But now I only have a taste for negation, I don't have *grace*] (*S* 38).

Romanian Transplant in Paris

Cioran left Romania twice in the 1930s, first for Germany (1933– 1935), then for France (1937–1940). In Berlin, with the support of an Alexander Humboldt Foundation grant, he discovered the expressionists, notably Oskar Kokoschka, who once described the themes present in his creations as "masochisme métaphysique" [metaphysical masochism] (*ML* 28). Cioran recalled this period fondly as one in which he discovered his "affinités avec le byronisme russe, de Petchorine à Stavrogine, mon ennui et ma passion pour l'ennui" [affinities with Russian Byronism, from Petchorin to Stravrogin, my ennui and my passion for ennui" [My affinities with Russian Byronism, from Petchorin to Stravrogin, my ennui and my passion for ennui] (*IEN* 132). Cioran then went to Paris on a fellowship from the French Institute of Bucharest for three years. With the exception of one year, 1940–1941, when he taught at the Lycée de Braşov, he chose to leave Romania definitively (after the fall of the fascist Legion in 1941) to spend the rest of his life in France.

Paris in the post-war period was, for Cioran, his "période mondaine" [society days]. He frequented the famous salon hosted by Madame Suzanne Tézanas du Montcel and devoted time to his friendships with Gabriel Marcel, Arthur Adamov, Eugène Ionesco, and Mircea Eliade. In 1949, he published his first book in French with Gallimard, *Précis de décomposition* [Handbook of Decomposition]. It quickly received the coveted Prix Rivarol (Le Prix de l'Universalité de la Langue Française). André Gide, Jules Romains, Jules Supervielle, and Jean Paulhan were just a few who made up the illustrious jury. Although the book sold few copies, it proved to be an immediate critical success with positive reviews by such prominent figures as Claude Mauriac in *La Table Ronde*, André Maurois in *Opéra*, and Maurice Nadeau in *Combat*. Despite rave reviews and despite the unequivocal French taste for ennui to which the national love and admiration for Baudelairean spleen attests, Cioran's splenetic essays and aphorisms were largely neglected for decades after he began publishing in French in the late 1940s. The press faulted him mainly for the rigorously negative tone that permeates his work. Even Eliade refused to endorse his friend's work. Speaking of *Des Larmes et des saints* [Tears and Saints], Eliade pronounced it an unpardonable affront to those who had once liked and admired Cioran:

> *Des Larmes et des saints* … est un tragique exemple de ce que peut signifier "la macération" de soi par le paradoxe et l'invective. Ce livre mélancolique abonde en passages exaspérants qui ont mis dans l'embarras jusqu'à ses admirateurs les plus enthousiastes: *ces passages sont, en tout état de cause, indéfendables*…. On a même l'impression qu'Emil Cioran les a écrits—*et publiés*—uniquement pour s'isoler jusqu'à l'absurde, pour devenir impénétrable dans sa solitude … certaines pages de son livre coupent tout lien vivant, toute communion avec le reste du monde, avec les gens qui l'aiment, le comprennent ou "l'admirent."

> [*Tears and Saints* ... is a tragic example of what might be "the maceration" of the self by paradox and invective. This melancholic book abounds in exasperating passages that confuse even his most enthusiastic admirers: *these passages are, in every case, indefensible....* We even have the impression that Emile Cioran wrote them—and published them—only in order to isolate himself to the point of absurdity, to become impenetrable in his solitude ... certain pages of his book cut him off from every live connection, from all communion with the rest of the world, with the people who love him, who understand him or who "admire" him.] (Eliade 39–40)

Once again Cioran tried to distance himself from others and, consequently, was hardly interested in seducing or entertaining the reader. In fact, he never claimed to write for others. In his notes to himself, published by Gallimard in 1997 as *Cahiers*, he wrote, "Il ne faut pas écrire avec l'idée de s'adresser aux autres. Il faut écrire pour soi-même, un point c'est tout" [One mustn't write with the idea of speaking to others. One must write for oneself, that's it] (347). Instead of responding to literary tastes and publicizing his work in the press and through publishers, Cioran's motives for writing had more to do with an internal necessity. "On peut toujours écrire et tout dire, mais si cet acte ne correspond plus à une nécessité intérieure, c'est de la littérature" [One can always write and say everything, but if this action no longer corresponds to an internal necessity, then it is literature] (*ML* 26). He did not want to be commended for having written "literature" (*E* 61). For Cioran, writing ought to function as "acts of aggression" designed to hurt rather than court the reader. He believed that "une œuvre n'existe que si elle est préparée dans l'ombre, avec l'intention d'un assassin qui médite son coup ... ce qui prime c'est l'intention de frapper" [a work doesn't exist unless it is prepared in the dark, with the intention of an assassin who premeditates his blow ... what counts is the intention to strike a blow] (*E* 14). Often the negativity in his writing focused on the author himself in self-flogging fashion. He wrote that "tous [mes] livres sont des suicides manqués" [all my books are botched suicides] (*E* 175), and he considered himself "un homme vaincu" [a vanquished man] suffering from "la sensation d'être une terrible quantité negligible" [the sensation of being a tremendous, insignificant quantity] (*OC* 829). Even his diatribes against others were veiled revelations about himself, as in "l'unique confession sincère est celle que nous faisons indirectement—en parlant des autres" [the only sincere confession is the one we make indirectly—in speaking of others] (*IEN* 59).

Cioran was a steadily prolific writer. After *Précis de décomposition* [Handbook of Decomposition] (1949), he published *Syllogismes de l'amertume* [Syllogisms of Bitterness] (1952), which was followed by *La tentation d'exister* [The Temptation to Exist] (1956), *Histoire et utopie* [History and Utopia] (1960), *La chute dans le temps* [The Fall into Time] (1964), and *Le mauvais démiurge* [The Bad Demiurge] (1969). Cioran refused to accept several awards that were offered to him during this period: Le Prix Sainte-Beuve (1957) for his essays, *La tentation d'exister*, Le Prix Combat by the Nouvelle Revue Française (1961) for *Histoire et utopie*, and the Prix (Roger) Nimier for the sum of his works. He could accept exclusion and criticism; he could not accept accolades. In a letter to his brother, Cioran explained why: "Toute la presse d'ici a parlé de mon refus d'un prix littéraire sans aucune importance à mon avis. Mais certains ne comprennent pas qu'on puisse renoncer à dix mille francs. Depuis longtemps, j'ai pris la décision de n'accepter aucune distinction de ce genre" [The press here speaks of my refusal to accept a literary prize without any concern for my own opinion. But certain people don't understand that one can renounce ten thousand francs. For a long time now, I have made the decision to never accept a mark of distinction of this type].[9] Cioran preferred the appellations "blasphemous," master of doubt and the absurd, and anti-Christian; yet, even these negative attributes were praised after some time. French students in the wake of May '68 heralded the rebellious character that Cioran represented for them. As he put it, "Ce sont les étudiants et les lycéens après 68 qui ont fait mon succès" [The students, both at the university and high school after 1968 have made me a success] (*ML* 30).

By 1970, Cioran was widely known in France and internationally as a truly original thinker devoted to expressing the most dire of psychological conditions and the most negative and hostile states of mind. Critics hailed him as an iconoclast, a man before his time, like the Marquis de Sade, a revolutionary *homme de lettres*, whose very notoriety pointed to a brilliance this century was not yet ready to receive. The bleakness of his writing manifested, according to some, an

---

[9] Letter to Aurel Cioran, 14 June 1977. Published in *Magazine Littéraire* 28.

unusually forceful resistance to the literary and artistic movements of his time. Between 1973 and 1987, Cioran published his final three collections of aphorisms and essays, *De l'inconvénient d'être né* [The Inconvenience of Being Born] (1973), *Essai sur la pensée réaction-naire* [Essay on Reactionary Thought] (later re-edited and published under the title *Exercices d'admiration* [Exercises in Admiration] in 1986) and *Écartèlement* [Drawn and Quartered] (1979). From 1987 until his death in 1995, Cioran renounced writing books for publica-tion altogether: "J'ai cessé d'écrire, je considère que ce n'est pas la peine de continuer. Maintenant j'ai compris que je ne voulais plus continuer cette comédie, parce que le fait d'écrire correspondait quand même à une sorte de nécessité, c'était une façon de me débarrasser de moi-même" [I stopped writing. I think it's not worth it to continue. Now I understand that I no longer wanted to continue this comedy, because the fact of writing corresponded to a sort of necessity, it was a way of relieving myself of myself] (*ML* 24).

Ennui and Writing

Relieving himself of himself appears to be the impetus behind his writing. However, the question of his relationship to the past and the fact that, in immigrating to France and writing exclusively in French, he was in part relinquishing his Romanian ties leads us also to believe that writing soothed his conscience and eased the pain of regret. As he said, "Je suis un univers de regrets" [I am a universe of regrets] (*OC* 186), and he gave a name to the quality of suffering he experienced: ennui. Ennui, the attenuation of time itself, created an empty space in his consciousness by virtue of the acuity of the anxiety it provoked: "L'érosion de notre être par nos infirmités: le vide qui en résulte est rempli par la présence de la conscience—que dis-je—ce vide est la conscience elle-même" [Erosion of our being by our infirmities: the resulting void is filled by the presence of consciousness, what am I saying?—that void is consciousness] (*IEN* 115). Ennui, brought on in moments of total solitude such as his recurrent insomnia, translated into his lexicon as the "utter rejection of and rejection by the world" (Gruzinska 71). For Cioran, ennui and solitude conspired to facilitate a sense of detachment, melancholy, exile, vertigo, emptiness, and even cruelty and ecstasy. It became a reassuring feeling, something as close to home as Cioran would ever know, and served to define his post-Romania existence: "Dans toute mélancolie, la douceur atténue les regrets et la nostalgie; elle confère à l'amour pour la solitude une pointe de délicatesse intime" [In all melancholy, the sweetness attenuates regrets and nostalgia, it confers a point of intimate delicacy on the love for solitude] (*LL* 49).

In Cioran's imagination ennui isolated him not only from others but also from his historical present and put him immediately in a different relation to the world around him. This metaphor is suitable for a man longing to create psychological barriers between himself and the reality of his past and present circumstances. Imagining himself as excluded from the present, outside social interactions, alone in a kind of ontological vacuum, gave Cioran a psychological alibi: "Souffrir c'est être totalement soi, c'est accéder à un état de non-coïncidence avec le monde, car la souffrance est génératrice d'intervalles; et quand elle nous tenaille, nous ne nous identifions plus avec rien, même pas avec elle; c'est alors que, doublement conscients, nous veillons sur nos veilles" [To suffer is to be totally oneself, to access a state of non-coincidence with the world, because suffering generates intervals; and when it tortures us, we no longer identify with anything, not even with suffering; it's then that, doubly conscious, we keep watch on our wakefulness] (*CT* 131). When it came to the question of his lack of engagement with the world, he had only to cite the debilitating effects of ennui as the excuse for his inactivity:

> Sur terre il n'y a pas pour moi d' "occupation" ni à vrai dire de "divertissement" […]. Une vie de rate ... de tristesses inutiles et épuisantes, de nostalgies sans objet et sans direction; un rien qui se traîne sur les chemins, et qui se vautre dans ses douleurs et ses ricanements. L'ennui me reprend, cet ennui que je connus dans mon enfance certains dimanches, et puis celui que dévasta mon adolescence. Un vide qui évacue l'espace, et contre lequel l'alcool seul pourrait me défendre.

> [On earth there is nothing for me for a profession nor, as a matter of fact, for a "diversion" […]. A life of a failure ... of useless and exhausting sadnesses, of nostalgia without an object and without direction; a nothing that languishes on the way, and wallows in its sorrows and its sneering laughter. Ennui comes back to me, this ennui that I knew in my childhood on certain Sundays, and then that which devastated my adolescence. A void evacuates the space, against which I have only alcohol to defend me.] (*C* 32, 24)

In Cioran's case, ennui was a shelter, a shelter from affective bonds, from work, from the present, and from a past he wished to disown. He *was* exiled in a sense greater than the physical and cultural exile that he also experienced. Cioran conceived his exile into ennui as "une chute irremédiable, une perte que rien ne peut combler" [an irreparable fall, a loss that nothing can assuage] (*E* 26). He lived ennui as a spiritual devotion to the void, the absolute consciousness of nothingness. He likened the saint's ecstatic visions to his own experience with the void: "Ce genre de négation peut aller au-delà du suicide, c'est vraiment le néant, on arrive à la conscience absolue du néant. Dans ces moments, on n'a que le choix de se suicider ou de devenir religieux" [This kind of negation might go beyond suicide, it is truly nothingness, one gets to the absolute consciousness of nothingness. In these moments, one has only the option of committing suicide or becoming religious] (*ML* 22). Narratives of certain saints and mystics describe the same leap into a void that he recounts from "the heights of despair":

> La béatitude de l'extase est presque insupportable. On a l'impression que tout est résolu et que le devenir n'a plus de sens. Ce sont des minutes extraordinaires qui rachètent la vie et que l'on n'aspire plus qu'à voir ressurgir. La déception est particulièrement pénible pour le croyant. Le mystique se sent abandonné, rejeté par Dieu, menacé de sécheresse spirituelle. Il sombre alors dans l'ennui, dans l'*acédia*, ce mal des solitaires qui comporte un aspect quasi démoniaque. Le danger pour eux n'est pas le diable mais le vide.

> [The bliss of ecstasy is almost unbearable. One has the impression that everything is resolved and that becoming has no meaning. These are extraordinary minutes that redeem life and that one hopes to see resurface. The deception is particularly painful for the believer. The mystic feels abandoned, rejected by God, threatened with being washed up spiritually. He thus sinks into ennui, into *acedia*, this evil of the solitary ones that carries with it an almost demonic aspect. The danger for them is not the devil but the void.]
> (*E* 16)

Only through suffering, renouncing desire, and embracing ennui could the saints experience ecstasy.[10] Cioran incorporated into his idea of ennui the discourse of a particular "science du regret." If spirituality can be a secular discipline, then Cioran's work would serve as an example of a lifelong dedication to its practice: "Il y a en moi une nostalgie de quelque chose qui n'existe pas dans la vie, ni même dans la mort, un désir que rien n'assouvit ici-bas, sauf à certains moments la musique lorsqu'elle évoque les déchirements d'un autre monde" [Within me there is a nostalgia for something that doesn't exist in life, nor even in death, a desire that nothing can assuage in this world, except at certain moments when music evokes the cleavages of another world] (*C* 76). Cioran suggested that one is only truly aware of existence, conscious of consciousness itself, when in pain.

Cioran embraced his psychic pain and wrote volumes of painstakingly well-crafted sentences about it, which makes one wonder as to the real depths of his despair. Those in a genuine state of depression find it hard to do anything. The most menial tasks seem insurmountable. Composing a poem, writing an essay, would seem impossible. A different quality of despair must have been at work in Cioran for him to develop an aesthetic from it and not be destroyed by it. His predisposition to intense anguish casts no doubt on the authenticity of his personal struggle with ennui. Writing provided an antidote to this struggle while it simultaneously kept the struggle alive within him. He could only write, in fact, during these sleepless nights: "Je n'ai jamais pu écrire autrement que dans le *cafard* des nuits d'insomnie, et durant sept années je pouvais à peine dormir. [...] J'ai besoin de ce cafard et aujourd'hui encore avant d'écrire je mets un disque de musique tsigane hongroise" [I was never able to write except in the *blues* of insomniac nights, and over seven years I could hardly sleep. [...] I need these blues and today before I write, I put on a disk of Hungarian gypsy music] (*E* 10). In place of letting time destroy him, Cioran ultimately came to a point at which he celebrated this feeling of time's horror, calling it "une chance extrême" [extreme luck] and "une aubaine" [a godsend] for it allowed him to further plumb its depths in writing (Gruzinska 71). The act of writing served as a kind of dis-

---

[10] Cioran, *Cahiers,* June 1958: "Le vide, plus j'y pense, plus je me rends compte que j'en ai fait un concept mystique, ou un substitut de l'infini, peut-être de Dieu" [The more I think about the void the more I realize that I've created a mystical idea of it or made it a substitute for the infinite or maybe for God] (*Cahiers* 26).

placement of nihilistic thoughts and negative energy, which would have otherwise led him to harm himself. Writing took the place of religion for Cioran who saw in the act itself "une rencontre avec Dieu, avec une autre solitude" [a meeting with God, with another solitude].[11] In other interviews, Cioran represented writing as an activity he took up "uniquement parce que j'étais un homme inoccupé, qui n'a jamais exercé de métier. Il fallait tout de même que je fasse quelque chose" [only because I was not a busy man, one who never practiced a profession. I had to do something in any case] (*E* 61). Cioran went as far as to say that "écrire est un vice, mais c'est un vice salutaire" [writing is a vice, but a salutary vice] (*E* 74).

For Cioran, writing was a perverse form of salvation, both the cause and its cure. "Si l'on continue cependant à vivre, ce n'est que par la grâce de l'écriture, qui en l'objectivant, soulage cette tension sans bornes. La création est une préservation temporaire des griffes de la mort" [If one continues to live, however, it is only thanks to writing, that in objectifying it, consoles this limitless tension. Creation is a temporary preservation from the claws of death] (*CD* 22). Writing became, according to one scholar, the cure of which "il ressentait si souvent la manifestation dévastatrice" [he felt so often the devastating manifestation]—a cure, that is, that never relieved the symptoms of the sickness (Zaharia 646). For him, the "work" that emerges from a sense of failure contains all the elements of the unattained, the unfinished, and the inexpressible. "La substance d'une œuvre c'est l'Impossible—ce que nous n'avons pu atteindre, ce qui ne pouvait pas nous être donné: c'est la somme de toutes les choses qui nous furent refusées" [The substance of a work is the Impossible—what we were not able to attain, what couldn't be given to us: it's the sum of all the things that were refused us] (*IEN* 116). Writing was the trace of this failure and ennui, the existential state associated with failure, "l'état poétique par excellence" [the ultimate poetic state] (Ianosi 65).

If Cioran was successful at one thing, it was in his ability to capitalize on his failure and to thread all his works together with it as a recurring theme. No other writer in France has reaped such benefits from a serious treatment of combined self-pity and self-abuse as

---

[11] Cioran explained this during the only television interview he allowed during his career. First televised on a Belgian station in 1971, it was shown for the first time in France after his death. Arte, 25 June 1995. Courtesy of l'Inathèque (Institut National de l'Audiovisuel) de France.

Cioran did in his essays and aphorisms. I wish to consider the reasons for both Cioran's pronounced efforts to create a private expression of nihilism, his choice of a literary form, the aphorism, and the French language, to articulate this expression. Understanding the negative tenor of Cioran's publications and his reputation as a misanthropic figure will help explain why he is the subject of so much speculation and derision.

Exile and the Lost Kingdom

Cioran considered himself an exile in many ways. He chose to remain in permanent exile from his native Romania. The feeling he described as ennui, the dissociation from the present, was further exacerbated by the perpetual and constant distance he felt in France from his Eastern European origins. He wrote that "Toute ma vie j'aurai vécu avec le sentiment d'avoir été éloigné de mon véritable lieu. Si l'expression 'exil métaphysique' n'avait aucun sens, mon existence à elle seule lui en prêterait un" [My whole life I have lived with a feeling of having been distanced from my true place. If the expression "metaphysical exile" were to have no meaning, my existence would give it one] (*IEN* 100). Besides the fact that he was already predisposed to nostalgia, he decided to exile himself from his mother tongue by switching languages in mid life. According to Cioran, he adopted a foreign language as his "patrie" over any physical space, for example, Romania or France.[12] He was at home nowhere. However, by virtue of his choosing French as his personal idiom, he found a place to rest: "On n'habite pas un pays, on habite une langue. Une patrie, c'est cela et rien d'autre" [One doesn't reside in a country, one resides in a language. A homeland is that and nothing else] (*AA* 21). "Exile" is a figure that recurs again and again in his work. Cioran often recalled his Romanian childhood, his origins, not so much as to stay connected to his past as to further detach himself. Nostalgia functioned as a kind of self-punishment: "Poursuivis par nos origines, nous le sommes tous; le sentiment que m'inspirent les miennes se traduit nécessairement en termes négatifs, dans le langage de l'autopunition, de l'humiliation assumée et proclamée, du consente-

---

[12] A biographical note that attests to his penchant for errancy: Cioran remained in France until his death in 1995, refusing to ever acquire property and preferring instead to live in modest *chambres de bonne* or residential hotels during the nearly fifty years of his life in Paris.

ment au désastre" [Pursued by our origins, we are all that; my own inspired a feeling that is translated into decidedly negative terms, in the language of self-punishment, in assumed and proclaimed humiliation, in the consent to disaster] (*HU* 11).

The creative act enabled Cioran to constantly relive this detachment from his past, origins, and childhood. It functioned as an act of mourning that he could perform as often as he wished; its repetition throughout his life can be seen as the symbolic elaboration of a single theme used to keep him in a state of mourning. Both his chronic misanthropy and his embrace of solitude speak to the fact that he identified himself tacitly as an exiled writer, living in France, but longing to be at close remove from his origins. As one critic put it, "He wants to be a total exile, pure, an exile without place of shelter, an exile that refuses to set down roots. Cioran would like to be a perpetual exile, an exile of the Universe, an exile of Time, a Prince of exile in a way" (Popescu 114). It was necessary for Cioran to identify himself as an exile, to cultivate the reputation of an iconoclast, and to refuse to belong to any of the literary or philosophical movements of his day. Indeed his own desire to remain tangential to the public intellectuals of the day and to refuse the cult of personality that he saw develop around Sartre, for example, contributed to his relative neglect over the decades. He once claimed, "Pour dire la vérité, j'ai vécu intensément, mais sans pouvoir m'intégrer à l'existence. Ma marginalité n'est pas accidentelle, mais essentielle" [To tell the truth, I have lived intensely, but without being able to integrate myself into existence. My marginality is not accidental but essential] (*E* 29–30). His misanthropy granted him the very marginalized status he desired in order to produce his work; yet, even more importantly, it masked a fear of having his previous allegiances discovered and bought him time out of the literary limelight for several decades. He went to great lengths to increase his infamy as an anti-social, politically apathetic intellectual at a time in Paris when intellectuals feared such damning descriptions and labored hard in the public spotlight to avoid them.

Cioran's work on nihilism, inseparable from his temperament and character, distanced him from others; yet, his intellectual projects kept him at close proximity to those public figures whose company he refused to keep. He wrote in French, the linguistic and cultural domain of his nemesis, Sartre, and he also engaged philosophical themes that were dear to Sartre—ennui, lassitude, the imperative of responsibility, or its absence. That Cioran's *Précis de décomposition* [Handbook of Decomposition] and Sartre's *l'être et le néant* [Being and Nothingness] were published in the same year and that both take on similar philosophical themes suggests that the two philosophers would have at least challenged each other publicly or privately.[13] These concerns alone would have made Cioran a friend of Sartre's—or at the very least, a rival—in the public eye. Yet, Cioran remained a stranger to Sartre and his intellectual milieu, and the reasons why he kept his distance underscore his attachment to the discourse around ennui that he produced in abundance over the years. A closer look at the differences between the philosophical projects with which Cioran and Sartre were respectively associated may help explain why Cioran saw himself as an outsider in regard to popular intellectual trends in France and more in line with a former self he would prefer to forget.

To be sure, Cioran detested the idea of engagement and Sartrian morality with its emphasis on the socially responsible writer and political and personal purposes put to aesthetic creation. Even from his early days in France in the 1940s, Cioran's virulent attacks on philosophical systems, their goal-oriented and praxis-driven character, pointed to a nearly visceral disdain of existentialism. More specifically, he dismissed Sartre's project as mere naive pretension to social revolution, as if, through the invention of certain key concepts that were then disseminated within a strictly intellectual milieu, the world would roll back centuries of exploitation and oppression. For Cioran, Sartre represented everything in French philosophy that was repugnant. He expressed disgust for Sartre's pretensions that philosophers (and writers in general) could and should change the course of history. Sartre's now famous statement from "Présentation des *Temps Modernes*" of 1945, "Je tiens Flaubert et Goncourt pour responsables de la répression qui suivit la Commune parce qu'ils n'ont pas écrit une ligne pour l'empêcher" [I hold Flaubert and Goncourt accountable for the repression that followed the Commune because they didn't write a word to prevent it] (13), was odious to Cioran if only because it repre-

---

[13] This is not to say that they did not cross paths over the four decades that they lived and wrote in the sixth *arrondissement* of Paris. In a recent study of Cioran's involvement with fascism, the author claims that Cioran who sought warmth and sustenance in the Café de Flore during the years of the Occupation, sat habitually at a table not far from the one Sartre claimed for himself every morning at 8 o'clock (Laignel-Lavastine 380).

sented a once-cherished belief he could no longer respectfully hold. As a member of the Young Generation in the 1930s in the capital city of Bucharest, Cioran had experienced the power intellectuals had to instigate social revolution, and he had believed that through rhetoric alone, the nation would rebuild itself and project a mystical idea of its past and future into the present situation. Such was the main impetus behind *Schimbarea la faţă a României* [Romania's Transformation]. Cioran was critical of the pretensions of Sartre who, in claiming to reveal truths about existence, ended up valorizing his own existence as the philosophizing subject. Whereas a philosopher such as Sartre would highlight subjective experience as an example of a universal psychological phenomenon as in the case of Roquentin in *La nausée* [Nausea], Cioran undermines the idea of the philosopher as exemplary of the human condition. He posits himself as a doubter, emphasizing his own insignificance and relativity as a subject in the world. However, he bears a resemblance to Sartre in one significant respect. Both philosophers believed that in order to effectuate coincidence with the self, the "pour-soi" and the "en-soi," existence and essence, one must be in a state of suffering, be it ennui or nausea. Cioran and Sartre come together on this conception of ennui and nausea as a degree zero point of consciousness. If Sartre saw this moment of metaphysical anguish as a problem to be understood and then seized as an occasion for expression, explanation, or at least, description, Cioran found an opportunity to surmount his own discomfort by delving deeper into suffering. Against Sartre's humanism and engagement, Cioran offered misanthropy and nihilism. This fundamental difference between the two philosophers manifested itself in quite disparate portraits of ennui. We find "nausea" and "ennui" depicted simultaneously in French; but whereas Sartre's ennui led to positive creation and ultimate social good, Cioran's ennui held no political or social value—it was experienced as pure indulgence:

> Je suis un fauve au sourire grotesque, qui se contracte et se dilate à l'infini, qui meurt et grandit en même temps, exalté entre l'espérance du rien et le désespoir du tout, nourri de fragrances et de poison brûlé par l'amour et la haine, anni-hilé par les lumières et les ombres. [...] Les ténèbres elles-mêmes ne brûlent-elles pas en moi?

> [I'm a fawn with a grotesque smile, who contracts and dilates infinitely, who dies and grows at the same time, ex-

alted between the hope of nothing and the despair of everything, nourished by fragrances and by poison, burned by
love and hate, annihilated by lights and shadows. […] The
shadows themselves, do they not burn within me?]

(*CD* 111)

Aesthetic creation never once offered Cioran the semblance of
self-coincidence, and he certainly harbored no illusions about the possibility of achieving transcendence through literature. For him, writing
was always a form of temporary relief from an experience he came to
view as essential to his everyday mode of existence.

Cioran claimed to have read only German philosophy, Nietzsche,
Schopenhauer, and Heidegger, as the basis for his philosophical ideas;
yet, he often made a point of denigrating his own neighbors, Sartre,
Beauvoir, and Merleau-Ponty, when citing his intellectual influences
in interviews. Despite his resistance to French philosophy, he chose
French and not German to express his ideas. He reasoned that con-
fronting his adversaries in their own language, refusing to integrate
into their philosophical community, and thereby insisting on remaining on the fringes would ultimately convey an unmistakable message
to his contemporaries in France. That is, his books would engage contemporary intellectual debate within the close-knit philosophical
community in France while simultaneously alienating him from this
same community. He positioned himself as the "anti-Sartre" who aspired to the opposite of humanistic bravado, the heights of despair that
led, not to freedom of choice and self-definition, but to ever-more
self-deception, darkness, and despair.

Given what we know about Cioran's hostility to France and its
public intellectuals of the 1930s and 1940s, it is curious that after
1947 he abandoned his native Romania and the Romanian language
for a life in France, speaking and writing exclusively in French.
Cioran quipped that it was because of the failure that he had experienced in trying to translate Mallarmé into Romanian. One possible
explanation is that the kind of structure and order represented by
French and France replaced for Cioran that for which he remained
nostalgic after he had left Romania. Yet, nostalgia and the desire to
return to Romania does not figure in his writing, correspondence, or
interviews. It was not that Cioran suffered from the pain that only real
exile engenders. Ambivalence toward Romania might describe the
combination, on the one hand, of the contempt he felt for Romanians

and, on the other, the pride of being able to share in a stereotypical Balkan propensity for self-pity. As Matei Călinescu cynically observed, "The Romanians, the French Cioran seems to believe, have not only failed (to enter History), but they have managed to demonstrate a vocation and even a genius for failure, the only vocation and genius that they have. On this account he feels proud of being a Romanian—of having 'with regard to pain, a professional competence'" (195). Disgusted by popular literary tastes in France, repelled by his own country's "genius for failure," Cioran identified instead with a former era of French grandeur—the eighteenth century—that embodied for him all the classic (lucid, sober) features of language as well as the sophisticated ends to which language can be put.

Choosing French and the Aphoristic Form

For Cioran, writing in the most polished and elegant French served the purpose of imposing constraints on his expression, constraints he very much desired and needed for his style. French functioned as a form of asceticism and discipline that he could practice.[14] He compared writing in French to wearing a "straitjacket" evoking both the restrictive and exacting nature of the French language as well as the pains he took to translate the highly enigmatic emotions and thoughts that characterize his work into a foreign language.[15] In many ways, it was the perfect idiom for him. French allowed him to maintain a distance between language and the torturous psychic conflict that resulted in a lifetime of insomnia, suicidal thoughts, and destruc-

---

[14] Cioran's decisive break with Romania and his switch to French as his primary language of expression were both professional and deeply personal. "Switching languages at the age of thirty-seven is not an easy undertaking. In truth, it is a martyrdom, but a fruitful martyrdom, an adventure that lends meaning to being. I recommend to anyone going through a major depression to take on the conquest of a foreign idiom, to re-energize himself, altogether to renew himself, through the Word. Without my drive to conquer French, I might have committed suicide. A language is a continent, a universe, and the one who makes it his is a conquistador" (Cioran, "Encounters with Paul Celan" 51).

[15] Cioran's choice of French was indeed deliberate. "The hardest experience" he had ever undergone, Cioran admits to it being the formative moment in his career as a philosopher and writer and that the uneasiness it created in him "led me to ponder the problem of style and the very *anomaly* of writing" (qtd. in Sontag 223). Elsewhere, he said that French was "l'idiome idéal pour traduire délicatement des sentiments équivoques" [the ideal idiom for delicately translating equivocal feelings] (*Oeuvres* 1723).

tive impulses. French created, rather than collapsed, the distances between word and thought while offering a constant reminder that he
would be forever linked, however obliquely, to his origins. The mark
of his nationality and his past (Romania in the shadow of the Iron
Guard), his Balkan accent, and his slightly awkward turn of phrase,
revealed itself in each utterance, spoken and written, in French.
Cioran's choice to express himself only in French signified the abandonment of the maternal idiom, a liberation from his old identity and
most importantly, from his past. As he said, "En une heure, ça a été
fini. Ce fut une réaction violente. J'ai rompu avec tout: avec ma
langue, avec mon passé, avec tout [...]. Le passage à une autre langue
ne peut se faire qu'au prix du renoncement à sa propre langue. Il faut
accepter ce sacrifice" [In one hour, it was over. It was a violent reaction. I broke with everything: with my language, with my past, with
everything [...]. The switch to another language cannot be done except
at the price of renouncing one's maternal tongue. One must accept the
sacrifice] (qtd. in Liiceanu 114).

French defined Cioran's relationship not only to language and
linguistic expression in general, but also to a particular aesthetic that
involved employing French as the appropriate expression for one who
believed in the correlation between effort and suffering and the practice of creating exquisite artistic forms out of torturous repetitive
workings. Even the difficulty and rigidity of the French language,
claimed Cioran, was something he ultimately overcame precisely as a
result of his need to break down his initial resistance to it:

> J'aurais dû choisir n'importe quel idiome, sauf le français,
> car je m'accorde mal avec son air distingué, il est aux an-
> tipodes de ma nature, de mes débordements, de mon moi
> véritable et de mon genre de misères. Par sa rigidité, par la
> somme des contraintes élégantes qu'il représente, il
> m'apparaît comme un exercice d'ascèse ou plutôt comme
> un mélange de camisole de force et de salon.
>
> [I should have chosen any other idiom, except French, be-
> cause I don't square well with its air of distinction, it is at
> odds with my nature, with my excesses, with my true self,
> and my kind of misery. By its rigidity, by the sum of its el-
> egant constraints that it represents, it seems to me like an
> ascetic exercise or rather like a mix of a straitjacket and a
> corset.] (*EA* 214)

For reasons of strict structure and convention, Cioran recycled forms long familiar such as those belonging to seventeenth-century salon culture and the *moralistes* through which to articulate his philosophical reflections. In French literary history, the aphorism and the maxim are associated most immediately with La Rochefoucauld and Pascal, who wrote in such forms in order to speak about principles of proper social conduct, in the case of the former, and to impart reflections on faith, in the case of the latter. These highly structured and elegant forms, which represented the seventeenth century's preferred mode of transmission for codified and prescriptive formulas of correct public and private, social and individual, behavior, was what Cioran chose to adopt, and not the content of moral counsel. If this was not the kind of content that interested Cioran, then what did obsolete literary forms provide to him that classic philosophical thesis lacked? Sanda Stolojan succinctly sums up Cioran's style thus: "Au spleen hypersubjectif d'autrefois se substitue un état de neurasthénie élégante, que seule la langue française, et par-dessus tout celle des écrivains et mémorialistes du XVIII siècle qu'a tant fréquentés Cioran, pouvait rendre" [He substitutes the hypersubjective spleen of another time with a state of elegant neuresthenia that only the French language, and with it all the writers and memorialists of the eighteenth century who Cioran knew well, could render] (*ML* 40). In other words, Cioran decided on some seventeenth-century literary forms to express a kind of noble neuresthenia associated with the eighteenth century—a version that was popularized by Baudelaire and others as "spleen" in the following century.

The aphorism allowed Cioran to erase those generic boundaries that are so necessary to literary classification in France and that serve to organize the French literary landscape, past and present. It is difficult to discern whether his writing falls under poetry or prose, autobiography or fiction, tract or personal manifesto, essay or epigram. Take, for example, this aphorism: "Nous mettons trop de passion dans nos négations. Mais toutes les négations ne deviennent-elles pas positives par notre excès?" [We put too much passion in our negations. But don't all these negations become positive by our excess?] (*LL* 67). Abstract and atemporal, difficult and provocative, this aphorism dramatizes the conflict between opposing extremes: the insult and the elegy, rage and laughter, the impassioned and the indifferent, vehemence and spleen. Unlike a maxim by La Rochefoucauld, an aphorism by Cioran might be cynical but it is not also disenchanted, as in "Si on n'a pas en soi la passion de l'insoluble, on ne peut pas se représenter les excès dont on est capable, la négation, l'impitoyable lucidité de la negation" [If one doesn't have in oneself the passion for the unsolvable, one cannot represent to oneself the excesses of which one is capable. Negation, the relentless lucidity of negation] (*LL* 187).

For Cioran, the resurrection of these forms placed him in a category by himself, outside the contemporary literary conventions and experiments in form, beside a philosopher like Nietzsche, whose choice of the aphorism was also considered a transgression of form in his time.[16] Cioran wrote that the aphorism *liberated* him from constraints; it allowed him more personal freedom of expression: "on est plus libre dans l'aphorisme—triomphe du moi désagrégé" [we are more free in the aphorism—triumph of the disarticulated self] (*AA* 115). Cioran's reappropriation of the aphorism, representing the height of elegance in literary form, to express the sentiments attached to the golden age of spleen—a dead nineteenth-century European ideal—once more ensured both the respect of the French reading public and his marginality as a philosopher with no interest in or pretentions to following the formal trends of the French republic of letters. Less admirable perhaps but nevertheless pertinent was the way in which Cioran went about constructing his perfect elocutions, laboring to distill them in the midst of some of the twentieth century's most trying times. As bombs were dropping not too far away and thousands of Jews were being rounded up in the infamous Vel d'Hiv *rafle*, Cioran sat ensconced at his desk in the rue Monsieur-le-Prince devoting himself to honing the sparest of lines, the perfect Ancien Régime formula such as, "vivre, c'est perdre du terrain" [to live is to lose ground] (*IEN* 115), "La lucidité complète, c'est le néant" [Complete lucidity is nothingness] (*ML* 327), or "exister est un plagiat" [existing is plagiarism] (*TE* 78).

---

[16] For extensive studies of Nietzsche and the aphoristic form, see Philippe Lacoue-Labarthes and Jean-Luc Nancy, *L'Absolu littéraire. Théorie de la littérature du romantisme allemande* (Paris: Seuil, 1978); Lucien Dällenbach, *La Question du fragment* (Geneva: University of Geneva, 1981) and *Fragment und Totalität* (Frankfurt: Suhrkamp, 1984); and Blanchot, "Nietzsche et l'écriture fragmentaire" and "*L'Athenaeum*" in *L'Entretien infini* (Paris: Gallimard, 1969).

Conclusion

Cioran fancied himself the "porte-parole" of twentieth-century ennui and devoted his life to suffering from it. "Ma mission est de souffrir pour tous ceux qui souffrent sans le savoir. Je dois payer pour eux, expier leur inconscience, la chance qu'ils ont d'ignorer à quel point ils sont malheureux" [My mission is to suffer for all those who suffered without knowing it. I must pay for them, expiate their consciousness, the possibility that they have had to ignore to some extent their unhappiness] (*IEN* 136). He considered his texts discharges of the negative energy that resulted from this relentless suffering. To live in a permanent state of grief was a condition for literary productivity. Cioran perceived himself as marginalized, rejected by his contemporaries and the public at large. It is clear from the published interviews and the collected volume of journals *Cahiers*, that Cioran, in addition to the *ressentiment* that figures in his public statements, felt great nostalgia for the past and, more specifically, for his formative years in Romania. Was he nostalgic for the halcyon days of his youth when he, along with Eugène Ionesco, Mihail Sebastian, and Mircea Eliade, were known as the Young Generation? Or the darker of those days marked by his fascination with the Iron Guard?

I would venture to guess that his philosophy of the void served to keep the nostalgia present, to render his ruined internal world forever alive, in fragments, as a never-to-be-recovered loss. Writing in French further emphasized the linguistic, geographical, political, and psychological exile he endured. Being *chez soi* neither in his physical environment nor in his language of choice allowed Cioran to develop his thought as a personal meditation, a deeply private movement of self-reflection on the universal themes of the experiences of time, memory, and nostalgia. The expression of this movement of thought is fittingly lyrical and errant: his "dépaysement" [homesickness] is reflected in the fragment. The irony is that his meticulous, obsessive attention to the accuracy of his French made him "the best stylist in France" (Codrescu 58) in a country that holds language at its highest level of patrimony. But for Cioran, this accolade represents a different kind of success. The triumph was not that he could "pass" as French. It was that he could *surpass* the French at two of their oldest games (*la belle phrase* and the *mise-en-scène* of ennui) and in this way he would also supersede his Romanian identity. As a friend of his once said, "Cioran est determiné à montrer aux Français qu'il peut écrire aussi bien qu'eux, et même mieux qu'eux" [Cioran is determined to show the French that he can write as well as them, and even better than them] (Liiceanu 49).[17] He was able to achieve the nation-less sovereignty he so desired through identification with the word and the form rather than with a place or a people. As he once wrote truthfully to his brother "dans n'importe quelle partie du monde, j'aurais eu la même vision des choses, le même tourment et le même dégoût. En soi, le fait de vivre à Răşinari ou à Paris n'a rien à voir avec ce qu'on est vraiment" [in any part of the world I would have had the same vision of things, the same torment, and the same disgust. The fact of living in Răşinari or in Paris has nothing to do in itself with who one really is] (Liiceanu 67).

Works Cited

Bollon, Patrice. *Cioran l'hérétique*. Paris: Gallimard, 1997.

Călinescu, Matei. "'How Can One Be What One Is?' Reading the Romanian and the French Cioran." *Salmagundi* 112 (Fall 1996): 192–215.

Cioran, Emil. *L'ami lointain, Paris-Bucharest* (with Constantin Noïca). Paris: Criterion, 1991.

_____. *Aveux et anathèmes*. Paris: Gallimard, 1987. (*AA*)

_____. *Cahiers 1957–72*. Paris: Gallimard, 1997. (*C*)

_____. *La chute dans le temps*. Paris: Gallimard, 1964. (*CT*)

_____. *Écartèlement*. Paris: Gallimard, 1979. (*Ec*)

_____. *Élan vers le pire*. Paris: Gallimard, 1988.

_____. "Encounters with Paul Celan." Ed. Benjamin Hollander. *Translating Tradition: Paul Celan in France*. San Francisco: ACTS 8/9, 1988.

_____. *Entretiens*. Paris: Gallimard, 1995. (*E*)

_____. *Exercices d'admiration*. Paris: Gallimard, 1986. (*EA*)

_____. *Histoire et utopie*. Paris, Gallimard, 1988. (*HU*)

_____. *De l'inconvénient d'être né*. Paris: Gallimard, 1973. (*IEN*)

_____. *Le livre des leurres*. Paris: Gallimard, Arcades, 1992. (*LL*)

_____. *Magazine Littéraire* "Cioran" 327 (1994). (*ML*)

_____. *Oeuvres Complètes*. Paris: Gallimard, 1995. (*OC*)

_____. *Précis de décomposition*. Paris: Gallimard, 1949.

_____. *Sur les cimes du désespoir*. Paris: l'Herne, 1990. (*CD*)

_____. *Syllogismes de l'amertume*. Paris: "Collection Folio" Gallimard, 1952. (*SA*)

_____. *La tentation d'exister*. Paris: Gallimard, 1956. (*The Temptation to Exist*. Trans. Richard Howard. Chicago: Quadrangle Books, 1986). (*TE*)

---

[17] See *Exercices d'admiration* 213.

_____. *Transfiguration de la Roumanie*. Trans. Alain Paruit. Paris: Editions de l'Herne, 2009.

Codrescu, Andrei, "E.M. Cioran, or God Doesn't Wear a Cane." *Essays on E.M. Cioran*. Costa Mesa: American Academy of Arts and Sciences, 1999: 57–63.

Eliade, Mircea. *Fragmentarium*. Trans. Alain Paruit. Paris: Editions de l'Herne, 1989.

"E.M. Cioran, 84, Novelist and Philosopher of Despair" *New York Times*, 22 June 1995: A13.

Gruzinska, Aleksandra. "From Musset to Cioran: Sampling and Taming Solitude." *Journal of the American Romanian Academy of Arts and Sciences* 20 (1995): 64–75.

Gruzinska, Aleksandra. "E.M. Cioran: Le temps humain et l'éternel présent." Essays on E.M. Cioran. Rasinari 1911–Paris 1995. Ed. Aleksandra Gruzinska. Costa Mesa, CA: American Romanian Academy of Arts and Sciences. 1999: 89–100.

Guiraud, Paul. *Codreanu et la Garde de Fer*. Paris: Éditions Francisme, 1940.

Ianosi, Ian. "Émile Cioran sur le dépassement de la philosophie par la poésie," *Cahiers Roumains d'Études Littéraires* 1 (1987): 118–33.

Laignel-Lavastine, Alexandra. *Cioran, Eliade, Ionesco: L'oubli du fascisme*. Paris: PUF, 2002.

Liiceanu, Gabriel. *Itinéraires d'une vie: E.M. Cioran suivi de Les Continents d'Insomnie*. Paris: Michelon, 1995.

Mutti, Claudio. *Les Plumes de l'Archange: Quatre Intellectuels Roumains face à la Garde de Fer*. Trans. from Italian by Philippe Baillet. Chalon-sur-Saône: Editions Hérode, 1993.

Petreu, Marta. *An Infamous Past: E.M. Cioran and the Rise of Fascism in Romania*. Chicago: Ivan Dee, 2005.

Popescu, Iulian. "Cioran ou la tentation de l'achronie," *Euresis: Cahiers Roumains d'Études Littéraires* 1–2 (1993): 114–18.

Said, Edward. "Amateur of the Insoluble." *Reflections on Exile and Other Essays*. Cambridge: Harvard UP, 2000. 24–30.

Sartre, Jean-Paul. *Situations II*. Paris: Gallimard, 1948.

Sontag, Susan. "A Note on the Author" (Introduction). *The Temptation to Exist*. By E.M. Cioran. Trans. Richard Howard. Chicago: Quadrangle Books, 1986: 7–29.

Vernescu, Flavia. "Émil Cioran: le philosophe et le styliste," *Dalhousie French Studies* 37 (Winter 1996): 73–80.

Zaharia, Constantin. "L'écriture fragmentaire de la mélancolie," *Critique* 617 (October 1998): 644–57.

Notes on Contributors

Monica Spiridon is a Professor of Semiotics and Twentieth-century European Culture at the University of Bucharest, Romania. She is the author of sixteen books of literary theory, comparative literature, and East-Central European intellectual history published inside and outside Romania, approximately one hundred academic studies published in scholarly periodicals, and two dozen book chapters. She is the vice-president of the International Comparative Association (2010–present) founder of the European Network of Comparative Studies (ENCS), and a member of the Executive Bureau (2003–2007). She is the chair of the Experts Panel for Literature of the European Science Foundation (ESF), a member of the European Pool of Reviewers, and an elected member of Academia Europea.

Ferdâ Asya is an Associate Professor of English at Bloomsburg University of Pennsylvania. Her research focuses on nineteenth-century and twentieth-century American literature with emphasis on the impact of the turn-of-the-century social and political issues on the fiction of the period. She has published articles on the works of American writers, multiethnic writers, and international writers. Her current research centers on the political aspects of the fiction of Edith Wharton and American expatriate writers in Paris.

Stephen Forcer is a Lecturer in French at the University of Birmingham, UK. He is the author of *Modernist Song: The Poetry of Tristan Tzara* (Legenda, 2006) and various article-length items on Dada and Surrealism in French literature and film. With Emma Wagstaff, he is currently co-editing a special issue of *Nottingham French Studies* on the French avant-garde.

Monique Yaari, Associate Professor of French, Department of French and Francophone Studies at the Pennsylvania State University, is a specialist in twentieth-century French literary and cultural studies. Her publications range across literature, the arts, and architecture, spanning modernism, postmodernism, and the historical avant-gardes. In addition to numerous articles, she is the author of *Ironie parado-xale et ironie poétique: sur les traces de Gide dans "Paludes"* (Sum-ma Publications 1988) and *Rethinking the French City: Architecture, Dwelling, and Display after 1968* (Rodopi 2008).

Monique Jutrin is a Professor of Literature and French Culture at the University of Tel Aviv, Israel. She is the founder of the Société d'étude Benjamin Fondane and the Director of the Cahiers Benjamin Fondane. She has published widely on Benjamin Fondane: *Benjamin Fondane ou le périple d'Ulysse* (1989), *Benjamin Fondane et les Cahiers du Sud* (1998), *Rencontres autour de Benjamin Fondane* (2003), *Une poétique du gouffre* (2005), and *Benjamin Fondane entre Jérusalem et Athènes* (2009). Her other publications include *Panaït Istrati/un chardon déraciné/écrivain français conteur roumain* (1970), *Marcel Schwob, cœur double* (1982), and *Lettres de Rachel Bespaloff à Jean Wahl* (2002).

Catherine Rossi holds a Ph.D. (*Les voies initiatiques chez Panaït Istrati et Harry Martinson/Rêverie, vagabondage, écriture* 2009) from the University of Bourgogne, Dijon, France. She is co-author of *Les haïdoucs dans l'œuvre de Panaït Istrati/L'insoumission des vaincus* (2002). Her research interests include Panaït Istrati, Harry Martinson, and Gaston Bachelard. She has recently published articles in *Francophonie roumaine et intégration européene* (Colloque International de Dijon), *Les Cahiers Gaston Bachelard* (France), and *Le Courrier International de la Francophonie* (Romania).

Ingrid Coleman Chafee is a retired Associate Professor of French, Morehouse College, Atlanta, Georgia. She has published articles and presented numerous papers on Ionesco and other writers of twentieth-century French theatre. She received her Ph.D. from Emory University, her M.A. in French from the University of Virginia, and her B.A. from the Western College for Women, Oxford, Ohio (now Miami of Ohio).

Ashby Crowder is a historian of twentieth-century Eastern Europe and an archivist at the US National Archives and Records Administration. He holds graduate degrees from Ohio University and the University of Maryland. He has published several articles in the field of contemporary Romanian history. They include "Romanian Reactions to Independent Unionism: Solidarnosc, East European Labor, and State

Socialism" (*Polish Review* 2007) and "Romanian Interpretations of the Prague Spring: Cadres, Diplomats, and the 1968 Crisis" (*Archives of Totalitarianism* 2008).

Jean-Jacques Thomas is the Distinguished Melodia E. Jones Chair at SUNY. An affiliated member of the University at Buffalo Poetics Program and Professeur Associé at the Centre d'Etudes Poétiques of the ENS (LSH–Lyon), he has published several books on poetry and poetics in French, Spanish, and English. With Hermes Salceda, he co-edited *Le Pied de la lettre* (Vigo/New Orleans: Presses Universitaires de Vigo/PUNM, 2009). He is the author of recent articles on Perec, Des Rosiers, Miron, Roubaud, Leiris, Emily Dickinson, Aimé Césaire, Charles Bernstein, Jean-Marie Gleize, Denis Roche, Pierre Alferi, Dany Laferrière, and the Oulipo. He is the general editor of *FPC* and the co-editor of *Formules*.

Anne Quinney is an Associate Professor of French at the University of Mississippi. She holds a Ph.D. from Duke University and a maîtrise from the University of Paris VIII. She has written numerous articles on French literature and philosophy, notably on Dumas, Blanchot, Sartre, Duras, Cioran, and Ionesco. She is the co-author of *Le goût de la révolte* (Mercure de France, 2008) and *Windows* (Nebraska 2003), a translation of J.B. Pontalis, *Fenêtres* (Gallimard 2000).